ARROYO C

Improving the Understanding of Special Operations

A Case History Analysis

Linda Robinson, Austin Long, Kimberly Jackson, Rebeca Orrie

Prepared for the United States Army
Approved for public release; distribution unlimited

For more information on this publication, visit www.rand.org/t/RR2026

Library of Congress Cataloging-in-Publication Data is available for this publication.
ISBN: 978-0-8330-9839-9

Published by the RAND Corporation, Santa Monica, Calif.
© Copyright 2018 RAND Corporation
RAND® is a registered trademark.

Limited Print and Electronic Distribution Rights

This document and trademark(s) contained herein are protected by law. This representation of RAND intellectual property is provided for noncommercial use only. Unauthorized posting of this publication online is prohibited. Permission is given to duplicate this document for personal use only, as long as it is unaltered and complete. Permission is required from RAND to reproduce, or reuse in another form, any of its research documents for commercial use. For information on reprint and linking permissions, please visit www.rand.org/pubs/permissions.

The RAND Corporation is a research organization that develops solutions to public policy challenges to help make communities throughout the world safer and more secure, healthier and more prosperous. RAND is nonprofit, nonpartisan, and committed to the public interest.

RAND's publications do not necessarily reflect the opinions of its research clients and sponsors.

Support RAND
Make a tax-deductible charitable contribution at
www.rand.org/giving/contribute

www.rand.org

Preface

The U.S. Army Special Operations Command asked the RAND Arroyo Center, a federally funded research and development center at the RAND Corporation, to examine how successful change has occurred in Army and U.S. Department of Defense (DoD) policy regarding special operations forces. The purpose of the project is to inform the command's development of options for policymakers and its articulation of how the varied Army special operations forces (SOF) capabilities can help to meet U.S. national security objectives. The command requested that the Arroyo Center review the history of key decisions on Army SOF development; analyze the principal factors in decisions and outcomes; develop an opportunity recognition framework; and derive recommendations for Army SOF and Army initiative planning and execution. We conducted in-depth historical and contemporaneous case studies to examine the formal and informal governmental processes by which capabilities were explained, proposals were advanced, and decisions reached concerning the formation, development, and employment of special operations capabilities at critical junctures. The research in this report was conducted from January to June 2016 and represents the state of affairs and our analysis at that time.[1]

This report contains the study results. The findings and recommendations should be of interest to the special operations community, congressional committees charged with oversight of the U.S. military,

---

[1] Since the writing of this report, Section 1208 has been codified into law as a permanent authority under United States Code, Title 10, Section 127e, which now enables the Secretary of Defense to expend up to $100 million for its authorized activities.

officials in DoD, and other departments and agencies with responsibilities in national security or international affairs. The study should also be of interest to a wider audience that includes officials, academics, or members of the public concerned with the interagency process for the development and promulgation of policy initiatives concerning the U.S. military.

The research conclusions reached do not necessarily reflect the official policy or position of the U.S. Army Special Operations Command, the Department of the Army, DoD, or the U.S. government. RAND research publications are peer reviewed and meet the quality-assurance standards established by the RAND Corporation to ensure that studies are objective, independent, and balanced. The standards are summarized and described in detail at www.rand.org/standards/summary.

This research was received and approved by the RAND Institutional Review Board (the Human Subjects Protection Committee). RAND operates under a Federalwide Assurance for the Protection of Human Subjects (FWA00003425) and complies with the Code of Federal Regulations for the Protection of Human Subjects under United States Law (45 CFR 46), also known as the Common Rule.

This research was sponsored by the U.S. Army Special Operations Command and conducted within the RAND Arroyo Center's Strategy, Doctrine, and Resources Program. The RAND Arroyo Center, part of the RAND Corporation, is a federally funded research and development center sponsored by the United States Army.

The Project Unique Identification Code (PUIC) for the project that produced this document is RAN167272.

Contents

Preface iii
Tables xiii
Summary xv
Acknowledgments xxxi
Abbreviations xxxiii

CHAPTER ONE
Introduction 1
Purpose of Study 1
Background 2
Research Approach 2
    Case Selection Criteria 3
    Analytic Framework 5
    Method of Assessing Outcomes and Deriving Lessons 7
Organization of This Report 8

CHAPTER TWO
Special Operations Capabilities: Creation of 6th Army Special Reconnaissance Unit 9
Overview 9
Catalyst 9
Stakeholder Analysis 10
Proposal Formation and Key Junctures 11
    Establishing the Alamo Forces 11
Decision and Outcome Analysis 14
Key Lesson 15

CHAPTER THREE
Creation of the Office of Strategic Services: SOF-CIA Precursor 17
Overview 17
Catalyst and Stakeholder Analysis 17
  Donovan at War and in Politics, 1905–1940 17
Proposal Formation and Key Junctures 18
  Coordinator of Information, 1941 18
Decision and Outcome Analysis 20
  Office of Strategic Services, 1942–1945 20
Summary of Lessons 21

CHAPTER FOUR
**Special Operations Capabilities: Creation of
U.S. Army Special Forces** 23
Overview 23
Catalyst 23
Psychological Operations 24
  Stakeholder Analysis: Advocates 24
  Stakeholder Analysis: Detractors 26
  Key Junctures 26
Unconventional Warfare 30
  Stakeholder Analysis 30
  Key Junctures 31
Decision, Outcome Analysis, and Lessons 34

CHAPTER FIVE
**Special Operations Capabilities: Special Forces
Expansion Under President Kennedy and
Contraction Through the Vietnam War** 37
Overview 37
Catalyst 37
Proposal Formation 38
Key Policy Initiatives 40
Stakeholder Analysis 42
Decision and Outcome Analysis 44
  Military Drawdown 44

Poor Relations 45
　　Conventionalizing the Vietnam War 48
　Summary of Lessons 50

CHAPTER SIX
CIA-SOF Cooperation in Southeast Asia, 1961–1975 53
　Overview 53
　Catalyst and Stakeholder Analysis 53
　　Laos, 1954–1962 53
　Key Junctures 55
　　South Vietnam, 1961–1975 55
　Decision and Outcome Analysis 58
　Summary of Lessons 61

CHAPTER SEVEN
Special Operations Capabilities: Creation of U.S. Special Operations Command and the Assistant Secretary of Defense for Special Operations and Low-Intensity Conflict 63
　Overview 63
　Catalyst 64
　　Operations Eagle Claw and Urgent Fury 64
　Proposal Formation and Stakeholder Analysis 66
　　Actors Inside the Pentagon 66
　　Actors in Congress 69
　　Actors in the Defense Industry 70
　Key Junctures 71
　Decision and Outcome Analysis 74
　Summary of Lessons 76

CHAPTER EIGHT
Special Operations Capabilities: Post-9/11 SOF Expansion 81
　Overview 81
　A Growing but Frustrated Community: SOF in the 1990s 82
　Catalyst 1: 9/11 86
　　The Window Opens: SOF Expansion 2001–2005 86
　　Stakeholder Analysis 87

Key Decisions 87
Outcomes 89
Big Changes: SOF Expansion 2006–2010 89
Catalyst 2: 2006 QDR 89
Stakeholder Analysis 89
Proposal Formation 90
Key Junctures and Outcomes 92
Fine Tuning: SOF Expansion 2010–2014 94
Catalyst 3: 2010 QDR 94
Stakeholder Analysis 94
Proposal Formation 94
Key Junctures and Outcomes 96
Summary of Lessons 96

CHAPTER NINE
Special Operations Capabilities:
  Special Mission Unit Expansion 99
Overview 99
Early Transformation: The 1990s 99
Initial Expansion and Change: 2001–2005 102
Catalyst 1: Afghanistan 102
Stakeholder Analysis 103
Key Decisions 104
Outcomes 106
Catalyst 2: Global Expansion, 2006–Present 106
Stakeholder Analysis and Proposal Formation 106
Key Junctures 107
Decision and Outcome Analysis 108
Summary of Lessons 109

CHAPTER TEN
Operational Authorities and Employment of SOF: Section 1208 111
Overview 111
Catalyst 112
Proposal Formation 113
Stakeholder Analysis and Key Junctures 114

Decision and Outcome Analysis 115
   How Section 1208 Has Grown 117
Addressing Congressional Issues 119
   Small Size, Low Cost 120
   Interagency Support and Coordination 121
Summary of Lessons 122

CHAPTER ELEVEN
Operational Authorities and Employment:
   The Global SOF Network Initiative 125
Overview 125
The Global SOF Network Framework 126
   Catalyst and Proposal Formation 126
   Decision and Outcome Analysis 129
   Stakeholder Analysis and Key Junctures 130
   Initiative 1: Theater Special Operations Command Empowerment 136
   Initiative 2: Regional SOF Coordination Centers 144
   Initiative 3: SOCOM National Capital Region 149
   Initiative 4: SOF Security Force Assistance Authority 153
Summary of Lessons 157

CHAPTER TWELVE
Operational Authorities and Employment:
   Irregular Warfare Directive 161
Overview 161
Catalyst 161
Proposal Formation 162
Stakeholder Analysis 163
Key Junctures 165
Decision and Outcome Analysis 167
Summary of Lessons 169

CHAPTER THIRTEEN
Operational Authorities and Employment:
   SOF and Plan Colombia 171
Overview 171

Catalyst.. 172
Proposal Formation.. 173
Stakeholder Analysis... 174
Key Junctures... 176
Decision and Outcome Analysis 181
Summary of Lessons... 182

CHAPTER FOURTEEN
Operational Authorities and Employment:
**   SOF Support to Syrian Fighters**.. 185
Overview... 185
Catalyst.. 186
Key Junctures.. 186
Proposal Formation and Stakeholder Analysis 193
Decision and Outcome Analysis 197
    "Some Options Have a Time Stamp on Them" 198
    Comprehensive Assessment Lacking 199
    Lack of Adequate Plan and Training Concept 201
    Negative Views of Unconventional Warfare............... 202
Summary of Lessons.. 204

CHAPTER FIFTEEN
Findings and Recommendations... 207
Findings: Synthesis of Case Study Lessons..................... 207
    Identify Whether a Propitious Policy Window Exists..... 208
    Understand and Leverage Established Processes to
        Initiate Proposals and Pursue Objectives 209
    Conducting Rigorous Proposal Development and Validating
        Its Substance Are Key Indicators of Success........ 209
    Map Stakeholders and Incorporate Them from the Outset
        to Solicit Input and Encourage Buy-in............... 210
    Cultivate Networks and Advocates at All Levels........ 211
    Provide Subject-Matter Expertise to Congress and Develop
        Relationships with Staff Through Authorized Engagements 213
    Address Bureaucratic Rivalry with Deliberate Strategies to
        Promote Synergy and Avoid Zero-Sum Outcomes 213

    Pursue Incremental Change as Part of a Long-Range Plan.............. 214
    Opportunity and Decision Analysis Framework........................... 215
    Recommendations 216
        Recommendation 1: Develop "Plain English" Explanations of
            Special Operations Terminology and Narrative...................... 217
        Recommendation 2: Further Develop the SOF-CIA Relationship
            and Reframe the Conduct of Unconventional Warfare............. 221
        Recommendation 3: Prepare SOF to Interact at the Policy Level....... 223
        Recommendation 4: Emphasize Pathways to
            Innovation and Excellence... 225
    Conclusion 226

Bibliography 229

Tables

10.1. Changes as a Result of Section 1208 Legislation 118
15.1. Decision Analysis Tool 216

Summary

Purpose of Study

Current political and budgetary constraints will likely complicate U.S. efforts to develop and implement a fully resourced national security strategy for some years to come. In consideration of these constraints and a challenging strategic environment, U.S. Army special operations forces (SOF) may constitute an effective and cost-sensitive capability, in combination with other irregular warfare (IW) capabilities that have been maintained by the services. However, Army SOF have not always been successful in making the case for employment of some of their capabilities to the policymaking audience. Therefore, the Army asked the RAND Arroyo Center, a federally funded research and development center at the RAND Corporation, to examine how the Army and Army SOF, as part of the joint SOF, might better articulate their value proposition and better contribute to formation of Army and U.S. Department of Defense (DoD) policy.

The purpose of the project is to examine how successful change has occurred in Army and DoD policy regarding SOF to inform future development of options for policymakers and to articulate ways in which the varied Army SOF capabilities can help to meet U.S. national security objectives.

Research Approach

We based our approach on the academic literature that examines how policy windows provide opportunities for new proposals to be generated and pursued within the government decisionmaking system.[2] We constructed detailed case histories of key decisions regarding SOF, relying on primary sources, including interviews with officials at all levels and such documents as concept papers, briefings, legislative records, and internal policy memoranda. Using these cases, we then analyzed the principal factors and actors affecting the decisions and outcomes. Each case produced lessons, which were then synthesized into broader findings on recurring themes and factors that influence outcomes. These findings were processed into an opportunity- and decision-analysis framework. Finally, we analyzed SOF's ability to act on the findings to derive recommendations to improve Army SOF and Army initiative planning and execution.

We selected a variety of cases to illustrate significant decisions regarding both the development and employment of special operations capabilities since World War II. We developed a common analytic framework to apply across the cases. For each case, we documented and analyzed the policy window or the events that created an opportunity for a proposal relating to special operations. The other elements studied include the proposal or initiative formation, the proponents and opponents, the array of stakeholders and the processes employed, the key junctures in the debate, and the eventual decision or outcome.

Following construction of each case study, the following criteria were applied to assess the case and derive the most pertinent lessons. These questions were used in this stage of the analysis:

1. Was the policy window recognized and exploited appropriately?
2. Was the necessary sense of urgency created where it did not already exist?

---

[2] Two excellent examples of this literature are Michael J. Mazarr, "The Iraq War and Agenda Setting," *Foreign Policy Analysis*, Vol. 3, No. 1, January 2007, pp. 1–23; and Julia M. Macdonald, "Eisenhower's Scientists: Policy Entrepreneurs and the Test-Ban Debate 1954–1958," *Foreign Policy Analysis*, Vol. 11, No. 1, January 2015, pp. 1–21.

3. Was the proposal formulated with a full view of all relevant objectives, constraints, and restraints?
4. Were all the potential supporters enlisted and opponents or factors of opposition addressed to the degree possible?
5. Were the right forums and formal and informal mechanisms and processes employed and followed?
6. Were necessary adaptations in language, content, and approach made to adjust to emergent factors?

We further narrowed the results to focus on those actions or factors that SOF may have the greatest ability to control or influence. In addition, the lessons drawn focus on those factors that appeared to be most critical to the decision and outcome (whether positive or negative). The lessons were then synthesized across the cases to identify the most common elements. These findings were then used to develop a tool for evaluation and preparation of future initiatives, recommendations for improving Army SOF, and Army initiative planning and execution.

Organization of This Report

The report is organized as follows: 14 case studies are presented following a common structure. The first section of each identifies the policy window or catalyst that created an opportunity for a proposal to develop, reform, or employ special operations capabilities. The proposal formation and advocate are described, followed by stakeholder identification and analysis. The progress of the proposal through the formal and informal bureaucratic processes is traced via the use of "key juncture" identification. Finally, the principal factors leading to the decision and outcome of the proposal are identified, and lessons of the case study extracted.

The final chapter synthesizes the case study lessons into broader findings and develops an opportunity- and decision-analysis framework. The current ability of SOF to act on the findings is then assessed to derive recommendations for specific changes in doctrine, organization, training, materiel, leadership, personnel, and facilities (DOT-MLPF), including development of policy-level narrative, outreach initiatives, and revisions to the internal process.

Cases

Thirteen cases were selected according to criteria we established, including the decisions' significance, scale and scope, involvement of interagency stakeholders, and representation across historical periods. Together, these 13 cases constitute a robust set of decisions regarding both the institutional development of special operations capabilities and the operational employment of those capabilities. While the 13 cases do not constitute a comprehensive history, they do represent major milestones in development of SOF and their post-9/11 use in counterterrorism (CT) and long-duration operations. The cases are arranged chronologically, so the study may be read as a history of significant decisionmaking regarding SOF.

The cases include

1. the development and expansion of special operations capabilities (Cases 1, 3, 6, 7, and 8)
2. SOF's relationship with the Central Intelligence Agency (CIA) and its common antecedent, the Office of Strategic Services (OSS) (Cases 2 and 5)
3. SOF's expansion of operational authorities and decisions regarding their employment in sustained operations (Cases 9–13)
4. expansion and contraction of the U.S. Army Special Forces in the Vietnam era (Case 4).

The cases, summarized briefly, include the following:

Case 1: The creation of the 6th Army Special Reconnaissance Unit/Alamo Scouts. This case is one of the earliest instances in which the Army recognized the need for units with special capabilities. While the Scouts predate the creation of Army SOF, this case illustrates the type of impetus created by war and challenges posed in wartime. The inability of existing forces to address the need created the opportunity for change. Like many of Army SOF's legacy units from World War II, the Alamo Scouts were born out of urgent necessity. However, establishing the unit was not straightforward. By leveraging measures that a commander could implement without higher approval, LTG Walter Krueger developed the Alamo Scouts Training Center to create his unit. After a year of embarrassing failures based on intelligence, he finally had an intelligence-collecting unit on which he, and the Army, could depend. While Krueger undertook development of the Scouts on his own, the absence of more senior-level resistance certainly played a part. The successes achieved demonstrated the initiative's value. The Army tacitly accepted the formation of this new capability and embraced it post facto.

Case 2: Creation of OSS. OSS was the organizational predecessor of much of the U.S. Army's special warfare capability. During World War II, it infiltrated officers into hostile territory across Europe, yet its existence was due almost exclusively to the political abilities of one man, William Donovan. Donovan was forced to contend with internal bureaucratic battles on multiple fronts and so achieved less than his grand ambitions for OSS. He nonetheless was able to outmaneuver adversaries to ensure a prominent role for special warfare in U.S. strategy.

Case 3: Creation of the U.S. Army Special Forces. The creation of U.S. Army Special Forces in 1952 provided the Army with psychological and unconventional warfare (UW) capabilities to fight behind enemy lines. Robert McClure, Russell Volckmann, and Aaron Bank successfully navigated the Army and policy processes to establish a permanent capability within the Army, rectifying the loss of skills and expertise that resulted from the post–World War II drawdown of forces and disbanding of OSS. Fighting against institutional, policy, and cultural barriers, these men, along with many other supporters, raised awareness through consistent advocacy until opportunities created by the Korean War, the contingency plans for the Soviet Union, and the deactivation of the Army Rangers highlighted the urgency of, and the opening for, establishing this new force.

Case 4: The expansion and contraction of the U.S. Army Special Forces in the Vietnam era. The case of U.S. Army Special Forces' expansion under President John F. Kennedy and their subsequent contraction after the Vietnam War provides examples of policy success and failure. The U.S. Army Special Forces embraced the policy window afforded by Kennedy's interest in UW but did not use the window to increase their support or improve their relationship with the conventional Army. After Kennedy's assassination, the U.S. Army Special Forces were left vulnerable to the policy agenda of the conventional military. While this arguably played a part in their contraction, the effect of changes in North Vietnamese tactics during the war and the overall drawdown of the military at the war's end represented major factors beyond the U.S. Army Special Forces' policy control.

Case 5: CIA-SOF cooperation in Southeast Asia, 1961–1975. Special warfare reached its Cold War apex in Southeast Asia, where thousands of SOF were employed in an array of efforts.[3] These efforts were foundational to U.S. Army Special Forces, whose expansions and adaptations were driven by demands within Southeast Asia. U.S. Army Special Forces also developed an extraordinarily strong relationship with the CIA in Southeast Asia, a reunion of sorts between the organizational descendants of OSS.

Case 6: Creation of U.S. Special Operations Command (USSOCOM) and the Assistant Secretary of Defense for Special Operations and Low-Intensity Conflict (ASD/SOLIC). The creation of USSOCOM and the ASD/SOLIC provides lessons regarding the role and influence of U.S. Congress and importance of informal processes to influence policy changes. By creating a unified combatant command responsible for all SOF and a civilian ASD to oversee SOF budget and policy issues, Congress was attempting to rectify what it determined was Pentagon neglect of SOLIC issues. The Senate Armed Services Committee conducted two years of intensive research on DoD organizational deficiencies, concluding that DoD

---

[3] In addition to special warfare, SOF were used in other roles, particularly special reconnaissance and intelligence collection operations. This chapter only covers special warfare operations in conjunction with the CIA.

suffered from a chain-of-command structure that discouraged interservice coordination and placed heavy planning and resourcing focus on the Soviet threat despite a rise in potential conflicts in the developing world. While these changes were set in motion by failures in Operations Desert One and Urgent Fury, the coalition built across congressional members and staff and civilian DoD officials was instrumental in achieving these fundamental reforms.

Case 7: Post-9/11 SOF expansion. Following the attacks of September 11, 2001, the U.S. SOF community expanded massively (although not instantly). From an end strength of roughly 38,000 in 2001, USSOCOM grew to roughly 63,000 in 2012.[4] While growth has tapered in subsequent years, the expansion was remarkable and unprecedented. While some expansion of SOF was no doubt inevitable given the size of the post-9/11 policy window, the form and scale of expansion was not a given. It is also striking that the expansion took place for more than a decade and thus crossed administrations and Congresses.

Case 8: Special Mission Unit (SMU) expansion. One of the major aspects of the post-9/11 SOF expansion was the increase in size, scope, and authority of SMUs. The transformation of this SOF community was the result of GEN Stanley McChrystal and his subordinates' focus on internal changes in SOF's own organizational culture and practices, including a special emphasis on the need to build partnerships. The expansion in resources and authorities required leveraging success from that transformation with senior leaders, most notably DoD Secretary Donald Rumsfeld. Finally, the successful transformation of this SOF community hinged on full interagency participation, which required giving stakeholders a reason to participate. McChrystal made an intelligence community representative one of his deputies, a level of commitment that helped cement the relationship. He also set the stage for an information-sharing relationship by opening task force files to the intelligence community.

---

[4] Jim Thomas and Chris Dougherty, *Beyond the Ramparts: The Future of U.S. Special Operations Forces*, Washington, D.C.: Center for Strategic and Budgetary Assessments, 2013, p. 31.

Case 9: Section 1208 authority. This case documents the creation of an SOF-specific authority that has been steadily expanded since its passage by Congress in 2005. Section 1208 of the Ronald A. Reagan National Defense Authorization Act for Fiscal Year 2005 created an authority to "provide support to foreign forces, irregular forces, groups, or individuals engaged in supporting or facilitating ongoing military operations by United States special operations forces to combat terrorism."[5] This authority—commonly called "Section 1208" instead of its official title, "Support of Special Operations to Combat Terrorism," has been progressively amended to permit USSOCOM to use increasing amounts of its appropriated operations funds for this purpose. Originally intended to support indigenous forces in UW, the revised language restricts the use to support of forces aiding U.S. CT operations. Congress required Chief of Mission concurrence and additional reporting, but it has been largely supportive of this post-9/11 program's performance.

Case 10: The Global SOF Network (GSN) initiative. GSN, a conceptual framework that USSOCOM advocated starting in 2011, was designed to strengthen USSOCOM's ability to respond to global contingencies and to develop a collaborative network among U.S. SOF and interagency and international partners. Led by then–USSOCOM commander ADM William McRaven, GSN comprised several initiatives that ranged in scope and ambition, some of which required DoD approval and changes to legislation and Executive-level documents. Approval and institutionalization of GSN efforts required significant DoD, state, and congressional interaction. The initiative comprised four main lines of effort: to increase Theater Special Operations Commands capability; establish Regional SOF Coordination Centers; strengthen USSOCOM's relationships among interagency partners in Washington, D.C., and beyond; and gain broad and flexible authority

---

[5] Public Law 108–375, Ronald W. Reagan National Defense Authorization Act for Fiscal Year 2005, October 28, 2004.

to conduct security force assistance more effectively.[6] Some of these endeavors succeeded, and some faced significant challenges.

Case 11: IW directive. The U.S. military's experiences in Afghanistan and Iraq after 9/11, and particularly its difficulties in grappling with insurgencies, led some U.S. officials to believe that institutional adaptations were required to enable the force to cope with the irregular aspects of warfare. ASD/SOLIC Michael Vickers led the effort to create DoD Directive 3000.07,[7] which was signed on December 1, 2008, by the Deputy Secretary of Defense. To arrive at a signable directive, Vickers and his team employed various methods to gain agreement among stakeholders and to leverage the influence of USSOCOM and senior DoD officials.

Case 12: Plan Colombia. The U.S. government engaged in a long-term effort to support the Colombian government's counternarcotics and counterinsurgency campaign against the Fuerzas Armadas Revolucionarias de Colombia, designated a foreign terrorist organization by the U.S. Department of State. As with many cases of SOF employment, this multifaceted effort involved many U.S. departments and agencies, including a very substantial role by U.S. SOF as the primary U.S. military force that provided extensive training, advice, and assistance to the Colombian military and in particular its special police and special operations units. The endeavor leveraged the consensus that existed for counternarcotics programs to provide aid to the Colombian military. Senior White House and State Department officials provided sustained support to maintain congressional funding for this effort for more than a decade, while accepting conditions that addressed public and congressional concerns about human rights abuses and level of U.S. forces in Colombia. Senior Colombian government officials also played significant roles in creating and maintaining support for the program.

---

[6] U.S. Special Operations Command, "Enabling the Global SOF Network," draft paper, March 2012a.

[7] Department of Defense Directive, "Irregular Warfare (IW)," Washington, D.C.: U.S. Department of Defense, number 3000.07, December 1, 2008.

Case 13: Support to Syrian fighters. Syria is another case in which the primary U.S. military actor has been U.S. SOF. The Syrian conflict, which began in March 2011 as an Arab Spring protest against Syrian President Bashar al-Assad's rule, bedeviled the administration of President Barack Obama as it morphed into a complex struggle involving a fractured resistance, rising jihadist groups, and a wide variety of actors supplying arms to one side or another. In late summer 2012, senior figures within the Obama administration endorsed a plan proposed by CIA Director David H. Petraeus to arm Syrian rebels. The president declined to approve the plan in fall 2012, but two years later proposed for the U.S. military to arm and train Syrian rebels to fight the Islamic State, which Congress approved. In 2015, the administration revised the program in reaction to poor results from its initial efforts. In addition, beginning in late 2014, the United States provided air support to Syrian Kurdish rebels fighting the Islamic State in northern and eastern Syria. The administration also furnished nonlethal assistance to civilian opposition groups beginning in 2012.

Findings

The synthesized lessons of the cases studies yielded the following findings of common factors that affected the decisions and outcomes of the case studied.

Identify if a propitious policy window exists. The case studies suggest the importance not only of correctly identifying a policy window that is propitious for putting forward a proposal regarding the use or development of SOF, but also of determining when it would be advisable to wait.

Understand and leverage established processes to initiate proposals and pursue objectives. Bypassing established procedures will likely antagonize superiors and other power centers. But proponents should not rely on formal process alone. The best practice appears to be to work within the system while actively cultivating allies in key nodes of the bureaucracy.

A proposal is most likely to succeed if development is rigorous and its substance is externally validated. This finding includes related elements—for example, the importance of conducting rigorous analysis internally. In some cases, the relevant audience lacked sufficient understanding of the requirements for successful special operations, and this basic knowledge deficit had to be addressed. Providing evidence of a policy gap greatly strengthens a proposal. Internally produced publications can also create the theoretical and evidentiary basis to strengthen proposals, but they need to be solidly constructed and address stakeholder concerns in accessible language. Public debate can be helpful in creating a supportive consensus for proposals.

Map stakeholders and incorporate stakeholders from the outset to solicit input and encourage buy-in. This finding encompasses a number of observations, including the need to show stakeholders how they may benefit from a proposal and how proponents should solicit and heed stakeholder input, engage in bargaining, and devise strategies for dealing with opposition. Proposals developed within staff may receive a warmer welcome than those originating outside.

Cultivate networks and advocates at all levels. Presidential support is a valuable asset, but paradoxically, it may not be sufficient. Senior military leaders' support is critical among both the services as well as the relevant operational commands. It is also important to cultivate relationships with midlevel managers and staff throughout the relevant departments, agencies, and congressional committees. Sometimes high-level advocates may be recruited explicitly to break through resistance. Such socialization is best conducted through established relationships.

Provide subject-matter expertise to Congress and develop relationships with staff through authorized engagements. Official liaison offices manage the U.S. military relationship with Congress; ASD/SOLIC is the DoD interlocutor on special operations policy matters. The offices' purviews and duties should be thoroughly understood, and a collaborative approach is usually preferable. An effort to place more serving or retired SOF personnel into congressional offices would pay enormous long-term benefits to the special operations community, creating a resident source of knowledge in a branch of government that touches virtually every aspect of special operations manning, training, equipment, employment, and funding.

Address bureaucratic rivalry with deliberate strategies to promote synergy and avoid zero-sum outcomes. For various reasons, some stakeholders are at least partly institutional rivals of SOF. While rivalry can be exacerbated by personalities or the personalization of issues, overlapping roles and missions or power dynamics (such as competition for resources) usually account for chronic tensions. Two particular tensions came to light in the case studies. First, CIA and SOF have competed and collaborated since their founding. The central lesson of the cases is that both communities have unique capabilities that are strongly synergistic for special warfare and UW in particular. The other chronic competition is between SOF and the military services, primarily because they compete for funds and, to some degree, missions.

Pursue incremental change as part of a long-range plan. Significant gains can be made at times through leveraging current authorities in creative ways. A close corollary is to accept partial gains because they do represent gains. A plan for evolutionary change can succeed with continuity of effort to build a coalition of supporters, coupled with evidence of the need for change and promised benefits.

Recommendations

This section summarizes recommendations made in Chapter Fifteen, derived from analysis of the current SOF ability to act on the findings identified. SOF leadership should consider the following initiatives.

Recommendation 1: Develop "plain English" explanations of special operations terminology and narrative. For the past decade, the special operations community has sought to refine its ability to communicate its unique requirements and capabilities in a manner that is well understood by interagency and external audiences. This endeavor is part of a more general effort to address what the community perceives to be a lack of understanding among geographic combatant commands, the interagency community, and in Congress regarding the utility and value of certain types of special operations. However, some of this effort has resulted in a veritable tsunami of new terms that may create more—rather than less—confusion, and whose relationship to other terms is unclear. Examples include *human domain* (versus *human terrain* and *human aspects* of military operations) and *gray-zone conflicts* (versus *hybrid warfare* or *IW*). Rather than coin new doctrinal terms, this study recommends using plain language for wide audiences, in particular relying on such readily understandable broad terms as *special operations, indigenous and partnered approaches*, and *precision targeting*. In addition, proposals may be best couched in terms of specific problems and specific special operations remedies, as well as reference to relevant past successful missions. The latter requires special operations leadership to promote a wider familiarization with the history of successful special operations missions among both governmental and public audiences.

Recommendation 2: Further develop the SOF-CIA relationship and reframe the conduct of UW. Interviewees described an intensive evolution toward greater familiarity and synergy between SOF and CIA than at any previous period in their history. This is not surprising from one vantage point: They both trace their lineage and missions to OSS. This synergy is particularly strong in the mission of UW. The historical case study notes that the CIA possesses unique assets and skills for phases 1–3 (preparation, initial conflict, infiltration) of UW and that SOF have primacy in terms of capabilities for planning and execution of phases 4–6 (organization, buildup, and employment). Thus, a cooperative approach readily suggests itself, which is that these forces enjoy the greatest success if they combine efforts in the conduct of UW. The historical record also suggests that most often, the President will prefer to authorize a UW mission under Title 50 authorities as a covert operation via a presidential finding. That finding may direct that the mission be carried out by DoD but, again, history suggests that the default entity is likely to remain the CIA. Presidents have daily interaction with the CIA, and the agency has refined the art of developing and maintaining relationships in Washington.

However, several additional steps might be taken to reframe how UW is presented and conducted. The study suggests that the conduct of UW may be most successful when experienced senior military officers at the O-6 level or higher are in command of the planning and operations, certainly at the point where the campaign becomes military in nature and of a scale that would severely strain the agency's capacity. The commanding officer can play this role in either entity, but the CIA would need to grant this authority to plan and execute a campaign and make the appropriate organizational adjustments.

Two additional adjustments may increase the utility of special operations for policymakers in a turbulent era without creating friction in the SOF-CIA relationship. When UW is reframed as support to resistance against an intervening or occupying power—in cases where UW is done in support of a duly constituted government—these efforts are not likely to require Title 50 authorities and may be carried out as traditional military activities.

Finally, and more generally, many special operations rely critically on the ability to conduct advance force operations—or operational preparation of the environment. The need to conduct such operations inside countries of interest to obtain information or create infrastructure is now part of the unclassified joint doctrine on special operations (Joint Publication 3-05);[8] this definition and explanation were promulgated openly in part to help educate policymakers and Congress about the vital nature of this activity. Without these early activities, it is not possible to compile full, honest, and realistic assessments of conditions, indigenous forces, and enemy formations. Additionally, without this ground truth, few viable options could be developed. The lack of authority to conduct such assessments reduces the number of sound options that can be provided to policymakers and increases the risk of any plan that is forwarded without it. The permission to conduct such assessments can be provided to SOF without a finding as a traditional military activity. Such proposed deployments will be sensitive due to their ability to interfere with bilateral relationships and other departments' and agencies' prerogatives, so special operations leaders need to prepare detailed proposals with provisions for notification and consultation.

---

[8] Joint Publication 3-05, *Special Operations*, July 16, 2014.

Recommendation 3: Prepare SOF to interact at the policy level. Perhaps the most important single focus of attention for Army SOF, considering the effects it could have for all other SOF activities, would be revisions to its personnel, leader development, and education practices to permit, motivate, and leverage SOF interagency knowledge and experience. The first step would be for special operations leadership, with support from the services' personnel divisions, to ensure that the most-talented special operations officers served two or more tours in Washington in a range of policy-relevant interagency assignments. Currently, the majority of SOF officers serve in only three locations: SOLIC, the Joint Staff special operations directorate, and the Army G-3 special operations directorate. Other opportunities should be sought in the Office of the Secretary of Defense, joint staff regional directorates, and the State Department's regional bureaus, as detailed policies and plans are discussed as the primary responsibilities in these offices. A formal program has been instituted in recent years whereby DoD and the State Department exchange personnel to serve as senior advisers, thus increasing interagency coordination. In addition, the White House national security staff is a major locus for policy deliberation and interagency coordination.

Investing in such opportunities requires a parallel commitment to use that officer's experience in subsequent positions. This sounds obvious, but both formal Army career promotion requirements and Army SOF's informal proclivity for routing their officers into a fixed path would need to be adjusted to motivate these interagency tours. Familiarity with Washington can also be an enormous boon for SOF officers in competing for such senior joint staff and interagency positions as in the joint staff directorates or as associate director for military affairs at the CIA.

Finally, the practice of sending officers out to assignments in non-SOF commands, in the interagency community, and internationally yields the same powerful benefits. Reducing staffing at SOF formations to enable more officers to serve in these positions would pay enormous long-term benefits in strategic-level knowledge for SOF, visibility and credibility for SOF, and the consequent understanding among wider audiences of what special operations can contribute to national security objectives.

Recommendation 4: Emphasize pathways to innovation and excellence. The special operations community, given its small size, has understandably focused on operations over institutional knowledge and processes during its first decades. The increasing use of SOF around the globe would put pressure even on a historically large force. However, that same expanding use creates a long-term requirement for the community to build the processes that will continue to develop its unique areas of military expertise. The nature of special operations, with a premium on flexibility of formations and agility in approaches, necessitates not only innovative material solutions but innovative thought leadership.

This decision would entail significant prioritization of and investment in knowledge-management systems, theoretical and applied research, and enhanced educational opportunities for operators by USSOC, Army SOF, and the services' personnel divisions. There are some excellent programs, including the master's degree program at the Naval Postgraduate School and the School of Advanced Military Studies' doctoral program in Fort Leavenworth, Kansas. In addition, senior service colleges and fellowships provide needed time for in-depth research and improved communications skills. Some programs such as those at Fort Leavenworth may push promising officers out of the current promotion track, in another sign of the undue rigidity of the personnel model.

Increasingly, senior leaders at the Pentagon and services are recognizing that knowledge is the coin of the future force, and SOF should associate themselves prominently in these initiatives. SOF should also lead in pressing for personnel reforms that prioritize the acquisition of this knowledge. In addition, SOF should be in the forefront of promoting a climate of experimentation and innovation grounded in sound practices. Openness to new ideas and an emphasis on crossfertilization are highly compatible with the core values of the community and can be productively highlighted to lead the force away from isolating practices and into a future of greater engagement.

Acknowledgments

We would first like to acknowledge the support of U.S. Army Special Operations Command (USASOC) G-5 and particularly Matt Erlacher, Ernesto Sirvas, and MAJ Kyle Packard, who provided excellent guidance and interface with the command throughout the project. The commanding general, LTG Ken Tovo, encouraged us to explore an array of currently pressing issues in the course of this study. We also acknowledge the USASOC G-9, particularly Robert Warburg, Larry Deel, and Damon Cussen, who supported this and other work to increase the utility of special operations forces (SOF) in the service of U.S. national security objectives at the strategic and operational levels. The USASOC headquarters staff provided us with assistance in obtaining data and access to serving and retired officers.

More than 50 serving and retired senior U.S. military and civilian officials agreed to provide lengthy interviews, at times multiple interviews, and in many cases assisted us with procuring documents or other primary-source data that enabled us to compile authoritative case studies on key policy decisions and debates involving SOF. Human-subject protection protocols require us to abide by the nonattribution terms of these interviews, but we would like to collectively thank all of the senior- and middle-level officials and officers at the U.S. Defense Department, the U.S. Department of State, the Central Intelligence Agency, and the U.S. Congress for their time and valuable insights.

The production of a RAND study is always the work of many hands. The study benefited enormously from the detailed reviews, thoughtful comments, and constructive suggestions made by RAND

Arroyo Strategy, Doctrine, and Resources Program associate director Michael Mazarr; as well as our distinguished peer reviewers, RAND senior policy researcher Sina Beaghley and Joseph J. Collins of the National Defense University. Their critiques greatly improved the final product. We would also like to thank the following colleagues for their substantial contributions: Madeline Magnuson, for exhaustive research on congressional testimony, congressional marks, and legislation pertaining to special operations forces; Jim Chiesa and Donna White for their superb editing assistance, Rhonda Normandin, Betsy Kammer, Darlette Gayle, Leah Hershey, Francisco Walter, Terri Perkins, Martha Friese, Francisco Walter, and Marcy Agmon for their administrative and programmatic assistance; RAND publications' Julie Amsden, Todd Duft, and Linda Theung for expert editorial work; and finally, the RAND Arroyo Center leadership, Tim Bonds and Sally Sleeper, for their guidance and oversight of this project.

Abbreviations

AFJI	*Armed Forces Journal International*
ASD ISA	Assistant Secretary of Defense for International Security Affairs
ASD/SOLIC	Assistant Secretary of Defense for Special Operations/Low-Intensity Conflict
ASTC	Alamo Scouts Training Center
CENTCOM	U.S. Central Command
CIA	Central Intelligence Agency
CIDG	Civilian Irregular Defense Group
COCOM	combatant command
CONOPS	concept of operations
CP	counterproliferation
C-T	Counter-Terror (team)
CT	counterterrorism
CTCC	Counterterrorism Coordinating Council
CW	conventional warfare
DCI	Director of Central Intelligence
DoD	U.S. Department of Defense
DOTMLPF	doctrine, organization, training, materiel, leadership and education, personnel, and facilities
DOTMLPF-P	DOTMLPF and policy

DSG	Defense Strategic Guidance
FAR	Forces Armées du Royaume
FARC	Fuerzas Armadas Revolucionarias de Colombia (Revolutionary Armed Forces of Colombia—People's Army)
FBI	Federal Bureau of Investigation
FY	fiscal year
GCC	Geographic Combatant Command
GCP-SO	Global Campaign Plan for Special Operations
GOFO	general and flag officer
GSCF	Global Security Contingency Fund
GSN	Global SOF Network
GWOT	Global War on Terror
HASC	House Armed Services Committee
IAPP	Interagency Partnership Program
ICD	Initial Capabilities Document
INCLE	International Narcotics Control and Law Enforcement
ISA	International Security Affairs
ISR	intelligence, surveillance, and reconnaissance
IW	irregular warfare
JCIDS	Joint Capabilities and Integration Development System
JCS	Joint Chiefs of Staff
JIATF	Joint Interagency Task Force
JROC	Joint Requirements Oversight Council
JSOC	Joint Special Operations Command
LP	legislative proposal
MACV	Military Assistance Command, Vietnam
MARSOC	Marine Special Operations Command

MFP	Major Force Program
MOS	Military Operations Center
NATO	North Atlantic Treaty Organization
NCR	National Capital Region
NDAA	National Defense Authorization Act
NSAM	National Security Action Memorandum
NSC	National Security Council
NSHQ	NATO SOF Headquarters
OCPW	Office of the Chief of Psychological Warfare
ODA	Operational Detachment Alpha
OMB	Office of Management and Budget
OPT	operational planning team
OSD	Office of the Secretary of Defense
OSS	Office of Strategic Services
P&O	plans and operations
PEO	Program Evaluation Office
PIFWC	Persons Indicted for War Crimes
PRU	Provincial Reconnaissance Unit
psywar	psychological warfare
QDR	Quadrennial Defense Review
REDCOM	U.S. Readiness Command
ROC	rehearsal of concept
RSCC	Regional SOF Coordination Center
SACSA	Special Assistant for Counterinsurgency and Special Activities
SASC	Senate Armed Services Committee
SFA	Security Force Assistance
SFOD-D	Special Forces Operational Detachment—Delta

SFOR	stabilization force
SMU	Special Mission Unit
SOCCENT	Special Operations Command Central
SOCSOUTH	Special Operations Command South
SOF	special operations forces
SOG	Special Operations Group
SOLIC	Special Operations/Low-Intensity Conflict
SOPAG	Special Operations Policy Advisory Group
TSOC	Theater Special Operations Command
UCP	Unified Command Plan
UN	United Nations
USAID	U.S. Agency for International Development
USASOC	U.S. Army Special Operations Command
US BICES/IIP	U.S. Battlefield Information Collection and Exploitation Systems/International Intelligence Programs
USPACOM	U.S. Pacific Command
USSOCOM	U.S. Special Operations Command
USSOUTHCOM	U.S. Southern Command
UW	unconventional warfare
WMD	weapon of mass destruction
YPG	Yekîneyên Parastina Gel

CHAPTER ONE
Introduction

Purpose of Study

The purpose of the study is to examine how successful change has previously occurred in U.S. Army and U.S. Department of Defense (DoD) policy regarding special operations forces (SOF) to inform future development of options for policymakers and to articulate ways in which the varied Army SOF capabilities can help to meet U.S. national security objectives. The analysis of these past decisions aims to enable the Army SOF to better understand the policy process; assist them in formation of appropriate, sound courses of action; and inform their engagement with other members of the U.S. government interagency community in a constructive manner. More generally, this study may inform future planning and execution by the Army SOF, the U.S. Army, and the joint special operations community.

To accomplish these objectives, we studied the history of key decisions on Army SOF development and employment, analyzed the principal factors in decisions and outcomes, developed an opportunity recognition framework, and derived recommendations to improve Army SOF and Army initiative planning and execution. The in-depth historical and contemporaneous case studies document a range of formal and informal governmental processes by which special operations capabilities were articulated, proposals were advanced, and decisions reached concerning the formation, development, and employment of special operations at critical junctures.

Background

Current political and budgetary constraints will likely complicate U.S. efforts to develop and implement a fully resourced national security strategy for some years to come. In consideration of these constraints and a challenging strategic environment, Army SOF may constitute an effective and cost-sensitive capability, in combination with other irregular warfare (IW) capabilities that have been maintained by the Army. The defense and foreign policy paradigm has already shifted and may shift further in the direction of recent defense strategy guidance to emphasize early intervention planning and synchronized campaigns that employ special operations and IW capabilities at low but persistent and flexible levels over long periods. This approach stands in contrast to reliance on crisis planning and large-scale force deployment.

These trends and opportunities notwithstanding, Army SOF have not always been successful in making the case for employment of their varied capabilities to the policymaking audience. Many capabilities beyond those used in counterterrorism (CT), particularly those used to support indigenous partners in places as varied as Colombia, the Philippines, and Europe, remain less well known to policymakers.

Research Approach

A large body of academic research analyzes government decisionmaking through a variety of lenses. Among them are studies that look at the role that military services have played in the decisionmaking process regarding the development and employment of military capabilities. This study draws on the literature of policy windows and stakeholder analysis to inform its approach.[1] This report contributes to that literature with a particular focus on how significant decisions have been reached concerning the development or use of U.S. SOF.

---

[1] Two excellent examples of this literature are Michael J. Mazarr, "The Iraq War and Agenda Setting," *Foreign Policy Analysis*, Vol. 3, No. 1, January 2007; and Julia M. Macdonald, "Eisenhower's Scientists: Policy Entrepreneurs and the Test-Ban Debate 1954–1958," *Foreign Policy Analysis*, Vol. 11, No. 1, January 2015, pp. 1–21.

The research team employed a case-study method to document and analyze past decisions regarding either the development or use of special operations capabilities. Examining past decisions provides an empirical basis for formulating recommendations for how the Army and Army SOF, as part of the joint SOF, can better contribute to formation of Army and DoD policy. The record of past decisions identifies leading indicators of windows of opportunity that demonstrate the utility of special operations and IW options and the factors that influenced the subsequent development, debate, and decisions regarding use of these capabilities.

Accordingly, this report examines the history of major U.S. decisions related to the development or employment of SOF. Each case study identifies the policy window or catalyst that gave rise to the initiative, the formation of proposals, the stakeholder interactions, and the eventual decisions or outcomes.

We constructed detailed case histories of 14 key decisions involving special operations capabilities, relying on primary sources, including interviews with officials at all levels and such documents as concept papers, briefings, legislative records, and internal policy memoranda. The interviewees included proponents and opponents of a given initiative as well as civilian officials from the Executive and Legislative Branches and military officials who participated in the proposal formation and decisionmaking process. In keeping with the requirements of human-subjects protection, the interviews were conducted on a nonattribution basis. One case study is included in a classified annex.

Case Selection Criteria

As an initial step in selecting the cases, we surveyed major decisive points in the history of Army and joint SOF that represented significant Army or U.S. government decisions that concerned either the development or the employment of special operations capabilities. We established the following criteria to select which decision points to study:

1. The decision concerned an issue of significant importance to SOF's development or employment.

2. The decision substantially involved U.S. government actors outside the special operations community, including the Pentagon, the White House, U.S. Congress, a military service, or another department or agency.
3. The cases would be selected from a range of historical periods.
4. The issues involved sufficient scale and duration to require the building and sustaining of a policy consensus (as opposed to shorter-term or more-routine missions debated and approved within the military chain of command or regular budget and program deliberations).

The 13 cases fulfill these criteria and together constitute a robust collection of significant examples of the institutional development of special operations capabilities and operational employment of those capabilities. While the cases do not constitute a comprehensive history, they do represent major milestones in development of SOF and their post-9/11 use in CT and long-duration operations. The cases are arranged chronologically so the study may be read as a history of significant decisionmaking regarding SOF.

The cases include

1. the development and expansion of special operations capabilities (Cases 1, 3, 6, 7, and 8)
2. SOF's relationship with the Central Intelligence Agency (CIA) and its common antecedent, the Office of Strategic Services (OSS) (Cases 2 and 5)
3. SOF's expansion of operational authorities and decisions regarding their employment in sustained operations (Cases 9–13)
4. expansion and contraction of the U.S. Army Special Forces in the Vietnam era (Case 4).

The cases on development of special operations capabilities include one from the World War II era, when the Army recognized the need to develop units with distinct capabilities. In this case, the catalyst was the pressure of World War II, and the deficit of reconnaissance forces in the Pacific theater. An enterprising Army commander used the authorities he possessed for training forces to develop the special capabilities and thereby a specialized unit, the 6th Army Special Reconnaissance Unit. The formation of the U.S. Army Special Forces occurred in the postwar period, catalyzed by concerns over possible Soviet encroachment and spurred by the actions of several Army and special operations leaders and presidential interest. The first historic period of the Army SOF expansion occurred in the Vietnam War, followed by an abrupt contraction as the war wound down and the U.S. military shied away from counterinsurgency. The failures and missteps in operations to rescue American hostages in Iran and Grenada catalyzed the formation of the joint U.S. Special Operations Command (USSOCOM), spurred by commission inquiry and congressional legislative action. The second historic period of expansion of SOF occurred in the period of the 9/11 attacks, spurred in part by DoD officials and studies recognizing the need for expanded capabilities.

The cases concerning the SOF-CIA relations include the World War II development of OSS, catalyzed by wartime needs and spurred by presidential interest. The SOF-CIA relationship developed during the Vietnam War, catalyzed by the enemy insurgency and spurred by the desire to combine U.S. capabilities for expanded covert action.

The cases focused on operational employment of SOF and the authorities that enable those operations, including the post-9/11 increase in CT capabilities and authorities. Section 1208 legislative authorities were catalyzed by operational deficits in Afghanistan and enabled by interagency and congressional support for SOF use of partnered forces. The Global SOF Network (GSN) initiatives were designed to increase the operational effectiveness of U.S. SOF in a variety of ways, catalyzed by expanding use of SOF and partially supported by DoD and Congress. Two cases focus on the policy and legislative decisions regarding long-term SOF missions in Colombia and Syria, catalyzed by security crises that affected U.S. interests and spurred by the U.S. policy and congressional desire to shore up friendly forces through SOF.

Analytic Framework

We developed a common analytic framework to apply across the cases. It is designed to yield factually grounded observations and is not intended to be employed as a tool to engage in bureaucratic gamesmanship, but rather to enable the special operations community to develop understanding, trust, and credibility as effective interagency partners. In each case, we documented and analyzed the event or other catalyst that created an opportunity—sometimes referred to as a *policy window*—for a proposal relating to special operations. The other elements studied included the proposal or initiative formation, the relevant stakeholders (including proponents and opponents), the formal processes and information measures employed, the key junctures in the debate, and the eventual decision or outcome. The analysis followed this basic framework:

1. Catalyst: How did the issue come to the attention of policymakers? What were the circumstances that created the policy window?
2. Proposal formation: What was the proposed course of action, who advocated it, and what initial actions did they take?
3. Stakeholder analysis: Who were the stakeholders and key interlocutors, and what were their positions, vantage points, and equities in the issue?
4. Key junctures: What were the key junctures and inflections points as the proposal wound its way through the process? Who opposed and aided, and why?
5. Decision and outcome analysis: What was the outcome, and what were the key factors influencing the outcome (i.e., the policy decision)?

A general caveat is to stipulate that our assessment of key factors responsible for a given outcome is a judgment based on the documents consulted and the participants interviewed. While a wide evidentiary base was developed to the degree the study parameters permitted, the judgment of which factors were considered most consequential may be debated or disproven through further research.

Method of Assessing Outcomes and Deriving Lessons

Following construction of each case study, the following criteria were applied to assess the case and derive the most pertinent lessons. The questions used in this stage of the analysis were the following:

1. Was the policy window recognized and exploited appropriately?
2. Was the necessary sense of urgency created where it did not already exist?
3. Was the proposal formulated with a full view of all relevant objectives, constraints, and restraints?
4. Were all the potential supporters enlisted, and opponents or factors of opposition addressed to the degree possible?
5. Were the right forums and formal and informal mechanisms/processes employed/followed?
6. Were the necessary adaptations in language, content, and approach made to adjust to emergent factors?

Each case study yielded numerous lessons, which were further narrowed to focus on those points of most value to the special operations community. Two questions were posed to this end: What actions or factors did SOF have the greatest ability to control or influence? Which factors appeared to contribute most directly to the decision and outcome (whether positive or negative)?

Each case study concludes with the lessons derived from that case. While each case study asked the same basic questions to elucidate the policy dynamics, because of the particular nature of each case, some issues appeared to be more pertinent than others. Thus, each case contains some variation in its organization, length, and lessons derived because of the substance of the issues involved and the order in which events occurred. Finally, while the cases did not produce uniform lessons, many did overlap or cluster around several more general points.

These individual case lessons were synthesized into broader findings for two purposes. First, we developed an opportunity- and decision-analysis framework that drew the broadest lessons across the cases to provide a tool for commanders and planners to use in asking key questions to assess future policy windows and development of proposals. We also analyzed the current forces' ability to act on the synthesized findings to derive a set of recommendations for Army SOF and Army future initiative planning and execution to include institutional measures to develop Army SOF knowledge of the policy process.

Organization of This Report

We present 13 case studies following a common structure; the 14th case is included in a separate annex. The first section of each case identifies the policy window or catalyst that created an opportunity for a proposal to develop, reform, or employ special operations capabilities. The proposal formation is described, followed by stakeholder identification and analysis. The progress of the proposal—through the formal and informal bureaucratic processes—is traced via the use of "key juncture" identification. Finally, the principal factors leading to the decision on and outcome of the proposal are identified, and lessons of the case study extracted.

The final chapter synthesizes the case-study lessons into overarching findings and develops an opportunity- and decision-analysis framework. The findings are then analyzed to derive recommendations for specific changes in doctrine, organization, training, materiel, leadership, personnel, or facilities (DOTMLPF) that would improve development of narrative, proposal formation, and interagency engagement.

CHAPTER TWO
Special Operations Capabilities: Creation of 6th Army Special Reconnaissance Unit

Overview

The creation of the 6th Army Special Reconnaissance Unit, also known as the Alamo Scouts, is one of the earliest instances in which the Army recognized the need for units with special capabilities. While the Alamo Scouts predate the creation of Army SOF, this case illustrates the type of impetus created by war and challenges posed in wartime. The inability of existing forces to address the need for battlefield intelligence created the specific opportunity for change. Like other Army SOF legacy units from World War II, the Alamo Scouts were born out of urgent necessity. However, establishing the unit was not straightforward. By leveraging measures that a commander could implement without higher approval, LTG Walter Krueger created a training center, Alamo Scouts Training Center (ASTC) that became the means to creating a unit. Krueger was the lone advocate in this initiative; he recognized the need for a capability and acted. The absence of senior-level resistance certainly played a part, as the Army tacitly accepted the formation of this new capability and embraced it post facto.

Catalyst

The urgent need for reliable intelligence and the inability of existing units to provide it in the Pacific theater provided the catalyst for the creation of the Alamo Scouts during World War II. After the United

States had suffered a year of embarrassing operational failures because of inaccurate intelligence and interservice rivalry, Krueger developed the ASTC to create an intelligence unit of his own on which he could depend for future operations. Although he did not have the authority to create the unit outright, he leveraged his authority as a unit commander to create new training centers that achieved his ultimate purpose.

Stakeholder Analysis

Krueger was not the obvious choice to command 6th U.S. Army in the South Pacific. At practically 62 years old, even he thought he would be considered "too old for active overseas service."[1] Originally joining the Army to fight in the Spanish-American War in 1898, Krueger had 45 years of experience at the time of his appointment. His posts and training included areas that would later benefit his command of the 6th U.S. Army, such as time spent mapping the central plains of Luzon in the Philippines and teaching at the Naval War College in Rhode Island, where he learned about amphibious warfare.[2] When the United States began preparing for war in 1941, the Army conducted the Louisiana Maneuvers, designed to "identify the strengths and weaknesses of U.S. Army leaders and to assess the equipment, training, and battle-readiness of their men."[3] Through these, Krueger established himself as a brilliant tactician with a no-nonsense approach to training.

The other notable stakeholder during this time was GEN Douglas MacArthur, commander of U.S. Army Forces in the Far East. MacArthur did not have a fruitful relationship with the Joint Chiefs of Staff (JCS) in Washington, D.C., particularly with ADM Ernest J. King, Chief of Naval Operations. The mutual dislike and distrust between MacArthur and the Joint Chiefs contributed to MacArthur's

---

[1] Lance Q. Zedric, *Silent Warriors of World War II: The Alamo Scouts Behind Japanese Lines*, Ventura, Calif.: Pathfinder Publishing of California, 1995, p. 33.

[2] "Krueger of the Sixth," *Newsweek*, February 4, 1946, pp. 58–61.

[3] Zedric, 1995, p. 37.

resistance to allowing OSS into the Pacific theater, convinced as he was of that office's ties to the Pentagon.[4] This also allowed MacArthur to remain in control of the intelligence network he himself had established.[5] The various commands within this network (including the Allied Geographical Section, the Allied Intelligence Bureau, the Allied Translator and Interpreter Section, and the Australian Coastwatchers) experienced acute rivalry, especially when the rival command was from a different U.S. armed service or nation (that is, an ally).[6] The competition resulted in intelligence stovepiping, at times obstructing the campaign in the region, and would go on to play a major contributing factor to Krueger's decision to create the Alamo Scouts.

Proposal Formation and Key Junctures

Establishing the Alamo Forces

On January 11, 1943, MacArthur sent a cable to Krueger, requesting his and the 3rd Army's transfer to the South West Pacific Area to "act as an independent echelon in command of all American combat units."[7] The Army denied MacArthur's request for the 3rd Army and instead provided a 6th Army headquarters that operated at approximately half strength.[8] Later that month, MacArthur established the 6th Army at Camp Colombia in Australia. Because MacArthur wanted to ensure that Americans controlled the force, not General Sir Thomas A. Blamey, the Australian commander of all Allied Land Forces, MacArthur ordered the unit to operate under the code name "Alamo Force."[9] The name was attributed to Krueger's ties to San Antonio,

---

[4] Larry Alexander, *Shadows in the Jungle: The Alamo Scouts Behind Japanese Lines in World War II*, New York: NAL Caliber, 2010, p. 40.

[5] Zedric, 1995, p. 38.

[6] Zedric, 1995, pp. 38–39; and Alexander, 2010, p. 41.

[7] Zedric, 1995, p. 33.

[8] Walter Krueger, *From Down Under to Nippon: The Story of Sixth Army in World War II*, Washington, D.C.: Combat Forces Press, 1953, p. 3.

[9] Zedric, 1995, p. 33.

Texas, and the mission there. MacArthur's reluctance to allow Blarney to control the new force had more to do with poor experiences from World War I in coordinating and politicking in an international command than any specific issue with the Australians or Blamey.[10]

"To Heck with This. I'll Form My Own Intelligence Unit!"

In the Pacific theater, intelligence posed a consistent challenge to mission success. During the second half of 1943, two key events finally convinced Krueger that he needed his own intelligence-collecting unit on which he could depend. On August 15, 1943, tens of thousands of American and Canadian troops landed on the island of Kiska in an attempt to retake it from the Japanese. However, the Japanese had already left the island weeks earlier, resulting in a confused invasion that led to the deaths of Allied forces from friendly fire and accidents.[11] The bungled invasion conveyed to Krueger a somber lesson on the importance of intelligence.

The second event occurred in fall 1943, when Allied forces planned to take New Britain, code named Operation Dexterity, which Krueger would lead. However, limitations to intelligence capabilities left gaps in estimates of enemy forces and in hydrographics, gaps that were critical for the Army and U.S. Navy, respectively.[12] To resolve both issues, ADM Daniel Barbey and Krueger agreed to send the 7th Amphibious Force, a newly created Army-Navy joint unit (although primarily under the control of the Navy) nicknamed "Amphibious Scouts."[13] Since the Scouts could collect information that both services needed, they agreed to share the intelligence afterward. Krueger briefed 1LT Milton Beckworth, one of the Army members of the unit, on the specific information he needed for Operation Dexterity. The Scouts scheduled the mission to last from October 6 to 16, but muddled communication with the boat captain slated to pick them up resulted in the Amphibious

---

[10] Interview with author and historian, Arlington, Va., March 30, 2016.

[11] Zedric, 1995, p. 41; and "Battle of the Aleutian Islands," History.com, 2009.

[12] Zedric, 1995, p. 39.

[13] Zedric, 1995, p. 39; Alexander, 2010, p. 41; and interview with author and historian, Arlington, Va., March 30, 2016.

Scouts' remaining on the island an additional 11 days, forcing them to fend off starvation and capture by the enemy.[14]

Subsequent events only made matters worse. Once Beckworth was picked up, the Navy did not allow him to return to Krueger to brief him on the intelligence he collected. Instead, the Navy took him to debrief Navy intelligence on New Guinea first. Then, the Navy put him on a boat, giving the captain instructions not to allow Beckworth to return to Australia, where 6th Army headquarters was. While Beckworth remained aboard the Navy ship, Krueger set his staff to begin drafting plans for the organization of a new, Army-only Scouts unit, fatigued by the disappointments of working with others' intelligence units.[15]

After four days aboard the ship, Beckworth dove overboard and made his way back to Krueger to debrief him. The entire episode disgusted and enraged Krueger, exclaiming to Beckworth: "to heck with this. I'll form my own intelligence unit!"[16] Following through on the work he began while Beckworth was captive to the Navy, on November 7, 1943, Krueger's Deputy Chief of Staff, COL George H. Decker, sent a letter to the Assistant Chief of Staff of G-2. Decker informed the Navy that, because of the failures of the past two Amphibious Scouts' missions and subsequent unwillingness to share intelligence they gathered with the Army, Krueger decided to withdraw all Army personnel from the Naval Amphibious Scout Training Center and from the "joint" unit.[17]

---

[14] Zedric, 1995, p. 40; and Alexander, 2010, p. 42.

[15] W. W. Culp, "A Recommended Plan for the Program for Training of Scouts," memorandum to Gen. Krueger, October 30, 1943; J. F. Polk, "A Plan for the Organization and Training of the Scouts," memorandum to Gen. Krueger, October 31, 1943; and Patrick C/S, "Planning for the Alamo Scout Training Center," memorandum to Gen. Krueger, November 1, 1943.

[16] Zedric, 1995, p. 41; and Alexander, 2010, pp. 42–43.

[17] Memorandum to Assistant Chief of Staff, G-2, G.H.Q., S.W.P.A., APO 500, "Naval Amphibious Scout Training Center," from Headquarters Alamo Forces, Office of the Chief of Staff, Col. G. H. Decker, Deputy Chief of Staff, November 7, 1943.

Decision and Outcome Analysis

To prevent further mismanagement à la Kiska or Operation Dexterity, Krueger wanted to maintain sole control over this new unit.[18] Krueger understood that, as an Army commander, he had full authority to conduct independent training as he saw fit even if he could not form a new unit outright, so he considered the possibility of creating a Scouts training center to create his intelligence unit.[19] He sent letters to the commanders of other units, seeking out how they initiated and conducted training, and tasked his G-2 to write up an order to establish a training facility. The most overt opposition came not from policymakers but from Krueger's own divisions, which were forced to give up some of their best men to the new training center.[20] On November 28, 1943, he established the ASTC to "train selected volunteers in reconnaissance and raider work."[21] By creating the ASTC, Krueger had his intelligence reconnaissance unit. The consistent success the Scouts experienced in the Pacific demonstrated validation for their creation or at least enough positive attention to stem any major objections.

From their creation in 1944 until the war's end in the Pacific in 1945, the Alamo Scouts conducted more than 100 successful missions, liberated two prisoner of war camps, killed more than 500 Japanese soldiers, captured approximately 60, and performed all of these feats without a single member being killed or captured. However, the greatest contributions the Scouts provided was in the intelligence they provided to the larger Allied units. Their efforts assisted with the victories on Los Negros, Biak, and more.[22]

---

[18] Krueger, 1953, p. 29.

[19] Zedric, 1995, p. 42.

[20] Interview with author and historian, Arlington, Va., March 30, 2016.

[21] Zedric, 1995, p. 42.

[22] Zedric, 1995, p. 251; and Alexander, 2010, p. 5.

Key Lesson

This case illustrates the ability of a commander to recognize an opportunity and use his existing authorities to create needed change. The need was urgent and obvious to those fighting the war in an environment burdened with poor intelligence and at times debilitating interservice rivalry. At least tacit support from the superior commanding officer—in this case, MacArthur—provided helpful top cover. Krueger's initiative also leveraged other experience: The concept of an intelligence reconnaissance unit did not present a new idea, as it followed the general direction of the Amphibious Scouts and so was likely to be more accepted.[23] However, Krueger did assume some risk, as he did not have the authority to address the need by directly forming such a unit. He only had the authority to affect training and the imperative to improve operations over which he commanded. He made a calculation that the results of improved intelligence would compensate for this technical overreach in wartime. Therefore, this case suggests a lesson for U.S. Army Special Operations Command (USASOC): In urgent circumstances, commanders should look for creative and unorthodox ways to use their existing authorities to address compelling needs, ideally when they can rely on at least tacit support from their superiors.

Leverage current authorities in creative ways. Instead of trying to directly pursue his ultimate goal, Krueger leveraged the areas in which he did have authority to dictate changes to establish the training center. However, he did so within an environment primed for such an opportunity, as the concept was familiar and the need was great. Pursuing such a creative path may not have proven as favorable outside of this wider context.

---

[23] Interview with author and historian, Arlington, Va., March 30, 2016.

CHAPTER THREE
Creation of the Office of Strategic Services: SOF-CIA Precursor

Overview

OSS is the organizational predecessor of much of the Army's special warfare capability. During World War II, OSS infiltrated officers into hostile territory across Europe, yet its existence was due almost exclusively to the political abilities of one man, William Donovan. Donovan was forced to contend with internal bureaucratic battles on multiple fronts and so achieved less than his grand ambitions for OSS. He nonetheless was able to outmaneuver adversaries to ensure a prominent role for special warfare in U.S. strategy.

Catalyst and Stakeholder Analysis

Donovan at War and in Politics, 1905–1940

In the decades before World War II, Donovan was uniquely positioned to create a U.S. intelligence service with special warfare capabilities. A graduate of Columbia University, Donovan became an accomplished attorney on Wall Street in the decade before World War I. When the United States entered the war, Donovan organized and led a battalion of the New York Volunteers 69th Regiment. For actions in Europe during the war, Donovan received multiple decorations, including the Medal of Honor.[1]

After the war, Donovan became politically active within the Republican party, becoming a U.S. attorney and later a senior official in the U.S. Department of Justice. In 1932, he ran for governor of New York and engaged in a public war of words with fellow New Yorker and Democratic presidential candidate Franklin D. Roosevelt. Donovan lost the race and returned to private practice on Wall Street.[2]

Yet Donovan was restless and bored by corporate law, so he traveled the world, and particularly Europe, for much of the 1930s. He closely observed fascist Italy, meeting dictator Benito Mussolini and touring the frontlines of Italy's war in Ethiopia. As the decade drew to a close, Donovan and Roosevelt began a rapprochement, as both were concerned about the growing potential for another world war. Roosevelt even considered bringing Donovan into his cabinet as Secretary of War, but ultimately Donovan became Roosevelt's unofficial envoy to the United Kingdom after the fall of France in 1940.

Proposal Formation and Key Junctures

Coordinator of Information, 1941

After a year as envoy, Donovan was ready to propose a more ambitious plan to Roosevelt. Donovan had spent much of the year engaged with British intelligence, and the British had convinced Donovan of the need for a robust U.S. intelligence effort. While the United States was not yet at war, Donovan envisioned an organization that would collect and analyze intelligence and then take covert action, principally in the sphere of propaganda, based on that intelligence.[3]

---

[1] Anthony Cave Brown, *The Last Hero: Wild Bill Donovan*, New York: Times Books, 1982; and Douglas Waller, *Wild Bill Donovan: The Spymaster Who Created the OSS and Modern American Espionage*, New York: Free Press, 2011.

[2] Brown, 1982; and Waller, 2011.

[3] Michael Warner, *The Office of Strategic Services: America's First Intelligence Agency*, Washington, D.C.: Center for the Study of Intelligence, 2000; and Waller, 2011.

Donovan's proposal in June 1941 was pushing on an open door with Roosevelt, who was enamored by skullduggery and intrigue. Donovan would later refer to Roosevelt as "a real cloak-and-dagger boy," so his proposal for the position of Coordinator of Information was well received by the President. Yet Roosevelt was practically the only person in Washington favorable to the proposal. As Donovan biographer Douglas Waller bluntly notes, "A bureaucratic firestorm erupted behind closed doors over Donovan's intelligence plan."[4]

Federal Bureau of Investigation (FBI) Director J. Edgar Hoover harbored a standing dislike for Donovan resulting from disagreements dating to Donovan's time in the Justice Department. But Hoover also opposed the plan because the FBI was already the premier U.S. civilian intelligence organization, with a massive counterintelligence operation that included overseas collection in Latin America. U.S. Army Chief of Staff GEN George Marshall was no more enthusiastic about the possibility that responsibility for military intelligence would be usurped by Donovan.[5]

However, Roosevelt was convinced both that a new intelligence coordinator was needed and that Donovan was the right man for the job. The position was initially vague and even unpaid, but it was a start for Donovan, who would report directly to the President. Donovan took to it with enthusiasm, but frequently ran afoul of other influential Washington figures. He butted heads with Nelson Rockefeller, and lost, over Latin America policy. At the same time, he recruited politically connected subordinates, including U.S. Marine Corps Capt. (and President Roosevelt's son) James Roosevelt and the Washington-savvy sister of U.S. Supreme Court Justice Felix Frankfurter.[6]

Within six months of becoming Coordinator of Information, Donovan was confronted by the intelligence shock of the Pearl Harbor attacks. He quickly began expanding the size of his organization, which numbered about 600 by the end of 1941. He also sought to

---

[4] Waller, 2011, p. 71.

[5] Waller, 2011.

[6] Waller, 2011.

expand activities from mostly intelligence collection and propaganda to more-active opposition to the Axis powers.

Decision and Outcome Analysis

Office of Strategic Services, 1942–1945

Even as Donovan's ambitions grew, he realized he could not achieve them on his own. He needed to integrate more with existing institutions, particularly if he wanted the access and resources needed for special warfare. In May 1942, he approached President Roosevelt with a request that his burgeoning organization be made a part of the military under the JCS. Roosevelt was concerned that this would spell the end of the organization, but Donovan felt he was doomed if he did not make the request. As Waller notes,

> His outfit was too vulnerable sitting out as a lonely White House agency with the military, State Department, and Justice now at his throat. Moreover, the military controlled the war and Donovan believed his spies and guerillas had little chance of operating in the combat theaters unless they did so under the control of the Joint Chiefs.[7]

Marshall, hostile to Donovan's organization, initially resisted taking it on but eventually acquiesced to the President, who personally renamed the organization OSS. For its first six months, OSS was in a sort of limbo, part of the military (Donovan was returned to service at his prior rank of colonel) but without a formal charter. Despite this, OSS contributed to the success of the first major U.S. European theater offensive, the invasion of North Africa.[8]

Following this success, Marshall finally gave Donovan a formal charter. Promulgated in December 1942, the charter noted OSS would not direct Army and Navy intelligence, but it would be coequal with

---

[7] Waller, 2011, p. 115.

[8] Warner, 2000; and Waller, 2011.

them. Further, it would have the authority to use military resources to conduct special warfare.

Yet, this success bred its own problems. As the organization continued to grow, reaching 4,500 personnel by August 1943, many felt Donovan's managerial style was no longer effective. He preferred to be at the front rather than in Washington, meaning crucial decisions that needed to be made piled up in his absence. He also believed in a loose, extemporaneous style of management, at least for this purpose. Faced with what one of his subordinates called "a Palace Revolt," Donovan made adjustments to his style (such as delegating decisionmaking in his absence) but not the substance. OSS would not become just another Washington bureaucracy.

As the war wound down in 1944, Donovan began to look ahead to establishing a permanent intelligence organization for peacetime. These plans faced some of the same bureaucratic opposition as he had faced earlier, particularly from the FBI, but also a concern about such an organization becoming "the American Gestapo." Donovan believed he could manage these concerns, but the death of President Roosevelt in 1945 derailed his plans. He was never able to establish a good relationship with the President's successor, Harry S. Truman, and OSS was disestablished in September 1945. Ultimately, the CIA and Army special warfare units rose from the ashes of OSS, but without Donovan in an official capacity.

By the end of the war, OSS had grown from one man's idea into an organization conducting intelligence collection and unconventional warfare (UW) on a nearly global scale. Its veterans proved the utility of "cloak and dagger" operations to a skeptical military and civilian establishment. While far from a perfect organization (and Donovan was a particularly poor organizer, as demonstrated by the "Palace Revolt"), OSS remains a byword for wartime innovation and flexibility.

Summary of Lessons

The OSS case demonstrates the extent to which a single policy entrepreneur can, in the right context, substantially change the course of special warfare policy. Donovan was almost uniquely qualified and was working with a president predisposed to support unconventional approaches, so the lessons from this case may have limited generalizability. Nonetheless, this case suggests two important lessons that underscore the need for policy entrepreneurs to cultivate relationships in Washington policy communities and the interagency environment.

Presidential views matter. The importance of the President in special warfare may seem obvious, but it is worth reiterating. Without Roosevelt's strong (although far from unlimited) support, Donovan would never have gotten the Coordinator of Information position, much less the creation of OSS. After Roosevelt's death, Truman's dim views of Donovan and OSS doomed the organization, although elements of OSS would return in CIA.

Presidential support is not enough; other support is also required. While Roosevelt's support was necessary, it was not sufficient for special warfare success. Donovan realized that, unless he made peace with Marshall and became a valued part of the military, his organization would never have the access and resources it needed. The demonstrated value of OSS, combined with Donovan's willingness to subordinate OSS to the Joint Chiefs, finally sold Marshall on the value of special warfare. Donovan was also careful to hire subordinates, including the President's son, who understood broader Washington politics to manage what today would be called the interagency process.

CHAPTER FOUR
Special Operations Capabilities: Creation of U.S. Army Special Forces

Overview

The creation of U.S. Army Special Forces derived from two distinct lines of effort: psychological and UW capabilities. These two lines of effort present valuable lessons for policy navigation in how they differed from and complemented each other. By establishing this unique force, Robert McClure, Russell W. Volckmann, and Aaron Bank established a permanent capability within the Army, rectifying the loss of skills and expertise that resulted from the post–World War II drawdown of forces. Fighting against institutional, policy, and cultural barriers, these men, along with many other supporters, created visibility through consistent advocacy until opportunities created by the Korean War, the contingency plans for the Soviet Union, and the deactivation of the Army Rangers created the urgency and the opening for establishing this new force.

Catalyst

The roots of the U.S. Army Special Forces can be traced to the numerous reconnaissance, intelligence, and special operations units created during World War II. These units included Darby's Rangers, the Devil's Brigade, and the Alamo Scouts. Arguably the most influential, however, was OSS, established in 1942 in conjunction with the Office of War Information (see case study in Chapter Two).[1] The drawdown following the end of World War II not only led to a loss of the units but also the capabilities they developed during the war. This is where the efforts to create the U.S. Army Special Forces began. Major advocates saw the loss of these capabilities after the war as a detriment to the United States, a loss that would play out over the beginning years of the Cold War.

The initial conceptualization of U.S. Army Special Forces did not surface with the same capabilities the command holds today. It began as two lines of effort that remained largely separate until the years immediately preceding the organization's genesis in 1952. Therefore, we describe the lineage and stakeholders of these two lines separately.

Psychological Operations

Stakeholder Analysis: Advocates

Although not credited with the title "father of the Special Forces," MG Robert McClure served as the new unit's central advocate for many years. Recognizing McClure as a rising star within the Army, GEN Dwight D. Eisenhower appointed him in 1942 to create the Information and Censorship Section of the Allied Force Headquarters during World War II.[2] This appointment would go on to shape his view and estimation of psychological warfare's (psywar's) importance in warfare. Although McClure supported both psywar and UW, his advocacy primarily lay with his background expertise in psywar. Only after becoming Chief of Psychological Warfare did he begin to truly expand his attention to include UW.

---

[1] The Office of War Information was established in June 1942 to officially "promote, in the United States and abroad, understanding of the status and progress of the war effort and of war policies, activities, and aims of the U.S. government" ("Administrative History," Records of the Office of War Information, Record Group 208, 208.1, June 13, 1942). The office is associated with propagating pro-American propaganda during World War II.

[2] Alfred H. Paddock, Jr., *U.S. Army Special Warfare: Its Origins*, revised ed., Topeka, Kan.: University of Kansas Press, 2002, p. 11.

An important aspect of McClure's advocacy within the Army was the respect he received as an authority figure on psychological operations following World War II. For example, when COL Ivan Yeaton presented the plans and operations (P&O) report *A Study of Psychological Warfare* in 1948, he felt the need to note that McClure had given his "complete concurrence" with the study's findings.[3] In a memorandum to the new Chief of Staff GEN Omar Bradley, Albert C. Wedemeyer, director of P&O, named McClure as an expert on the subject of psywar whose expertise should be consulted in the matter.[4]

McClure's ability to secure the chief's position suggests the heavy influence of Secretary of the Army Frank Pace, Jr. Shortly after becoming secretary in 1950, Pace wrote a memorandum to the Army Chief of Staff signaling his interest in psywar and the progress of the capability within the Army.[5] With a background in law, Pace joined the Army for a short duration in 1942, where he served in the Air Transport Command before returning to law.[6] Later in his career as chief of the Bureau of the Budget, he assisted with President Harry S. Truman's tightening of the defense budget.[7] His nomination for Secretary of the Army came on the heels of the National Security Council (NSC) 68 approval, which refocused U.S. national security from an all-out war with the Soviet Union to the more likely conduct of proxy wars in the Third World. Pace entered his new position agreeing that the military

---

[3] Department of the Army, Plans and Operations Division, Washington, D.C., Summary Sheet and Study to Chief of Staff, subject: A Study of Psychological Warfare, from Lt. Gen. A.C. Wedemeyer, Director of Plans and Operations, 10 February 1948, Record Group 319, P&O Division, 1946-48, 091.3-091.7, Section I, box 28, P&O 091.412 TS (15 January 1948), National Archives.

[4] Department of the Army, Plans and Operations Division, Washington D.C., Memorandum for the Chief of Staff, 18 March 1948, from Lt. Gen. A.C. Wedemeyer, Director, Plans and Operations, Record Group 319, Plans and Operations Division, 1946–48, 091.3-091.7, Section I, box 28, filed with P&O 09.412 (30 November 1948), National Archives.

[5] Paddock, 2002, p. 63.

[6] "Frank Pace Jr., Former Secretary of the Army and Executive, Dies," *New York Times*. January 10, 1988.

[7] James Bryant Gibson, "Super-Rangers: The Early Years of Army Special Forces 1944–1953," thesis, Chapel Hill, N.C.: University of North Carolina at Chapel Hill, 2008, p. 11.

could be smaller than it was during World War II but still capable of defeating the spread of communism throughout the world.

Psywar saw a number of other advocates during McClure's campaign. Eisenhower proved an early supporter for keeping psywar capabilities that the military acquired during World War II. Wedemeyer, a close friend of McClure's, served to boost McClure's ideas across many of the initial hurdles. Despite the lack of progress under Pace's predecessor, Gordon Gray, the latter was also a champion for the capability within the Army.

Stakeholder Analysis: Detractors
Other prominent stakeholders in this case did not share these sentiments. The largest was the new civilian agency, the CIA, which subsumed part of OSS. Following the war, the War Department and NSC began shifting covert responsibilities to this new agency, which enthusiastically took on these roles. McClure fought against the initial policies to create the psywar office and later the Special Forces. Clear delineations between the responsibilities for each remained murky, and the two often butted heads.

In general, the Army had a strong aversion to such "sneaky" tactics as psywar. During McClure's first psywar office staff meeting, he warned his men that others in the Army not familiar with psywar would perceive them as "long-haired, starry-eyed" individuals.[8] In particular, Secretary of the Army GEN Kenneth Royall's tenure stood as a noteworthy hurdle for the psywar campaign. In June 1948, he famously declared he did not want the Army "even to know anything about [covert operations]."[9]

Key Junctures
Interwar Years
Following the end of World War II, two developments hindered any immediate establishment of a special group for psychological operations within the Army. The first was the creation of the Central Intel-

---

[8] Paddock, 2002, p. 94.

[9] Paddock, 2002, p. 57.

ligence Group—the direct predecessor of CIA—in January 1946 and the subsequent handoff of OSS's clandestine capability to it by the War Department. This began a precedent of looking to the civilian agency as the proper wielder of clandestine activities during peacetime. NSC reinforced this notion with the passage of NSC 4/A at the end of 1947, granting the CIA responsibility for covert psychological operations.[10] The second development was the military's overall drawdown. Retaining the psywar capability within the service during peacetime was an unpopular option, and, even then, the various aspects of the capability were split among different functions in the Army.[11]

Despite the dilution of responsibilities within the Army and the CIA's assumption of the capability during peacetime, proponents of creating a psywar division received major support from Eisenhower, then–Chief of Staff of the Army. In 1947, Eisenhower indicated to the director of P&O his desire for the War Department to keep alive parts of psywar. In a memorandum he wrote in November of that year, he offered to do more work toward a psywar division and suggested that McClure lead it. However, these recommendations were not accepted.[12] While Eisenhower's advocacy did not lead to the desired changes, they assisted with keeping the ideas in the view of top leadership.

Advocacy during the interwar years, although persistent, attained few results. Bradley guardedly supported Wedemeyer's plan to incorporate psywar at the strategic level.[13] Incoming Secretary of the Army General Royall would prove a major hurdle in the policy effort. However, a continuous stream of reports and studies continued to nudge along the process in the face of opposition. These included *The Army's Role in Current Psychological Warfare* by Wallace Carrol for Under Secretary of the Army William Draper in February 1949. By conceding a civilian consultant (who would later become the next Secretary of the

---

[10] Andrew Green, "National Security Council Directive 4-A" in Jan Goldman, ed., *The Central Intelligence Agency: An Encyclopedia of Covert Ops, Intelligence Gathering, and Spies*, Vol. 1, Santa Barbara, Calif.: ABC-CLIO, 2015, p. 266.

[11] Paddock, 2002, pp. 44–45.

[12] Paddock, 2002, pp. 49–50.

[13] Paddock, 2002, pp. 55–56.

Army) to oversee a psywar office, Wedemeyer and Carrol began to win over Royall.[14]

Royall, with his stark opposition to psywar, was an aberration among Army secretaries during this time, but with Gordon Gray's succession to the position, support in the Army for a psywar division began to revive. However, his interest in the topic did not result in much progress within the Army, partially because of unresolved policy issues and his awareness of political sensitivities on the subject.[15] It was to be during Pace's term that advocacy in the leadership lent itself to the desired policy changes because of the opening of two policy windows: the hot war in Korea and the Cold War in Europe.

The Cold War: Korea and the European Theater

In the lead-up to the Korean War, Pace outlined not only his interest in psywar but also his concern for the dearth of capability despite the developments on the peninsula.[16] During this time, McClure was brought back into the fold by MG Charles L. Bolte, the G-3, as McClure was still considered the expert on psywar.[17] After a particularly scathing memorandum from Secretary Pace to Chief of Staff GEN J. Lawton Collins on the need for a permanent division, Bolte timed his recommendation to the Chief of Staff for the creation of a Psychological Warfare Division. McClure likely had a hand in the recommendation's approval, given his conferences with the Deputy Chiefs of Staff, Vice Chief of Staff, Secretary Pace, the Assistant Secretary of State for Public Affairs, and members of the Joint Staff during this time.[18] Thus, McClure gained his Office of the Chief of Psychological Warfare (OCPW).

The Korean War proved a boon in gaining support for psychological operations, but the Cold War in the European theater also receives credit in providing McClure and others with a window of opportu-

---

[14] Paddock, 2002, pp. 57–58.

[15] Paddock, 2002, pp. 60–62.

[16] Paddock, 2002, pp. 90–91.

[17] Paddock, 2002, p. 91.

[18] Paddock, 2002, p. 63.

nity to act.[19] In April 1950, NSC published NSC 68, advocating "all means short of war" to contain and counter the Soviet Union, which included political, economic, and psychological warfare.[20] Unlike in Korea, psywar efforts in the European theater remained as a contingency plan, but also forced OCPW to juggle its resources to ensure Europe was prepared in the event of Soviet expansion across the Iron Curtain. The Army also had to compete with the U.S. Air Force in both Korea and Europe as the new service argued for its own role in psywar, which McClure characterized as redundant and expensive.[21]

Looking Beyond OCPW

Despite McClure's victory at creating the new OCPW, its inclusion as a subsidiary of the G-3 posed problems with his larger goals. In his first weekly staff meeting in October 1950, McClure stated that OCPW should have its own division and such a division would have three parts: psywar, cover and deception, and UW.[22] Once established in his new role with OCPW firmly implanted in the Army structure, McClure successfully lobbied the General Council for an amendment to OCPW's mission to include special operations.[23] The expansion of OCPW responsibilities would go on to have a major effect on the role and organization of what later became the Special Forces. Throughout this, Secretary Pace continued to be a strong supporter of McClure, writing letters and memoranda that strengthened the new office within the Army and its addition of special operations responsibilities.

---

[19] Samuel A. Southworth and Stephen Tanner, *U.S. Special Forces: A Guide to America's Special Operations Units*, Cambridge, Mass.: Da Capo Press, 2002, p. 19.

[20] "NSC 68: United States Objectives and Programs for National Security: A Report to the President, Pursuant to the President's Directive of January 31, 1950," Washington, D.C., April 7, 1950.

[21] Paddock, 2002, p. 116.

[22] Paddock, 2002, p. 94.

[23] Paddock, 2002, p. 94.

Unconventional Warfare

Efforts to maintain a UW capability within the Army started at the same time as those for psywar. However, UW faltered because of the lack of senior leadership advocacy and an Army culture that opposed this type of warfare.

Stakeholder Analysis

Stakeholders for a UW capability within the Army were largely the same as those for psywar, with two important additions: Colonel Bank and Captain Volckmann. Both had UW experience from World War II that shaped their understanding of its importance in war. Bank served in OSS in Europe, while Volckmann raised a local guerrilla force in the Philippines. As a result of their experiences, both were convinced following the conclusion of the war that UW should remain within the Army's response repertoire. However, their advocacy potential remained largely untapped until McClure brought them aboard OCPW.

Similarly with psywar, the military held a cold aversion to UW. After the dissolution of OSS in 1946, most military commanders believed conventional methods were adequate for combatting future enemies.[24] Traditional military minds called guerrilla warfare "illegal and dishonorable."[25] By 1947, even the JCS expressed doubts about the feasibility of "special forces." Despite this, Chief of Staff Eisenhower again proved to be a reliable supporter of maintaining capabilities acquired during World War II. In 1948, he commissioned Volckmann to begin writing new Army doctrine for the conduct of guerrilla warfare.[26]

---

[24] Mike Guardia, *American Guerrilla: The Forgotten Heroics of Russell W. Volckmann*, Havertown, Pa.: Casemate Publishers, 2010, p. 169.

[25] Department of the Army, Office of the Chief of Psychological Warfare, Washington, D.C., Summary Sheet for Chief of Staff, subject: J. Lawton Collin's Conference at the Infantry Center, 5 April 1951, from Col. Edward Galvin, Acting Chief of Psychological Warfare (summary sheet prepared by Lt. Col. Russell W. Volckmann), 16 April 1951, Record Group 319, Army-Chief of Special Warfare, 1951–54, TS Decimal Files, Psy War 337 (16 April 1951), National Archives, p. 23.

[26] Guardia, 2010, p. 160.

Key Junctures
Interwar Years

Similarly to psywar, UW faced early interagency opposition along the same two themes outlined above. In May 1948, NSC 4/A, the document granting the CIA authority to conduct psychological operations, expanded to NSC 10/2 to include other such covert activities as paramilitary activities and political and economic warfare against the Soviets.[27] Secretary of the Army Royall's statement in June 1948 concerning his disdain for covert affairs within the Army extended to UW as well. On top of this, the JCS sent a memorandum in August to Secretary of Defense James Forrestal suggesting that U.S. UW capabilities should fall under the responsibility of the CIA during peacetime and under the national military establishment only during war. Thus, the JCS was backing away from the idea of the military's having a guerrilla warfare corps.[28] According to Bank, the military was scared of being accused of engaging in cloak-and-dagger activities and attempted to pass the buck to the CIA.[29]

In contrast to the evolution of psywar capabilities, by mid-1948, internal Army studies and documents that might have raised awareness of the need to create a UW capability ceased.[30] At Secretary Forrestal's behest, the JCS conducted *Study of Guerrilla Warfare*, published in March 1949. Although the study concluded that the JCS "should retain strategic and broad policy planning functions of guerrilla warfare" and that the Army "should be assigned primary responsibility for all other guerrilla warfare function," only the CIA really continued to develop a UW capability.[31] Despite the capability falling to the CIA in practice,

---

[27] Paddock, 2002, p. 68; and Andrew Green, "National Security Council Directive 10/2," in Jan Goldman, ed., *The Central Intelligence Agency: An Encyclopedia of Covert Ops, Intelligence Gathering, and Spies*, Vol. 1, Santa Barbara, Calif.: ABC-CLIO, 2015, pp. 267–268.

[28] Paddock, 2002, pp. 67–68.

[29] Aaron Bank, *From OSS to Green Berets*, New York: Simon and Schuster, 1987, pp. 160–161.

[30] Bank, 1987, p. 160.

[31] Bank, 1987, p. 162; and Paddock, 2002, pp. 69–70, 74.

the Army retained a coordinating relationship with the civilian agency in this regard, assisting with the training of personnel for UW.[32]

The Korean War

While psywar advocacy maintained attention in the interwar years, UW in the Army remained undeveloped. Months after the beginning of the Korean War, Volckmann completed his guerrilla warfare doctrine document originally commissioned by Eisenhower. It was the Army's first document detailing the conduct and techniques of conducting guerrilla warfare and would "set the precedent for all future counterinsurgency doctrine."[33] However, even with the visibility created by this and an article written by MAJ Robert B. Rigg (veteran of IW operations in China and Iraq) calling for the Army to devote more attention to UW, their appearance in late 1950 did not give the Army enough time to digest them, since conventional forces' participation in UW in Korea began to wane in early 1951.[34] Real progress would not occur until Volckmann and Bank joined McClure within OCPW.

Bringing UW into the OCPW

McClure brought on Volckmann in January 1951 and then Bank in March to assist with the effort to create a UW capability within the Army.[35] According to Bank, he believed an OSS structure was the best means for this capability, while Volckmann initially leaned toward a Ranger-style organization given his own experiences in the Pacific.[36] McClure agreed with Volckmann, believing that the Army might be more receptive to the UW idea if it appeared familiar.[37] However, both

---

[32] Paddock, 2002, p. 72.

[33] Guardia, 2010, p. 163.

[34] Andrew J. Birtle, *U.S. Army Counterinsurgency and Contingency Operations Doctrine 1942–1976*, Washington, D.C.: Center of Military History, U.S. Army, 2006, pp. 104–105.

[35] Bank, 1987, p. 154.

[36] Bank, 1987, pp. 165–166.

[37] Bank, 1987, p. 167.

Bank and Volckmann agreed that the European theater would be the focus of this new UW force.[38]

Two key events ultimately paved the way for the special forces concept as conceived of by Bank and Volckmann. The first began with Volckmann's attendance at Chief of Staff Collins's conference at Fort Benning as the representative from OCPW. His subsequent analysis of Collins's comments and his own recommendations laid out the structure and responsibilities of the U.S. Army Special Forces.[39] Volckmann sent his memo to Chief of Staff Collins with this request:

> the interpretation that has been placed on these statements of General Collins be confirmed or commented on in order that appropriate action may be initiated by the Assistant Chief of Staff, G-3, to initiate the directives necessary to accomplish the desire of the Chief of Staff.[40]

This spurred the need for additional studies, including "Army Responsibilities in Respect to Special (Forces) Operations," which was largely written by Volckmann and later approved by Collins. This was a "classic illustration of the manner in which one achieves visibility for a project in the Pentagon bureaucracy."[41]

During this time, the major hurdle to establishing a permanent UW force lay in the lack of openings within force capacity. An opening emerged when, in mid-1951, Far East Command deactivated its Ranger companies in Korea, and the Chief in Command, Europe, indicated he saw no use for Rangers in his theater.[42] This could provide Bank and Volckmann with the force spaces they needed. In August of that year, GEN Maxwell D. Taylor, Army G-3, held a conference to determine the future use of the Rangers. This was Bank's prime opportunity to sell the OSS-styled special forces that he wanted, and McClure pro-

---

[38] Bank, 1987, p. 166.

[39] Guardia, 2010, p. 173.

[40] "GEN J. Lawton Collins's Conference at the Infantry Center," April 5, 1951.

[41] Paddock, 2002, pp. 123–124.

[42] Bank, 1987, p. 172.

vided support, telling him, "Here's your golden opportunity. Go get it!"[43] Following Bank's briefing, Taylor announced he would deactivate the Rangers, as recommended in Bank's briefing, and requested Bank and the OCPW provide him with a current study on the concept and a Table of Organization and Equipment.[44] Bank and Volckmann now had the troop spaces they needed and Taylor's interest in their special forces concept to move forward.

Decision, Outcome Analysis, and Lessons

The creation of the U.S. Army Special Forces was a case of advocates McClure, Volckmann, and Bank, along with many others, achieving the creation of a unit that restored World War II capabilities to the Army by carefully navigating institutional, policy, and cultural barriers that existed following the end of that war. By priming stakeholders with consistent dialogue through studies and papers, they were able to place the issue at the forefront of the Army's mind until policy windows emerged for their respective lines of effort (although psywar advocates experienced greater success than UW for many years). Taken together, the two components of this case study reveals lessons for a policy success that emphasizes patience through a slow but rewarding process, including focusing on incremental steps in pursuit of the ultimate objective. This case study suggests the following lessons:

Create visibility through official publications. One of the distinct differences in the trajectory of the psywar and UW initiatives immediately after World War II was that the former garnered visibility, currency, and comprehension among key stakeholder audiences through internal studies, personal letters, and memoranda, and the latter did not. Supporters of psywar presented a constant stream of documents that helped develop its concept even during the antagonistic tenure of Secretary Royall; this, however, did not occur for UW. The lack of top leadership advocacy was part of the reason for this lack in

---

[43] Bank, 1987, pp. 171–172.

[44] Bank, 1987, p. 174.

UW's part. Following Chief of Staff Eisenhower's departure from the Army, UW did not have a strong advocate again until after McClure turned his attention and that of top leadership supporters' to the issue.

Do not force a window of opportunity. Although the two efforts did not blossom at the same opportunity, neither may have succeeded without a policy window favorable to the capability sought. For psywar, the concerns about the Soviets in Europe and the initiation of hostilities in Korea revealed just how much the Army had lost after its drawdown following World War II. The strain of contracting and then expanding rapidly within a matter of years convinced many of the need for a permanently established capability. For UW, the capability stalled on the inability to secure the force spaces needed to establish the command that Bank and Volckmann had in mind. Once the question of Ranger deactivation rose, the team jumped at the opportunity to suggest an alternative use for the spaces.

Partial gains are still gains. A phased approach to building organizations and new capabilities may be more successful in achieving the objectives. While McClure may have had UW as a component of a psywar division from the start, he did not begin pushing for this addition until the OCPW was firmly established and held senior support. Attempting to pursue all of the components he ultimately wanted may have ended less successfully or taken longer to accomplish.

CHAPTER FIVE
Special Operations Capabilities: Special Forces Expansion Under President Kennedy and Contraction Through the Vietnam War

Overview

The case of special forces expansion under President John F. Kennedy and their subsequent contraction after the Vietnam War provides examples of policy success and failure. The special forces embraced the policy window afforded by Kennedy's interest in UW but did not use the window to increase their support or improve their relationship with the conventional Army. After Kennedy's assassination, special forces were left vulnerable to the policy agenda of the conventional military. While this arguably played a part in their contraction, changes in North Vietnamese tactics during the war and the overall drawdown of the military at the war's end fell out of special forces' policy control.

Given the breadth and complexity of policies and events during the 1960s, we do not in this case attempt to cover the full history of special forces during the Vietnam War. Instead, we attempt to draw broad themes through specific examples and stakeholders that highlight lessons for USASOC today.

Catalyst

Coming off of the two World Wars and an arguably successful campaign in Korea, the conventional military had proven to be the most consequential tool in the national security arsenal, but the world was beginning to change as the conflicts the United States confronted became increasingly unconventional and embedded within populations. Kennedy entered the White House as insurgency, insurrection, and uprisings in the Third World were on the rise. To complicate these and other similar issues, Soviet Communist Party Secretary Nikita S. Khrushchev announced on January 6, 1961, that the Soviet Union would support "just wars of liberation and popular uprisings," warning that he would support proxy wars against the West in the Third World.[1] Kennedy attempted to refocus the U.S. Army to face this different kind of threat.

Proposal Formation

During the early 1960s, U.S. Army Special Forces had a number of prominent advocates. First and foremost, Kennedy, whose name now boldly emblazes the renamed U.S. Army John F. Kennedy Special Warfare Center and School, was the major advocate for the forces during his administration. His enthusiasm for UW and guerrilla warfare began even before his short tenure as president. He opposed President Dwight D. Eisenhower's defense policy, particularly the concept of "massive retaliation" that relied on the superiority of technology and nuclear weapons to deter any threat from the Soviet Union.[2] Kennedy sought more flexible options, stating that massive retaliation invited communist tactics that allowed for expansion without raising the offensive to induce nuclear war.[3] Spurred by this initial concern for the lack of flexible responses, Kennedy's preference and admiration for special forces and other unconventional units only grew as he interacted with and relied on them more and more.

---

[1] Charles M. Simpson, *Inside the Green Berets: The First Thirty Years*, Novato, Calif.: Presidio Press, 1983, p. 54.

[2] Richard H. Shultz, Jr., *The Secret War Against Hanoi: The Untold Story of Spies, Saboteurs, and Covert Warriors in North Vietnam*, New York: Perennial, 1999, pp. 4–5.

[3] John F. Kennedy, *A Compilation of Speeches During His Service in the U.S. Senate and House of Representatives*, Washington, D.C.: U.S. Government Printing Office, 1964.

Kennedy was not the only one in his administration who held such views on guerrilla warfare. He surrounded himself with similarly oriented advisers. McGeorge Bundy, Kennedy's special assistant for national security affairs, stood as a prominent advocate for covert action and later went on to chair the 303 Committee, which came to oversee all covert operations after the Bay of Pigs incident.[4] Others included Brig Gen Edward Lansdale, who presented the UW case in his January 1961 report cataloguing the issues in Vietnam and advocating an unconventional solution to the problems.

Other advocates for the techniques employed by the special forces present more of a mixed case. Some authors argue that advocates were found among the older generation of defense experts. These included Maxwell Taylor, who later chaired the Special Group (CounterInsurgency), and Walt Rostow, Bundy's successor, who wrote a book about addressing the causes of communist insurgency before they took root and ensured that the President saw the report from Lansdale.[5] Driven by his desire to downsize and streamline the giant military, Secretary of Defense Robert McNamara also played a part in Kennedy's early initiatives.[6] However, these men also held responsibility for some of the policies that contracted the special forces' operations during the Vietnam War and placed greater emphasis on the conventional military. Contending authors argue that they simply followed the orders of the President, and after Kennedy's death, had more room to return to what historically won the day: the conventional military. Another possibility is that black-and-white did/did-not support descriptors do not capture the nuances in their positions. What is clear is that advocacy for the special forces at senior levels dried up after Kennedy, leaving the forces in general neglect and vulnerable for employment in missions for which they were not designed.[7]

---

[4] Shultz, 1999, p. 6.

[5] Shultz, 1999, p. 7.

[6] John K. Singlaub with Malcolm McConnell, *Hazardous Duty: An American Soldier in the Twentieth Century*, New York: Summit Books, 1991, p. 263.

[7] Of note are the stark contradictions between Shultz's narrative of these men in *The Secret War Against Hanoi* (Shultz, 1999) and their depiction by Susan Marquis in *Unconventional*

Key Policy Initiatives

Kennedy gave a number of notable speeches and took actions that bolstered support for the special forces. Beyond his general advocacy, three key policy initiatives in particular proved pivotal for the expansion.

The first, the transfer of covert operations responsibility from the CIA to the Pentagon, sprang from frustration at the lack of progress by the civilian agency. On January 28, 1961, Kennedy held his first NSC meeting, where participants discussed Lansdale's report from Vietnam. Kennedy questioned if guerrilla operations could be conducted in North Vietnam. When CIA Director Allen Dulles responded that the agency had organized a small number of teams to work in the border regions from South Vietnam and Laos, Kennedy redirected them to expand their operations into North Vietnam.[8] Two months later, Kennedy asked for a progress report on this initiative, only to find that nothing had yet been accomplished. Frustrated, Kennedy issued National Security Action Memorandum (NSAM) 28, ordering the CIA to begin launching operations into North Vietnam.[9] That same spring, the Bay of Pigs operation failed spectacularly and was seen as yet another CIA failure by the administration and the military.[10] As a result, Kennedy penned NSAM 55, 56, and 57, which transferred responsibility for conducting UW from the CIA to the Pentagon. If the CIA could not conduct the missions Kennedy wanted, the special forces could. Other operations such as the Village Defense Program in Vietnam were moved from the agency to military control. Kennedy also created the 303 Committee, which gave the White House control over covert action, including paramilitary operations.[11] In Septem-

---

Warfare: Rebuilding U.S. Special Operations Forces (Washington, D.C.: Brookings Institution Press, 1997).

[8] Shultz, 1999, pp. 2–3; and Simpson, 1983, p. 144.

[9] *Guerilla Operations in Vietnam Territory*, National Security Action Memorandum No. 28, March 9, 1961.

[10] Shultz, 1999, p. 19.

[11] Shultz, 1999, pp. 19–22.

ber, 5th Special Forces Group was reactivated and assigned to South Vietnam.[12]

The second key policy initiative comes from a story often repeated in the history of the special forces. One month after 5th Special Forces Group deployed to Vietnam, Kennedy visited the U.S. Army Special Warfare Center in Fort Bragg, North Carolina. COL William Yarborough, commander of the center, took a calculated risk and chose to wear the green beret during the presidential visit. In 1956, GEN Paul Adams, then-commander of Fort Bragg, had banned the wearing of the green beret on base. Although he no longer commanded, Adams's ban remained in place in 1961.[13] Yarborough's risk paid off. The special forces and their headgear impressed Kennedy. After his visit, Kennedy wrote to Yarborough. The following year, the President also sent a memorandum to the Army, stating, "The Green Beret is again becoming a symbol of excellence, a badge of courage, a mark of distinction in the fight for freedom."[14]

Kennedy's third key policy initiative regarding the special forces resulted in the expansion of their capacity and the role of counterinsurgency. He directed Secretary McNamara to expand the forces, created the Special Group (Counter-Insurgency), and even directed the Army to include counterinsurgency training in curricula at all levels.[15] Kennedy had a number of other notable speeches and policy decisions that also played a role in increasing the capacity of special forces. For example, his speeches to Congress and the graduating class at the U.S. Military Academy/West Point highlighted his assessment of the importance of counterinsurgency and UW.

Kennedy's advocacy was resolute and produced tangible changes for the special forces during the early 1960s. However, Kennedy and his fellow advocates failed in their inability to change how the conventional Army perceived the units. Advocacy within the Army was

---

[12] Southworth and Tanner, 2002, p. 109.

[13] Simpson, 1983, pp. 31–32.

[14] John F. Kennedy, "Green Berets," John F. Kennedy Presidential Library and Museum web page, undated.

[15] Marquis, 1997, p. 14.

generally scant. When the Kennedy administration dispersed, support at the senior level for special forces dried up, possibly playing a role in the forces' contraction and near disappearance following the Vietnam War.

U.S. special forces did not immediately begin to contract following President Lyndon B. Johnson's entering the White House, but the loss of Kennedy's advocacy certainly allowed more space for their detractors. The forces continued to grow in the mid-1960s, expanding to seven component groups by 1966.[16] However, this did not last long. Their contraction did not occur wholly as a result of special forces policy failure but rather because of a change in the way the North Vietnamese fought and a general military drawdown as the war drew to a close. However, the poor relationship between the conventional Army and special forces contributed to the former's lack of understanding or appreciation of the role of UW. Thus, the contributions of the special forces in the Vietnam War were gradually sidelined as emphasis on the conventional Army increased.

Stakeholder Analysis

Overall, the conventional Army's opinion of the special forces during the 1960s was very low. When asked why Yarborough was not as successful in advocating for special forces after Kennedy, a number of special forces veterans from the Vietnam era whom we interviewed converged on the opinion that there was not much more he could have done, given that the majority of the Army was against him and losing his most senior advocate.[17] While Johnson did not oppose the special forces and continued expanding them after entering office, his advocacy did not match Kennedy's interest or commitment.

A few stakeholders in the Army received mixed reviews of their opinions toward special forces. First was GEN Creighton Abrams.

---

[16] Clancy, 2002, p. 205.

[17] Interview with former member of U.S. Special Forces and historian, Arlington, Va., April 6, 2016.

MG Jack Singlaub, chief of the Special Operations Group (SOG),[18] recalled Abrams as being "very anti–Special Forces."[19] Juxtaposed to this, MG Michael Healy, who served as commander of the 5th Special Forces Group in Vietnam for almost two years, asserted that "the idea that General Abrams was anti–Special Forces is just so much baloney."[20] The point was hotly contested during the trial of COL Robert Rheault and others within 5th Special Forces Group, which will be discussed in greater detail below.

Another notable detractor who received mixed reviews of his opinion toward special forces was GEN William Westmoreland, Abrams's predecessor in commanding U.S. forces in the Vietnam War. Westmoreland was another commander influenced by his conventional military experiences from World War II and the Korean War. Singlaub recalls having "fantastic relations with General Westmoreland," and yet, Westmoreland wrote in his own memoirs that he "had serious reservations about how much the covert operations accomplished" during the war.[21] While Westmoreland may not have held the same disdain for special forces as Abrams, he "didn't do anything spectacular for them."[22]

The mainstream opinion of the Army reflected these two commanders' opinions. While some nuance of opinion existed, most agreed

---

[18] SOG, led by the Military Assistance Command, Vietnam (MACV), was a covert program comprising special forces, U.S. Navy SEALs, U.S. Air Force special operators, and marines (Tom Clancy, Carl Stiner, and Tony Koltz, *Shadow Warriors: Inside the Special Forces*, New York: G. P. Putnam's Sons, 2002, p. 200; and Marquis, 1997, p. 16). The tactics of the program shifted during the war, but its primary purpose was to harass the North Vietnamese and collect intelligence. SOG operated in North and South Vietnam and against the Ho Chi Minh Trail. It was the "largest and most complex covert operation" since OSS (Shultz, 1999, p. ix).

[19] Interview with MG John K. Singlaub, 1996.

[20] Lewis Sorley, *Thunderbolt: General Creighton Abrams and the Army of His Times*, Bloomington, Ind.: Indiana University Press, 2008, p. 278.

[21] Interview with MG John K. Singlaub, 1996; William Childs Westmoreland, *A Soldier Reports*, Cambridge, Mass.: Da Capo Press, 1989, p. 106.

[22] Interview with former member of U.S. Special Forces and historian, Arlington, Va., April 6, 2016.

that UW, such as the missions of the special forces, would never be a factor determining victory or defeat in the war.

Decision and Outcome Analysis

The contraction of the special forces during the second half of the 1960s drew heavily from the overall downsizing of the U.S. military after 1968. However, additional factors associated with the conventional Army also contributed through two distinct themes: the poor relationship between the conventional Army and the special forces and the conventionalization of the Vietnam War. Neither of these themes produced discrete events that ignited policy to restrict the special forces specifically. Instead, a slow evolution of the themes exacerbated by failures and eventual withdrawal from the war produced the special forces contraction.

Military Drawdown

The policies leading to the expansion and subsequent contraction of the special forces loosely mirrored the evolution of the conventional military. Under Kennedy, defense spending as well as the number of active Army units increased.[23] Johnson promised to continue the trend, but with less defense spending. After an initial drop in Army personnel after 1962, their numbers swelled as the war in Vietnam conventionalized in the mid-1960s. At its height in 1968, the Army had 1.5 million active soldiers.[24] This time frame also boasted the largest number of special forces soldiers to date.

The contraction for the Army and thus the special forces began not long after they reached their maximum. While special forces possessed seven component groups in 1966, these reduced to three by 1968.[25] Similarly, the rest of the Army and total U.S. military forces began to

---

[23] John Ulrich, *Defense Drawdowns: Analysis with Implications*, Carlisle, Pa.: U.S. Army War College, 2012, pp. 9–10.

[24] David Coleman, "U.S. Military Personnel 1954–2014," historyinpieces.com, undated.

[25] Clancy, Stiner, and Koltz, 2002, p. 205.

decline after 1968. These bottomed out in 1974, when the Army had lost roughly 50 percent of its active personnel.[26] Special forces, in comparison, contracted by approximately 70 percent.[27] While the contraction ratio for Special Forces was slightly more severe, this should not indicate a conscious targeting of the forces. Given the force structure of the time and the comparable size of the special forces relative to the total Army, the numbers can prove misleading.[28]

Poor Relations

In conjunction with the evolution of force buildups and drawdowns associated with war, relations between the conventional Army and special forces also hampered the latter. A general misunderstanding of the value of UW pervaded the conventional Army's attitudes toward these forces during the Vietnam era. The conventional Army maintained poor relations with special forces, partly as a result of biases in favor of such conventional methods as those described above but also as a result of special forces' freedom of operation in Vietnam and how special forces interacted with conventional soldiers.

Special forces often operated independent of the Army, particularly within the Village Defense Program and SOG.[29] For example, after Operation Switchback, which transferred supervision of the Village Defense Program from the CIA to MACV, the CIA's funding for the program—and, by extension, for the special forces—remained in place. In a program called "Parasol-Switchback," funds were funneled directly to the special forces instead of through normal Army channels. This allowed the forces to bypass some of the Army's resource stipulations, provided Special Forces the flexibility they needed, and

---

[26] Coleman, undated. Data in this source are from the Defense Manpower Data Center, Office of the Secretary of Defense, DoD. Figures through 1976 are for the count at June 30 of that year. Figures for 1977 through 2013 are for September 30 of that year. Figures for 2014 are through March 31.

[27] Interview with former member of U.S. Special Forces, Arlington, Va., April 26, 2016.

[28] Interview with U.S. Army John F. Kennedy Special Warfare Center and School historian, April 27, 2016.

[29] Marquis, 1997, p. 20; and Clancy, Stiner, and Koltz, 2002, p. 206.

even saved the U.S. government hundreds of millions of dollars over the course of the war.[30] However, concerns of "he who pays commands" ruffled the conventional Army about this setup.[31] Parasol-Switchback also created closer oversight for instances of graft and corruption than for the conventional military's work with other Vietnamese units. Along with chagrin at the Special Forces for operating with too much freedom because of the funding, the conventional Army saw the reports of corruption as indicative of the poor performance and management of the Special Forces.[32]

Similarly, the conventional military had a negative view of the freedom of operation employed by SOGs. ADM Ulysses Simpson Grant Sharp, U.S. Pacific Command (USPACOM) chief from 1964 to 1968, expressed concern that if an SOG operation went wrong, he might be blamed, so he preferred to "keep SOG reined in."[33]

The efforts to increase Special Forces capacity and utility in the war effort led not only to a detriment in the quality of the soldier but also affected the perception of the conventional Army toward this group at large. Attrition rates at the training center when Kennedy entered office in 1961 hovered around 90 percent, suggesting the center acted as a powerful quality-control mechanism for the forces. In 1962, this percentage dropped to 70, and, by the mid- to late 1960s, it further declined to as low as 30 percent. A drop in quality was not only evidenced by the numbers graduating, but also by those being accepted to the training. For the first time, the training center accepted thousands of first-term Army recruits—those of lower ranks and less military experience—to serve within the Special Forces.[34] Such throughput contradicted the integrity of the forces as outlined in the later-produced

---

[30] Simpson, 1983, p. 165.
[31] Simpson, 1983, p. 166.
[32] Simpson, 1983, pp. 168–169.
[33] Shultz, 1999, p. 280.
[34] Simpson, 1983, p. 68; and Marquis, 1997, p. 20.

SOF truth: Their quality is more important than quantity.[35] Additionally, the frequency of high-stress missions in areas without support dealt a heavy toll on the psychology of the Special Forces. As MG (ret.) James Guest described, "that kind of stress sometimes leads to bizarre behavior. . . . When they came back into a base camp, they often just let it all hang out in ways that upset the others."[36] The rest of the Army began to derisively call the Special Forces "snake eaters" as a result of their dress and behavior.[37] (The term also referred to their survival training, which included foraging for food.)

One highly publicized incident in particular further tarnished relations between Special Forces and the conventional Army. In June of 1969, Thai Khah Chuyen, a North Vietnamese, was killed while in the custody of the 5th Special Forces Group.[38] Two months later, the Army charged Colonel Rheault, along with several others from SOG, with premeditated murder and conspiracy to commit murder.[39] However, Secretary of the Army Stanley Resor dropped the charges. Despite the CIA's involvement with the mission, the agency refused to allow its officers to stand trial, a decision that was made in coordination with the White House.[40] Abrams relieved Rheault of his command, leading to the end of the officer's career in the Army. The defendants accused Abrams of being anti–Special Forces, adding to the bruises on both of their reputations.[41]

---

[35] John Collins, "U.S. Special Operations—Personal Opinions," presented to the 1st Battalion, 1st Special Warfare Training Group, Camp Mackall, N.C., December 11, 2008.

[36] Clancy, 2002, p. 206.

[37] Southworth and Tanner, 2002, p. 114.

[38] Simpson, 1983, p. 183.

[39] Associated Press, "Green Beret Chief Held in Slaying of a Vietnamese," *New York Times*, August 6, 1969.

[40] James M. Naughton, "White House Confirms That Nixon Was Involved in Decision to Drop Charges Against Green Berets," *New York Times*, October 2, 1969.

[41] Marquis, 1997, p. 20.

Conventionalizing the Vietnam War

The decision to conventionalize the war did not stem only from the Pentagon's preference for conventional warfare (CW). At the same time, the tactics of the North Vietnamese Army transitioned from those associated with guerrilla warfare to those pertaining to a more conventionalized, structured force.[42] Assessing that the South Vietnamese government did not have the power to push back the communist forces, Westmoreland and Taylor advocated sending more troops; this was out of the hands of the Special Forces. Not only did this downplay the past role and successes the Special Forces displayed, but it also led to their misuse, decreasing their effectiveness.

When MACV took over the Village Defense Program from the CIA, it "understood neither the nature of special operations nor the special requirements of counterinsurgency."[43] As Westmoreland took command of the MACV in 1964, he constructed a plan for victory that emphasized conventional tactics and downplayed SOG contributions. He saw SOG and operations into North Vietnam as a sideshow that risked galvanizing China to enter the war.[44] As a result, MACV enacted changes that hampered success in terms of the mission's original intent. For example, MACV wanted to repurpose a portion of the Special Forces for more direct action and surveillance missions. It accomplished this by moving the administrative and training responsibilities to the Vietnamese Special Forces. These units did not have the skills nor leadership of U.S. Special Forces; they also maintained the general contempt by the Vietnamese for the local populations the U.S. Special Forces had been working with, undoing much of the early successes the program achieved.[45] Even worse, MACV expanded the program's camps into areas with strategic military objectives not based on the political and demographic realities on the ground.[46] This often

---

[42] Singlaub, 1991, p. 272.

[43] Clancy, Stiner, and Koltz, 200, p. 173.

[44] Shultz, 1999, pp. 275–277.

[45] Clancy, Stiner, and Koltz, 2002, p. 174.

[46] Clancy, Stiner, and Koltz, 2002, pp. 174–175.

placed the camps in remote and dangerous parts of the country, isolating them and sentencing them to constant attack.[47] The changes caused the Village Defense Program to slowly become more offensive in nature. Establishing camps for military missions without the presence of locals defeated the whole purpose of counterinsurgency strategy, and the program transformed into a conventional mission.[48]

While the Village Defense Program became conventionalized, SOG, without senior advocacy, became a victim of burdensome bureaucratic processes. Officially, MACV ran SOG. In reality, SOG was led by the Special Assistant for Counterinsurgency and Special Activities (SACSA) and reported directly to the chair of the JCS within the Pentagon.[49] SACSA kept close hold of the SOG's operations and made information available to others on a "need to know" basis.[50] The long-term teams sent to North Vietnam endured dithering in Washington, D.C., as senior officials waffled between what the mission for those teams should be and what they could and could not do. At the same time, the teams were subjected to tight scrutiny by senior commanders.[51] However, SOG had no advocate within the military at a rank above that of SACSA, resulting in a string of losses when it came to interagency policy struggles concerning them or Vietnam.[52] Indifference pervaded senior leadership and, as a result, SOG "was an orphan in the chain of command."[53]

---

[47] Southworth and Tanner, 2002, p. 111.
[48] Simpson, 1983, p. 109.
[49] Shultz, 1999, p. xii.
[50] Simpson, 1983, p. 146; and Shultz, 1999, p. 290.
[51] Shultz, 1999, p. 57.
[52] Shultz, 1999, pp. 300–301.
[53] Shultz, 1999, p. 280.

Summary of Lessons

Special Forces expansion under President Kennedy and subsequent contraction through the Vietnam War was a case of, on the one hand, missing some of the opportunities a policy window afforded. On the other hand, it was an example of a policy environment out of the Special Forces' control. Although Special Forces enjoyed widespread popularity during the Kennedy administration and cultivated those relationships, they did not use this time to improve relations with the conventional military or other detractors, suggesting an overreliance on the supporters they had at the time. However, certain developments during the Vietnam War fell beyond the control of the Special Forces, providing a powerful reminder that policy decisions sometimes remain outside of a group's political influence. This case study suggests the following specific lessons:

Take advantage of policy windows when they open. Before President Kennedy visited Fort Bragg in 1961, he had already expressed an interest in UW and covert warfare. His first visit to the U.S. Army Special Warfare Center and School afforded the Special Forces an opportunity to make the case for why they could help resolve Kennedy's concerns about the Third World. During the early 1960s, the Special Forces enjoyed growth, positive publicity, and the benefits of the most senior advocate in the U.S. government.

Cultivate personal relationships with potential senior advocates. In particular, Yarbrough's calculated risk to wear the banned green beret on base for the President's visit paid off by raising the Special Forces' visibility with the president and thus earned his enduring support. The decision to make the beret the official headgear was an incidental benefit that symbolized the presidential endorsement of the need for such specialized capabilities.

Senior advocacy should also come from the military and not just civilian leadership. During Kennedy's administration, the Special Forces failed to use the opportunity to improve relations with the conventional Army or find other potential supporters within the Pentagon's senior leadership. Once the Green Berets lost their core advocate, they lay vulnerable and exposed to those whom Kennedy never convinced. Special Forces need to have continuing advocacy within the Army and not only seek it within senior civilian circles.

Sometimes, policy decisions are superseded by realities of conflict. Although Special Forces could have worked to improve relations with the conventional Army, the change in North Vietnamese tactics and the overall military drawdown as U.S. forces evacuated Vietnam were factors largely or wholly beyond the ability of Special Forces to influence.

CHAPTER SIX
CIA-SOF Cooperation in Southeast Asia, 1961–1975

Overview

Special warfare reached its Cold War apex in Southeast Asia, where thousands of SOF were employed in an array of efforts.[1] These efforts were foundational to U.S. Army Special Forces, whose expansions and adaptations were driven by demands within Southeast Asia. SOF also developed an extraordinarily strong relationship with the CIA in Southeast Asia, a reunion of sorts between the organizational descendants of OSS.

Catalyst and Stakeholder Analysis

Laos, 1954–1962

Active U.S. military involvement in Southeast Asia began in 1954 as the First Indochina War came to an end. Before 1954, the U.S. military had observed that war while providing substantial military aid. Following the 1954 Battle of Dien Bien Phu and the subsequent negotiated end of French colonialism in Indochina, that role began to change. This new role catalyzed close SOF-CIA interaction.

---

[1] In addition to special warfare, SOF were used in other roles, particularly special reconnaissance and intelligence collection operations. This chapter only covers special warfare operations in conjunction with the CIA.

The first arena for this new role was in the newly established (or reestablished) Kingdom of Laos. The country was officially neutral but, because of an internal struggle between communist and noncommunist factions, this was a polite fiction rather than reality. The U.S. government sought to provide clandestine military support to the Royal Laotian Government and so established a Program Evaluation Office (PEO) inside the U.S. mission. PEO was notionally involved in evaluating economic assistance but, in reality, provided covert support to the Laotian military (known by the acronym FAR, from the French *Forces Armées du Royaume*).

The PEO and CIA stations in Laos were both small and cooperated with some frequency. A notable success was a combined CIA-PEO effort to train Scout Ranger units for the Laotian army. According to CIA historian Thomas L. Ahern, Scout Rangers "evolved into FAR's 1st and 2nd Parachute Battalions. The most effective units in the army."[2]

From 1959 to 1961, U.S. Army Special Forces augmented PEO. Initially appearing out of uniform, these Special Forces detachments trained and advised the Laotian army, which was fighting against the communist Pathet Lao. By late 1960, more than 100 Special Forces soldiers were advising at the battalion level. PEO's relationship with the CIA remained strong in this period but was informal, as both sides contributed resources to different aspects of the operations.

One area of contention emerged when the CIA sought to arm and support nongovernmental forces in the fight against the Pathet Lao. These surrogates were principally drawn from mountain-dwelling tribesmen, such as the Meo and Hmong, ethnically distinct from the lowland-dwelling Lao peoples. Special Forces officers in some areas believed that tribal units should have Special Forces personnel in command, with the CIA in support. This led to tension between Special Forces and the CIA, the latter believing it was better positioned to manage the complex relationships at the local, national, and interna-

---

[2] Thomas L. Ahern, Jr., *CIA and Rural Pacification in South Vietnam*, Washington, D.C.: Center for the Study of Intelligence, 2001, declassified 2006, p. 6.

tional level that such surrogate relationships required. The result was ad hoc support by Special Forces to CIA surrogate programs.[3]

This support was nonetheless often effective, as recounted by Ahern in detailing his own experience as a young case officer cooperating with a Special Forces captain in Thakek. This program sought to expand the surrogate program to ethnic Lao recruits, diversifying away from sole reliance on ethnic minorities. Ahern and Captain Sidney "Sid" Hinds were able to cooperate in part because Hinds was eager to work with troops willing to fight: He was officially responsible for advising a relatively lethargic Laotian army unit. Ahern and Hinds were able to convince Hinds's superior officers to let Hinds split his efforts between the regular army unit and the irregulars that the CIA was supporting.[4] However, in July 1962, an international agreement reestablished Laotian neutrality, leading the U.S. government to withdraw Special Forces personnel from Laos even as CIA paramilitary operations continued.

Key Junctures

South Vietnam, 1961–1975

Even as Special Forces involvement in Laos wound down with the Geneva agreement, it began to expand in neighboring South Vietnam. The 5th Special Forces Group was established in 1961 to address the growing demand for special warfare capabilities in South Vietnam. The group established its operations base at Nha Trang, where it advised and trained South Vietnamese personnel, including South Vietnamese Special Forces.

These Special Forces units soon became integral to a burgeoning CIA program known as the Civilian Irregular Defense Groups (CIDGs). CIDGs grew out of a contact between the CIA and "a young volunteer [David Nuttle] . . . doing economic development work among the Rhade, the principal tribe around the Darlac provincial

---

[3] Ahern, 2001, p. 70.

[4] Ahern, 2001, p. 107.

capital of Ban Me Thuot."[5] Nuttle spent considerable time with the Rhade, spoke their language, and had vast knowledge about the tribe's attitudes. He returned to Saigon and, circulating in the relatively small expatriate community, met a CIA officer from Saigon station's Military Operations Section (MOS). In April 1961, he had a long discussion with MOS chief Gilbert Layton, who believed the Rhade could be mobilized in their own defense. He suggested that this might be done by providing for their needs, which the Vietnamese government had ignored. Layton proposed investigating the potential for such a counterinsurgency program to chief of Station William Colby, who agreed and negotiated an agreement to begin such a program with the Vietnamese government.[6]

Layton began exploring opportunities with the Rhade using David Nuttle, known to the Rhade as "Mr. Dave," and a Special Forces medic (SFC Paul Campbell, known as "Dr. Paul") as his interlocutors. The two spent the summer in the Central Highlands of South Vietnam, with Campbell providing Rhade villagers with medical treatment as they sounded out local leaders. In fall 1961, the two returned and suggested that the area around the town of Buon Enao should be the first site for the new program.

This program brought in a U.S. Army Special Forces Operational Detachment Alpha (ODA), along with a South Vietnamese Special Forces ODA, to support the villagers. The program combined economic and medical development with the training of village defense forces. It expanded rapidly, drawing in more U.S. and Vietnamese Special Forces over the course of 1962. The CIA's Layton was a skillful manager, finding underused resources to support the nascent program. In April 1962, there were 40 villages incorporated into CIDGs around Buon Enao with about 1,000 village defenders and a 300-man strike

---

[5] Thomas L. Ahern, *Undercover Armies: CIA and Surrogate Warfare in Laos, 1961–1973*, Washington, D.C.: Center for the Study of Intelligence, 2006, p. 44.

[6] Ahern, 2006, pp. 44–62; Francis J. Kelly, *Vietnam Forces: U.S. Army Special Forces 1961–1971*, Washington, D.C.: Center of Military History, Department of the Army, CMH Pub 90-23-1, 1973, pp. 20–33; and 5th Special Forces Group Headquarters, 5th Special Forces Group Headquarters, *U.S. Army Special Forces Participation in the CIDG Program Vietnam, 1957–1970*, Houston, Tex.: Reprint by Radix Press, 1996, pp. 83–124.

force. By July, the program had more than 4,000 armed villagers across the Central Highlands. In August, more than 200 villages had joined the CIDGs, and in November, it had armed 23,000 men. In less than a year, a small army was created using only 24 U.S. ODAs and a few CIA personnel.[7]

As the program grew, so did overall U.S. military presence in South Vietnam. Part of this expansion was by way of establishing a special warfare branch in the operations directorate of the newly created MACV. MACV then successfully argued that it and the CIA should jointly control the CIDG program, which was using Army troops supported by CIA logistics.

In June 1962, as the program grew, decisionmakers in Saigon and Washington concluded the expansion was such that the program was no longer covert action. This conclusion in turn led to a decision to transfer the program entirely to MACV. The transfer was referred to as Operation Switchback and was somewhat contentious.

Attitudes varied in both the military and the CIA. Some at the CIA felt the transfer was required to prevent overburdening the agency's Saigon station. CIA Director John McCone favored transfer of the CIA's counterinsurgency programs to the military. Officers at the working level in CIA headquarters and Saigon station were split. Some agreed with McCone in wanting to divest such a relatively overt program in favor of intelligence collection and more clandestine activity. Others believed MACV would distort the program and lacked the CIA's political acumen.

The ostensible beneficiary of Operation Switchback, MACV commander GEN Paul Harkins, was not in favor of the transfer to his command. He believed the program was not ready to transition, and the CIA should continue to run it. Harkins recognized the value of the CIA's skill in navigating South Vietnamese politics and Saigon station's ties to South Vietnamese leaders. The commander of Special Forces in Vietnam, COL George Morton, was also against transfer for similar

---

[7] Ahern, 2006, p. 57; Kelly, 1973, pp. 26–29; 5th Special Forces Group Headquarters, 1996, pp. 85–89.

reasons. However, he did also worry about logistics, as he would be losing the CIA's uniquely flexible support.[8]

Decision and Outcome Analysis

Following Operation Switchback, the CIDGs under MACV began to look more like an offensive program, with an emphasis on expanding numbers over political deftness. In 1964, a handful of CIDG units mutinied, killing dozens of South Vietnamese Special Forces trainers and temporarily taking U.S. Special Forces advisers hostage. This mutiny was eventually defused by Special Forces and CIA officers. The official history of the U.S. Special Forces confirms the decline of the program:

> By the end of 1964 the Montagnard program was no longer an area development project in the original sense of the term. There was a shift in emphasis from expanding village defense systems to the primary use of area development camps or centers (CIDG camps) as bases for offensive strike force operations.[9]

Even as CIA involvement in the CIDGs ended, the agency was exploring other possibilities for paramilitary counterinsurgency programs. In 1964, CIA officers in Kien Hoa province partnered with the Vietnamese province chief Major Chau to form a unit of "deserters and small time crooks."[10] This unit, termed a Counter-Terror (C-T) team, would give the province chief an "action arm" to execute missions against insurgent leadership.

As Ahern describes it, this program also called for CIA cooperation with Special Forces:

> The Station had as yet no facilities of its own to teach the requisite skills, and resorted once again to informal, local arrangements

---

[8] Ahern, 2006, pp. 97–99, 102–103.
[9] Kelly, 1973, pp. 33–34.
[10] Ahern, 2006, p. 141.

with MACV. Thus, the first C-T team got its instruction from the US Special Forces team stationed at Mac Hoa in Kien Tuong Province. Its commander, Major Al Francisco, allayed Station concerns about the students' aptitudes by getting them through a rigorous training program.[11]

From this modest beginning, the CIA began to create C-T teams across South Vietnam. In 1965, it centralized training for its cadre at Vung Tau and, by November 1964, the program had 1,900 indigenous personnel across the country.[12] At Vung Tau, a coastal city, the CIA began to rely informally on U.S. Navy SEALs to provide advice and training to C-T cadres.[13]

The continued expansion of the C-T teams, which were subsequently renamed Provincial Reconnaissance Units (PRUs), began to outstrip the CIA's ability to provide advisers and oversight in the field. In many instances in 1965–1966, the CIA took to supplementing its officers in the field through informal arrangements with the military. In 1966, for example, the U.S. Marine Corps contingent in Quang Nam province provided "two second lieutenants and a sergeant whose specialty was long-range reconnaissance."[14]

In 1967, the CIA sought to formally acquire the support for PRUs it needed from the military, and in July of that year, MACV commander Westmoreland approved the initial detail of four officers and 40 noncommissioned officers as PRU advisers.[15] As former PRU adviser Andrew Finlayson notes,

> Ideally, these DoD assignees were to be skilled in the special warfare tasks needed by a PRU advisor. With this in mind, the bulk of the PRU advisors came from the U.S. Army's Special Forces,

---

[11] Ahern, 2006, pp. 141–142.

[12] Ahern, 2006, p. 187.

[13] Ahern, 2006, p. 299.

[14] Ahern, 2006, p. 271.

[15] Ahern, 2006, p. 299.

the Navy's Seals [sic], and the U.S. Marine Corps' Force Reconnaissance Companies.[16]

In addition to providing field advising to PRU cadres, U.S. military personnel detailed to the program also provided a crucial link to U.S. military support. Finlayson notes, "The PRU relied heavily on the Americans who accompanied them on dangerous missions to provide radio contact with U.S. supporting units, especially medevac helicopters and artillery units."[17] This combination of indigenous personnel with U.S. advisers and supporting units proved highly effective in many (although not all) provinces.

PRUs acquitted themselves well during the chaos of the 1968 Tet Offensive, and the CIA sought to expand the program further that year. The goal was to grow from 3,500 indigenous personnel to 6,000 while also providing PRUs more firepower.[18] This expansion would require further detailees from MACV, again heavily drawn from the special operations community.

However, the post–Tet Offensive shifts in U.S. domestic politics and the adoption of a policy of rapid "Vietnamization" of the war was the beginning of the end for CIA-SOF cooperation on PRUs. Both the CIA and MACV began to curtail involvement in PRUs, which became a South Vietnamese police program in 1969. Military advisers were instructed not to accompany PRUs on field operations as of November 1969 and, by 1970, only 17 CIA personnel were involved in the program.[19]

---

[16] Andrew R. Finlayson, *Marine Advisors with the Vietnamese Provincial Reconnaissance Units, 1966–1970*, Quantico, Va.: History Division, U.S. Marine Corps, 2009, p. 8.

[17] Andrew R. Finlayson, "A Retrospective on Counterinsurgency Operations: The Tay Ninh Provincial Reconnaissance Unit and Its Role in the Phoenix Program, 1969–70," *Studies in Intelligence*, Vol. 51, No. 2, 2007.

[18] Ahern, 2006, p. 317.

[19] Finlayson, 2007; and Ahern, 2006, pp. 363–366.

Summary of Lessons

CIA-SOF cooperation in Southeast Asia was a major developmental milestone for both organizations. Born from the ashes of OSS, both organizations were only a decade old when U.S. involvement in Southeast Asia began to grow. While the initial experience of cooperation was positive, the end of both wars and subsequent effect of the wars on U.S. domestic politics meant the special warfare would draw down significantly in the late 1970s. The success of this early period suggests one central lesson.

CIA and SOF synergy. The central lesson from CIA and SOF cooperation is that both communities have unique capabilities that are strongly synergistic for special warfare. The CIA's flat organization and flexibility make it extraordinarily effective in initiating paramilitary special warfare programs. It was able to exploit local circumstances, such as Nuttle's insight on the Rhade tribe or Major Chau's "deserters and small time crooks," to generate early success.

However, the CIA's flexibility is enabled in part by its small size, so as its special warfare programs grew, it simply did not have the personnel to support expansion. With CIDGs and PRUs in particular, the programs simply could not have expanded without SOF participation. SOF provided the crucial military advisory expertise to these programs at the tactical level as well as a critical link to such U.S. military enablers as medevac and fire support.

In terms of the seven phases of UW, the CIA was extraordinarily capable in phases I–III (preparation, initial contact, infiltration), although it benefited from the assistance of such SOF personnel as Campbell, the special forces medic. In phase IV (organization), the CIA began to increasingly rely on SOF, with phases V–VI (buildup and employment) dominated by SOF personnel on the ground.

However, the different outcomes for CIDGs and PRUs highlight the importance of an ongoing role for the CIA, even in these later phases. Once CIDGs became an MACV-only program, it began to suffer under the yoke of a vast military bureaucracy (as Special Forces Colonel Morton had feared). In contrast, PRUs remained a CIA program even during buildup and employment and thus was effective until both the CIA and SOF drew down as part of Vietnamization.

CHAPTER SEVEN
Special Operations Capabilities: Creation of U.S. Special Operations Command and the Assistant Secretary of Defense for Special Operations and Low-Intensity Conflict

Overview

The creation of USSOCOM and the ASD/SOLIC provides several data points to consider in analyzing how to influence policy changes in Congress. By creating a unified combatant command (COCOM) responsible for all SOF and a civilian assistant secretary of defense to oversee SOF budget and policy issues, Congress was attempting to rectify what it determined was Pentagon neglect of SOLIC issues. The Senate Armed Services Committee (SASC) conducted two years of intensive research on DoD organizational deficiencies, concluding that DoD suffered from a chain-of-command structure that discouraged interservice coordination and placed heavy focus in planning and in resourcing on the Soviet threat despite a rise in potential conflicts in the developing world. Further, the events at Desert One, the failed hostage-rescue operation in Iran in 1980, and Urgent Fury, the U.S. invasion into Grenada in 1983, while fundamentally different in outcome, both displayed that a lack of service integration and communication was a critical issue that needed to be addressed.

Without the disaster at Desert One, Congress would likely not have turned with such urgency to DoD reform debates that resulted in the Goldwater-Nichols DoD Reorganization Act of 1986. Without the Goldwater-Nichols Act and the significant effort that went into researching and passing that legislation, the Nunn-Cohen amendment to the Fiscal Year (FY) 1987 National Defense Authorization Act (NDAA), which created USSOCOM, may not have had the analysis, support, or leverage against Pentagon and White House opponents that was required for adoption and implementation.

This case study details the conditions that drove Congress's concern with Pentagon handling of SOF and broader SOLIC issues, the strategy that SOLIC proponents adopted along several key decision points, the key players involved, and the results of their efforts.

Catalyst

Operations Eagle Claw and Urgent Fury

After the Vietnam War ended, support for special operations waned within DoD. The pervasive attitude among military leadership was that Vietnam represented an aberration in American warfighting, and that preparing for smaller-scale insurgencies—and the operations required to be successful in those conditions—would be an ineffective use of resources.[1] Accordingly, in the 1970s, the Pentagon focused increasingly on conventional planning for the Soviet adversary, and resourcing, support, and attention to SOF dropped significantly.

Nonetheless, the 1970s were not without key advances in the special operations community. Despite institutional resistance to the creation of additional special operations units, an elite Army Special Mission Unit (SMU) was created in 1977. Special operations advocates, such as GEN Edward Charles "Shy" Meyer, who served as the Army's deputy chief of staff of operations in the late 1970s and became the Chief of Staff of the Army in 1979, had long advocated for increased support to special operations and briefed senior military officials on the importance of developing a high-end counterterrorist unit. These proposals did not gain traction until October 1977, when President

---

[1] William G. Boykin, "Special Operations and Low-Intensity Conflict Legislation: Why Was It Passed and Have the Voids Been Filled?" Carlisle Barracks, Pa.: U.S. Army War College, 1991.

Carter learned that the West German counterterrorism unit GSG-9 conducted a successful hostage rescue operation in Mogadishu. Carter immediately directed Secretary of Defense Harold Brown and National Security Adviser Zbigniew Brzezinski to create similar capabilities in the United States, and the SMU proposal, submitted to Chief of Staff of the Army Bernard Rogers just months before by General Meyer, was expedited and implemented less than a month later.[2]

In April 1980, U.S. SOF suffered a heavy loss during Operation Eagle Claw, a special operations mission to rescue the 53 hostages held captive at the U.S. Embassy in Tehran. Two helicopters collided at a rendezvous location known as Desert One, killing eight service members. The incident was not only an operational failure, but its effect on how the public—both domestic and international—viewed the competency of the U.S. military was significant. The errors, largely from lack of interservice coordination and planning and from extreme compartmentalization of information among the various units involved, were documented in a final report produced by the Holloway Commission.

The commission's panel of senior active and retired flag officers, led by retired Chief of Naval Operations ADM James Holloway, found that the lack of an effective command and control structure and inadequate interservice coordination led to the failure in Iran. The commission made two key recommendations: that DoD create an elite SMU, complete with permanently assigned staff and assigned forces; and that the JCS establish a Special Operations Advisory Panel (later the Special Operations Policy Advisory Group [SOPAG]) comprising senior military officers, both active and retired, with deep experience in special operations.[3] While both of these recommendations were implemented over time after the report was published, the deficiencies underscored by the Eagle Claw disaster were not adequately addressed and again came to light in 1983 in Grenada.

Although the U.S. joint operation to evacuate Americans from Grenada after a coup occurred in October 1983 was lauded as a mili-

---

[2] Marquis, 1997.

[3] Joint Chiefs of Staff, Special Operations Review Group, *Holloway Commission Report*, 1980.

tary success by the Ronald Reagan administration, there was strong opposition to that characterization within the military. The operation, known as Urgent Fury, was constrained by poor intelligence, tactical mobility issues, inadequate communication and coordination between the services, and conventional commanders' inexperience with how to execute special operations missions. An example of this inexperience was the decision to order SOF units to conduct their operation at daybreak, although darkness is a critical element in special operations planning. Colin Powell, then–senior military assistant to Secretary of Defense Caspar Weinberger, noted that "fractured command and control, interservice parochialism, and micromanagement from Washington" had plagued U.S. forces during Urgent Fury.[4] These issues together galvanized concern and urgency among SOF advocates and would later play a critical role in influencing Congress to take action on SOF reform.

Proposal Formation and Stakeholder Analysis

Actors Inside the Pentagon

While Desert One impinged on the national discussion of special operations and of defense reform more broadly, it was not enough to elicit action from the U.S. military or the government to revitalize special operations in a meaningful way. Throughout the early 1980s, various initiatives to strengthen special operations and CT capabilities at the Pentagon—sometimes even from within the SOF community—were met with silence and inaction.[5]

Noel Koch, the Principal Deputy Assistant Secretary of Defense (PDASD) for International Security Affairs (ASD ISA) from 1981 to 1986, was a notable and influential exception to SOF resistance within DoD. Koch had originally been recruited to the Pentagon to

---

[4] James R. Locher, III, *Victory on the Potomac*, College Station, Tex.: Texas A&M University Press, 2002; and Colin L. Powell with Joseph E. Persico, *My American Journey*, New York: Random House Ballantine Publishing Group, 1996, p. 292.

[5] Marquis, 1997.

lead the Near East, Africa, and South Asia office within ASD ISA, but for bureaucratic reasons, he was not ultimately selected for it.[6] When Koch threatened to leave, he was offered the PDASD position instead. Together with his military assistant, former 5th Special Forces Group commander COL George McDonald, and ISA analyst Lynn Rylander, Koch led efforts within the Pentagon to address the institutional challenges SOF faced, often under heavy opposition from senior officials. These efforts frequently relied on leveraging the team's extensive network to push SOF reform issues and on forceful maneuvers to gain access to DoD leadership.[7]

Koch, who had spent six years enlisted in the Army and served in Vietnam, was influenced in part by those experiences and the counsel of both Rylander and McDonald. Also, through his PDASD duties, Koch had become increasingly concerned that terrorism would present a problem for DoD over time, yet the military was not oriented to confront it.

Koch also pushed forward several key initiatives that assisted in creating high-level access to decisionmakers and bringing SOF issues to the public. First, Koch and his team established the Special Planning Directorate, with Koch at the helm, designed to circumvent the bureaucratic—and often SOF resistant—layers within OSD policy, directly reporting to the Under Secretary of Defense for Policy and the Deputy Secretary of Defense. This allowed far more access to both the Deputy Secretary and the Secretary of Defense, enabling Koch and his team to advocate more effectively for special operations.[8] Koch was able to establish this directorate by directly appealing to DoD leadership, who were concerned Koch would leave his job since he was perceived to be well connected in the Reagan administration; Koch was already angered by not being chosen for the original position for which he was recruited. Capitalizing on residual presidential-level interest in SOF from Desert One, Koch led frequent briefings starting in early 1982 to

---

[6] Interview with former Office of the Secretary of Defense (OSD) official, September 30, 2016.

[7] Marquis, 1997.

[8] Marquis, 1997.

Secretary Weinberger on outstanding special operations requirements, thus enabling access for his team to directly advocate for SOF issues to DoD leadership.[9]

Second, Koch established SOPAG as directed by the Holloway Commission. Koch recruited retired general and flag officers, largely with experience in special operations. The preference for retired officers was to increase the likelihood that members would speak more freely and not be subject to pressure from their home service as much as an active-duty officer might be.[10]

Third, in 1983, at Secretary Weinberger's request, Koch and his team wrote a classified memorandum that addressed the implications of unmet support requirements the SOF community had of the armed services. Aiming to reach Congress and the wider interested public regarding the issues the memorandum had highlighted, Koch and Rylander also composed an unclassified version of the memorandum, but they were unable to gain the required sign-offs from the rest of DoD to submit the memorandum to the Secretary; Koch went directly to Paul Thayer, the Deputy Secretary of Defense. Despite Koch's bypassing of many layers of signatures, Thayer signed the memo on October 3, 1983. While only a nonbinding memorandum, it had several meaningful implications, including that the services could no longer make resource decisions affecting SOF without coordinating with OSD ISA and gaining approval from the Secretary of Defense.[11] Further, in response to the memorandum, the Joint Special Operations Agency was established in January 1984. With no command and control responsibilities, no resources, and only a two-star general officer as its lead, it served largely as an advisory organization without actual authority, but it did provide a much-needed SOF advocacy arm within the Joint Staff.[12] These efforts and Koch's divisive tactics were met with significant opposition, and Koch resigned in 1986, but not before he

---

[9] Marquis, 1997.

[10] Marquis, 1997.

[11] Marquis, 1997.

[12] Boykin, 1991.

had elicited attention from the public, including Congress, on SOF issues as he intended.

Actors in Congress

By 1984, Congress had begun to take notice of—and act on—the Pentagon's neglect of special operations. In addition to concern about SOLIC capabilities after Desert One and Urgent Fury, many in Congress were increasingly concerned about the U.S. ability to counter terrorism after the October 1983 bombing in Lebanon that killed 237 Marines.[13] In particular, Congressman Dan Daniel, chairman of the Readiness Subcommittee of the House Armed Services Committee (HASC), was an early and vocal supporter of SOLIC issues. Daniel had been motivated by the experiences and counsel of his friend and constituent LTG Sam Wilson, a highly regarded special operations expert, member of the Holloway Commission, and onetime lead of SOPAG, and Daniel's staff member Ted Lunger, a former member of the U.S. Army Special Forces. Daniel's influence, driven by the persistence and advocacy of both Wilson and Lunger, proved to be one of the most meaningful factors in establishing USSOCOM and ASD/SOLIC. Further, the House of Representatives convened a special panel, chaired by Congressman Earl Hutton, to oversee SOF reform and improvement efforts.[14] On the Senate side, in April 1984, Senator Strom Thurmond read on the Senate floor a critical speech written by Noel Koch, which publicly communicated Koch's criticisms of DoD's handling of SOLIC issues.[15] Koch and Rylander, capitalizing on this small but powerful show of support for their agenda, began to increase and leverage their network on Capitol Hill, increasing their interaction with Congress and assembling influential advocates for eventual action. However, Congress's cadre of special operations advocates did not expand meaningfully until 1985.

---

[13] Interview with former congressional staff, February 10, 2016.

[14] James R. Locher, III, "Congress to the Rescue: Statutory Creation of USSOCOM," *Air Commando Journal*, Vol. 1, No. 3, Spring, 2012.

[15] Marquis, 1997.

Although certain members of Congress, particularly Daniel, had for years steadfastly supported SOLIC reform, and SOF had achieved some gains through the early 1980s, Congress had largely refrained from mandating Pentagon support to SOF. However, in 1985, Congress began to show its frustration with the Pentagon through legislative action, with HASC and Senator Sam Nunn each offering legislation aimed at withholding certain procurement funds until the Pentagon displayed more commitment to SOF programs. Further, Daniel offered an amendment to the 1986 NDAA stating that SOF reform should be one of the "highest defense priorities" and that OSD should increase its oversight authority over SOF.[16] Each of these events further expanded SOF advocates' coalition of supporters and reinforced their argument that SOF reforms were urgently required.

Actors in the Defense Industry

During the same time, staff and members on both sides of the political aisle became increasingly exposed to reports of inadequate SOF capabilities and support through staff outreach conducted by Daniel and Lunger as well as through a series of articles published by Ben Schemmer, editor and owner of *Armed Forces Journal International* (AFJI). Schemmer, a longtime advocate of strengthening SOF capabilities who was frustrated with the Pentagon's lack of progress on SOLIC reform, began a campaign in AFJI by publishing 45 articles and letters to explain challenges facing SOF. These were aimed at reminding the readership—which included Pentagon leadership and members of Congress—of SOF equities and that SOF was still undersupported. The audience of officials and members of the public who were becoming interested in SOF issues was active and growing.[17] Authors of the published articles included Koch, who wrote regularly on SOF capabilities and the services' views of SOF, and Daniel, who went so far as to propose a sixth service. Schemmer had widespread credibility on defense issues throughout Congress, which he used to advance SOLIC reform issues. For example, Senator William Cohen was reportedly influenced

---

[16] Marquis, 1997, pp. 129–130.

[17] Marquis, 1997.

to take on SOLIC reform after a direct call from Schemmer.[18] In January 1986, Senator Cohen even published an article in AFJI titled "A Defense Special Operations Agency: Fix for a SOF Capability That Is Most Assuredly Broken." Cohen's article signaled that the Senate had joined the House in registering deep dissatisfaction with how DoD was supporting SOF.[19]

While the influence of the articles is debated, the AFJI series enabled public debate and education that otherwise was difficult if not impossible because of the Pentagon's hesitance to share SOF information. Koch was allowed a public platform to voice concerns ignored by the Pentagon, and articles published by members of Congress carried an implicit warning: If the Pentagon will not fix the problem, Congress will.

Key Junctures

A significant turning point for SOLIC reform effort came in October 1985, when the SASC report *Defense Organization: The Need for Change* was released. The 645-page report, which detailed gaps and deficiencies throughout DoD and the National Command Authority, took years to research and write.[20] The work of the research team, led by SASC staffer James Locher, was widely influential and served as the analytical basis for the landmark Goldwater-Nichols DoD Reorganization Act of 1986. Although it was not focused specifically on SOF, the report showed clear concern for SOLIC reforms, making several observations about the special operations community, including that it needed a "strong . . . multifunctional, organizational focus for low-intensity warfare and special operations." The decision not to target

---

[18] Interview with former congressional staff, February 10, 2016; and Locher, 2012.

[19] William S. Cohen, "A Defense Special Operations Agency: Fix for an SOF Capability That Is Most Assuredly Broken," *Armed Forces Journal International*, January 1986.

[20] Sam Nunn, Barry M. Goldwater, and James R. Locher, III, *Defense Organization: The Need for Change: Staff Report to the Committee on Armed Services, United States Senate*, Washington, D.C.: U.S. Government Printing Office, October 16, 1985.

special operations issues in the ensuing Goldwater-Nichols legislation that acted on the content of the report was deliberate and forward looking: The SASC decided that SOF reform did not have enough supporting senators nor sufficient analytic rigor at that time to be included in such a contentious bill, as it would be at greater risk of being weakened or negotiated away than if it was included in a less-contentious piece of legislation.[21]

A week prior to the release of the report, Senators Goldwater and Nunn, frustrated with both the Pentagon's and Congress's inaction on DoD reforms, took to the Senate floor to deliver eight speeches on the past errors and miscommunications that were caused by inherent flaws in existing military structure, such as Urgent Fury, and also warning of dangerous implications—including Americans dying unnecessarily—if drastic steps to reform the Pentagon were not taken.[22] The tenor and passion in those speeches set the stage for the Goldwater-Nichols Act debate, which occupied the Senate's attention into spring 1986.

The Goldwater-Nichols Act, which aimed to address interservice coordination and competition issues highlighted by Desert One and Grenada, strengthened the role of the chairman of the JCS, removed operational responsibility from the services, and specified that the chain of command between the combatant commands and the President runs through the Secretary of Defense, among other changes to DoD organization. The Goldwater-Nichols Act passed the Senate unanimously in April 1986 and was taken up by HASC, allowing SASC staff to turn to SOLIC reform and the upcoming NDAA.

In June 1986, Daniel submitted House Resolution 5109, his measure to reform SOLIC. The resolution, which sought to establish a National Special Operations Agency with civilian leadership and budgetary authority, was considered more provocative than the ultimate Nunn-Cohen legislation and did not earn wide support throughout the SOF advocate community because the Daniel language would functionally remove SOF from key OSD and NSC policy processes and iso-

---

[21] Interview with former congressional staff, February 10, 2016; and Locher, 2012.

[22] Evan Thomas and Bruce van Voorst, "Drums Along the Potomac: The Military Establishment Is Besieged by Some of Its Staunchest Supporters," *Time,* October 21, 1985.

late SOF from the rest of DoD.[23] However, its far-reaching proposals, perhaps by design, generated response from the Pentagon, which proposed a USSOCOM under the JCS that would have an advocacy role for SOF issues on the Defense Resources Board.[24] SOF reform advocates felt that the Pentagon's proposal was not robust enough as it did not give the command true authority, budget control, and leadership by a sufficiently high-ranking individual. The relatively radical proposals within the Daniel bill also allowed Locher and his team to propose a more palatable, but still consequential, alternative in the form of the Nunn-Cohen amendment.

After facing down the Pentagon in the passage of Goldwater-Nichols in the Senate, the SASC turned to SOLIC reform in April 1986. The issues uncovered throughout the research for the SASC's Defense Organization report gave Congress little confidence in the Pentagon's ability to direct substantive organizational change without the threat of legislation, including on SOLIC reforms. Because of the research completed to compose and pass Goldwater-Nichols, SASC had cultivated momentum and credibility in organizational issues and seized the opportunity to move forward on what they viewed as a closely related issue in SOLIC reform. Further, the Goldwater-Nichols Act directly addressed the role of combatant commands, which influenced the direction of SOLIC reform.[25] SASC staff, led by Locher, spent months analyzing the state of SOF capabilities, along with organizational and operational deficiencies, and educating members of the Senate who had little exposure to or interest in SOLIC issues.[26] SASC determined that the annual NDAA was the optimal vehicle to attach an SOLIC reform measure to, as its details could largely be negotiated in conference with the House instead of during a full Senate debate,

---

[23] Locher, 2012.

[24] Marquis, 1997.

[25] Interview with former congressional staff, February 10, 2016.

[26] Locher, 2012.

and the measure would have a much greater chance of reaching the Senate floor than a stand-alone bill would.[27]

Generating a coalition of support in the Senate for SOLIC reform was relatively easy for Locher and his team for several reasons: The SASC had earned credibility on organizational issues post–Goldwater-Nichols and had generated momentum to continue to reform DoD to be better able to meet future national security challenges; the Pentagon was no longer trusted to be transparent or to fix internal issues on its own given its hollow protests to Goldwater-Nichols reforms; and highly influential members such as Senators Goldwater, Cohen, Nunn, and Levin were supporters of SOF reform. Further, the events in Operation Eagle Claw, having motivated the Goldwater-Nichols reforms, had generated urgency throughout Congress that much needed to be done, including within special operations, to reorganize DoD to prevent such a disaster from occurring again.

Decision and Outcome Analysis

In July and August 1986, Cohen organized a series of hearings on SOF capabilities in an attempt to prepare for the upcoming SOLIC reform debate on the NDAA. Several DoD officials testified, including ASD ISA Richard Armitage and chairman of the JCS William Crowe. Although many agreed that changes were necessary, the DoD position was that those changes could be and were being made from within the Pentagon, and the USSOCOM concept could be a viable solution.[28]

Also during this series of hearings, LTG Sam Wilson, to whom members of Congress accorded an unmatched reputation and credibility on SOF issues, appeared before the SASC. In his testimony, Wilson maintained that binding legislation to rebuild SOF would be necessary. Several other senior SOF experts also appeared before the SASC, including GEN Shy Meyer, but the pivotal testimony was delivered on

---

[27] Interview with former congressional staff, February 10, 2016.

[28] Interview with former congressional staff, February 10, 2016; and Boykin, 1991.

August 5, 1985, by recently retired MG Richard Scholtes, the former commander of Joint Special Operations Command (JSOC).[29]

Scholtes, who had led JSOC during Urgent Fury, delivered the majority of his testimony in a closed classified session. He described to lawmakers that his forces in Grenada had suffered casualties in part because of mismanagement and lack of understanding of SOF on the part of conventional planners and commanders. This testimony was so compelling that Senator Cohen called for an additional private meeting that afternoon with Scholtes and several other key senators, including Sam Nunn, John Warner, and James Exon.[30] As a result, Cohen directed Locher to rewrite the Nunn-Cohen measure overnight from a "Sense of the Senate" resolution expressing a majority opinion into binding legislation. On August 6, 1985, with 26 cosponsors, the Nunn-Cohen amendment was adopted by unanimous consent into the Senate version of the FY 1987 NDAA.[31]

Although both the House and the Senate were motivated to pass SOLIC reforms, their approaches were quite different. The Senate's version of the legislation was driven by Goldwater-Nichols reforms and sought to create a COCOM. The House's version included a senior civilian overseeing the USSOCOM organization and created specific budgetary and resourcing authority within that entity. Daniel asked Wilson to participate in the negotiations, which was a critical decision: Wilson, having the trust and confidence of both sides, mediated the disagreements between both teams. He convinced HASC of the merits of a military-led command integrated into the National Command Authority's policymaking structure, and he negotiated with the SASC to include Daniel's provision to establish the creation of an SOF-specific major force program (MFP) budget line, now called MFP-11, by the Senate. Conference negotiations lasted nearly a month.

The conference version of the NDAA passed the Senate on October 15, 1986. Although Secretary Weinberger and the White House voiced strong objections to the Nunn-Cohen legislation, neither dis-

---

[29] Boykin, 1991.

[30] Interview with former congressional staff, February 10, 2016; and Boykin, 1991.

[31] Marquis, 1997.

sent nor threat of veto was of significant concern: President Reagan and the Pentagon had also opposed the Goldwater-Nichols legislation but had not followed through, and the SASC was confident none of the Nunn-Cohen language encroached on the President's authority.[32] The FY 1987 NDAA was signed by President Reagan on November 14, 1986.

The final bill created a unified COCOM overseeing all SOF, led by a four-star flag officer, created the position of ASD/SOLIC, and established MFP-11 for SOF-unique funding needs.[33] While MFP-11 only composes a portion of USSOCOM's total funding (it relies on the services to fund personnel, service-issued equipment, base support, and other service-common needs), it provided USSOCOM a funding line of its own for SOF-specific needs that grew to roughly $10 billion in the post-9/11 years. The challenges to implement SOLIC reforms throughout DoD remained for many years—some argue that it was not until the events that followed 9/11 that forced DoD collaboration and support to special operations. However, the story of how Congress felt compelled to legislate the creation of USSOCOM describes how the long-term cultivation of influential advocates, even if small in number, combined with a public message of urgency, can be leveraged into fundamental change if timed while a policy window is open. Further, the legislative creation of USSOCOM also highlights the criticality of engaging with and providing information to congressional staff members, who often hold significant influence over legislative language and members' willingness to engage on a policy issue.

Summary of Lessons

The case of the creation of USSOCOM and ASD/SOLIC illustrates SOF advocates' success in overcoming strong institutional resistance to create fundamental change in policy and organizational structure. The establishment of these two organizations was greatly enabled by SOF

---

[32] Interview with former congressional staff, February 10, 2016.

[33] Boykin, 1991.

advocates who collaborated across institutions over time to develop a deep network of credible voices that helped to correctly identify an appropriate policy window and message of urgency that ultimately underscored to Congress the criticality of greater SOLIC support. Further, SOF advocates continually modified and iterated their approach to achieve incremental gains, even compromising certain provisions to forge a collaborative solution.

While many lessons may be drawn from this case, specific lessons highlighted below explain examples in which SOF and SOF advocates had the most control over and actions that were clear sources of successful change.

Adopt a phased approach to major change. Locher stated that the passage of Goldwater-Nichols was the most influential factor in the creation of USSOCOM and ASD/SOLIC. Goldwater-Nichols enabled USSOCOM advocates to develop credibility and subject-matter expertise about DoD structure and organization, which contributed to the broad support the SASC received when it introduced Nunn-Cohen. Further, the SASC waited for the optimal vehicle to pass Nunn-Cohen legislation, which was the later NDAA. SOF reform may not have been successful if advocates had pushed the measure forward before conditions were conducive.

Provide subject-matter expertise to Congress. Doing so when resident knowledge on SOF issues was low (since the Pentagon was hesitant to share that information widely) was extremely valuable. Current and former special operations personnel served important roles as outside experts to inform congressional thinking on the path to the creation of USSOCOM and ASD/SOLIC. Ted Lunger, who worked for Representative Dan Daniel, was a former U.S. Army Special Forces officer. Ken Johnson, a former member of 5th Special Forces Group, helped to write the Defense Reorganization report, and helped to shape Locher's thinking on SOF issues.[34] To refine their thinking on SOLIC reform, both Senator Cohen and his lead staff member, Chris Mellon, spoke with several former special operators.[35] Throughout the drafting

---

[34] Interview with former congressional staff, February 10, 2016.

[35] Marquis, 1997; and Boykin, 1991.

of Nunn-Cohen, Locher and others quietly met with active-duty SOF personnel to gain a better understanding of the support and capabilities challenges that SOF were facing.

Senior SOF leaders can also be valuable policy advisers. While the members of SOPAG were influential and offered observations from their experiences to congressional staff, the influence of LTG Sam Wilson in particular was critical to crafting and passing Nunn-Cohen: Not only did he play a central role in NDAA negotiations between the House and the Senate, he also served as a continual source of credible, senior-level information on special operations challenges.

Well-grounded research supplements practitioner testimony. In the case of DoD reorganization, congressional staff had spent years researching management and organizational issues at the Pentagon and published a widely read and authoritative report on the subject, earning its authors credibility on defense-reform issues. On SOLIC reform, the articles published by AFJI provided a forum to generate ideas, provide expertise openly, and bring SOF issues to public debate.

Create public debate on needed reforms. By bringing key SOF capability deficiencies into the public eye, Congress was able to gain further critical information to understand and convey the urgency of the situation, create networks of supporters throughout both houses of Congress and inside both parties, and leverage the Pentagon to acknowledge certain deficiencies in support to SOF. This was accomplished by members voicing their own opinions in hearings and in floor speeches, calling for hearings to gain testimony from outside experts and government and military officials, and by offering legislation to generate debate on SOF issues with the Pentagon.

Cultivate an SOF network for ongoing, informed support. Lynn Rylander, Noel Koch's key adviser, had close relationships with House and Senate staff. Rylander and Locher, formerly colleagues in OSD, maintained open communication on challenges SOF reform faced within the Pentagon after Locher moved on to Capitol Hill.[36] The close and continuing relationship between LTG Sam Wilson and his representative, Dan Daniel, was also a key factor in how SOF advo-

---

[36] Interview with former congressional staff, February 10, 2016.

cacy influenced legislative change. Developing and maintaining long-term relationships built on trust and education is critical at all levels, senior to staff.

In the case of the Nunn-Cohen amendment and the House SOLIC reform legislation, the congressional coalition that actively supported SOF issues was never large. Instead, a small number of influential members of Congress built support from the momentum and goodwill generated after the passage of Goldwater-Nichols and from individual influence and established authority on defense issues.[37]

Develop relationships with congressional staff. In Congress, influence is often carried by key staff members. Because staff often have limited "bandwidth," they tend to rely on outside experts to gain detailed understanding of issues before they approach the members they support. Investing time in relationships with staff members, such as relevant committee staff or members' personal staff advisers on defense issues, can prove beneficial in advancing policy goals, as evidenced by the experience of SOPAG members, Noel Koch and his office, and other SOF advocates who developed strong relationships with such staff as Ted Lunger and Jim Locher.[38]

Identify opportune policy windows and act quickly. Policy windows may be fleeting, so networks and advocacy efforts must be well in place to move quickly and create critical change at the right time. Leveraging wide-ranging networks—such as on Capitol Hill or within DoD—can help SOF to understand when conditions may be conducive to push for such changes. By waiting to address SOLIC reforms until after Goldwater-Nichols legislation was complete, SOF advocates were able to effectively achieve the changes it required in a way they might not have been able to if they had acted earlier. When the appropriate legislation emerged to support the creation of USSOCOM and ASD/SOLIC, the SOLIC community was well prepared to argue for the requirements and employed credible voices at the right time to gain a foothold into the policy discussion.

---

[37] Interview with former congressional staff, February 10, 2016.

[38] Interview with former congressional staff, February 10, 2016.

CHAPTER EIGHT

Special Operations Capabilities: Post-9/11 SOF Expansion

Overview

Following the attacks of September 11, 2001, the U.S. SOF community expanded massively (although not instantly). From an end strength of roughly 38,000 in 2001, USSOCOM grew to roughly 63,000 in 2012.[1] While growth has tailed off in subsequent years, the expansion was remarkable and unprecedented. While some expansion of SOF was no doubt inevitable given the size of the post-9/11 policy window, the form and scale of expansion was not a given. It is also striking that the expansion took place over more than a decade and thus crossed administrations and Congresses.

This chapter spans five parts. First, it briefly recaps the developments in SOCOM and the SOF policy community in the 1990s, which set the stage for post-9/11 expansion. The next three parts describe each of the three major phases of SOF expansion: the immediate post-9/11 period (2001–2005), the critical 2006 Quadrennial Defense Review (QDR) and after (2006–2010), and finally the 2010 QDR and after (2010–2014). The chapter concludes with key themes from the case.

---

[1] Thomas and Dougherty, 2013, p. 31.

A Growing but Frustrated Community: SOF in the 1990s

SOF policy triumphs of the 1980s, culminating in the creation of SOCOM and its MFP-11 budget, were impressive but only the first in a series of battles to establish a strong SOF policy community. The 1990s were a critical development period for SOCOM, ASD/SOLIC, and SOF generally. Yet it was also a time of significant policy frustration, particularly as the SOF policy community tried to push policy options for which there was no window.

One of the first major developments for SOCOM in this period was creating an organization and staff with SOF credentials and experience. SOCOM was not created from the ground up as a "blank slate." Instead, the former U.S. Readiness Command (REDCOM) was redesignated as SOCOM and the last commander of REDCOM, GEN James Lindsay, became the first SOCOM commander.

While Lindsay had some SOF experience, REDCOM had been charged with providing general purposes forces for contingencies. The organization and staff reflected this charge, and it took some time to adjust to the SOCOM role as personnel rotated in and out.[2] Equally important, SOCOM had to establish relationships with the service SOF components—USASOC; Air Force Special Operations Command; and Naval Special Warfare Command. This developmental period was inevitable, but it meant that the most powerful institutional advocate for SOF, SOCOM, was heavily occupied with internal matters during the first half of the 1990s.

Similarly, ASD/SOLIC had to generate an initial organization and staff. In contrast to SOCOM, ASD/SOLIC did start with a mostly blank slate. However, it encountered friction within its parent organization, OSD, where at least some officials viewed the new entity as something foisted on them by an interventionist Congress encroaching on Executive prerogatives.[3] ASD/SOLIC was placed under the Under-Secretary of Defense for Policy, where it competed with regional offices for influence. SOCOM and ASD/SOLIC also sometimes found them-

---

[2] Interview with former senior military officer, March 16, 2016.

[3] Interview with former DoD civilian, March 10, 2016.

selves in competition as they sought to come to grips with their respective responsibilities.

Finally, SOF, like the rest of the military, were adjusting to the end of the Cold War. This major geostrategic shift meant both a change in possible adversaries and declining overall resources for defense. As an example, 10th Special Forces Group could no longer focus on missions conducted behind the front lines of an advancing Warsaw Pact.

The U.S. invasion of Panama in 1989 (Operation Just Cause) did allow SOF units to execute operations in conjunction with conventional forces under an improved command and control structure. The overall commander of the operation, LTG Carl Stiner, was an experienced special operator and ensured SOF were able to operate appropriately under a designated task force (Task Force Black). He further ensured the task force would be well led by appointing JSOC's then–MG Wayne Downing to command it.[4] The operation was an overall success, although there were a few command and control issues, such as the incompatibility of the existing Joint Deployment System with special operations requirements.[5] The operation allowed SOF to enter the 1990s on a high note.

By the mid-1990s, SOCOM and ASD/SOLIC had established themselves sufficiently to begin forming a policy community within the Executive Branch. SOF also adapted to the post–Cold War environment by focusing on new missions or refocusing on existing ones. The major new mission for SOF in the 1990s was counterproliferation (CP), as fears of "loose nukes" following the dissolution of the Soviet Union multiplied in Washington policy circles.[6] In 1998, SOCOM commander GEN Peter Schoomaker noted in testimony to Congress:

---

[4] Harry S. Brown, "The Command and Control of Special Operations Forces," thesis, Monterey, Calif.: Naval Postgraduate School, December 1996, p. 62.

[5] Ronald H. Cole, *Operation Just Cause: The Planning and Execution of Joint Operations in Panama February 1988–January 1990*, Washington, D.C.: Joint History Office, Office of the Joint Chiefs of Staff, 1995, p. 23.

[6] Interview with former senior military officer, April 12, 2016.

> The asymmetric challenge with the gravest potential facing the U.S. today is the threat posed by the global proliferation of WMD [weapons of mass destruction] and their means of delivery. . . . Today, counterproliferation (CP) has been given top operational priority at USSOCOM. CP includes actions taken to locate, identify, seize, destroy, render safe, or transport WMD. We are pursuing several approaches to address the WMD threat, including working with the geographic CINCs to determine how best to bring SOF's capabilities to bear in support of theater CP objectives.[7]

CP gave SOF both a clear mission and a set of resources to pursue it, but it was not the only mission.

A second significant mission in the late 1990s was CT, with the al Qaeda organization recognized as a growing threat. Here, the SOF policy community inside the Executive Branch was much less successful in gaining authorization to conduct operations. It is thus useful to compare CT with CP in terms of the SOF policy community's ability to recognize and exploit policy windows.

CP had broad bipartisan support in the Legislative and Executive Branches. In the legislature, well-respected Senators Sam Nunn and Richard Lugar promoted legislation passed in 1991 to assist the Soviet Union (and its successors) in dismantling and securing nuclear weapons and materiel. In the Executive Branch, proliferation was routinely noted as the most serious threat facing the United States.

In some ways, the CT threat was similar to CP. It was routinely listed by the intelligence community as one of the top threats to the United States along with CP. Osama bin Laden and al Qaeda were often designated as the most serious CT threat to the United States and were believed to be seeking WMDs as well, as CIA Director George Tenet noted in 1999.[8]

---

[7] Peter Schoomaker, "Testimony to Senate Armed Services Committee," 1998, p. 8.

[8] George Tenet, "DCI Statement: Current and Projected National Security Threats, State of the Director of Central Intelligence George J. Tenet Before the Senate Armed Services Committee Hearing on Current and Projected National Security Threats," Central Intelligence Agency website, speeches and testimony archive, February 1999, p. 2.

While SOCOM and the SOF policy community were able to gain resources to develop their CP capabilities and authorities with little controversy, they did not gain equivalent authorities to conduct operations against al Qaeda. As scholar Richard Shultz has detailed, there was enormous resistance at senior levels within DoD (both military and civilian) to operational use of SOF for CT in an offensive role (i.e., not hostage rescue or incident response). The reasons for this resistance varied from viewing CT as law enforcement or intelligence rather than military problem to risk aversion after the battle of Mogadishu in 1993.[9]

In short, while there was a wide-open policy window for CP, there was no window for offensive CT in the late 1990s. Moreover, efforts by the SOF policy community to press such options despite this lack of a window may have increased rather than decreased resistance. As Shultz notes, those who continued to advocate for offensive CT by SOF were increasingly portrayed as "pariah cowboys."[10]

Shultz highlights the military's antipathy to one of the most vociferous proponents of an aggressive CT policy, NSC staffer Richard A. Clarke:

> "Anything Dick Clarke suggested, the Joint Staff was going to be negative about," said one. Some generals had been vitriolic, calling Clarke "a madman, out of control, power hungry, wanted to be a hero, all that kind of stuff." In fact, one of these former officials emphasized, "when we would carry back from the counterterrorism group one of those SOF counterterrorism proposals, our job was to figure out not how to execute it, but how we were going to say no." By turning Clarke into a pariah, the Pentagon brass discredited precisely the options that might have spared us the tragedy of September 11, 2001.[11]

---

[9] Richard M. Shultz, "Showstoppers," *Weekly Standard*, January 26, 2004.

[10] Shultz, 2004.

[11] Shultz, 2004.

Shultz may be overstating the case to some degree, but the central point is that those seeking to push through a closed policy window may have made the challenge more rather than less difficult.

At the end of the 1990s, the SOF policy community had become organized and capable, with resources flowing from the CP mission supporting at least some SOF forces even in lean budgetary times. Yet, it was also a frustrated community, as summed up by Schoomaker in remarks to Shultz about offensive CT: "But Special Operations was never given the mission. It was very, very frustrating. It was like having a brand-new Ferrari in the garage, and nobody wants to race it because you might dent the fender."[12]

Catalyst 1: 9/11

The Window Opens: SOF Expansion 2001–2005

The frustration of the SOF policy community came to a definitive and terrible end in 2001. Within days of the attacks, plans to use SOF against al Qaeda and the Taliban in Afghanistan were in development. While there were frustrations in the development and execution of these plans, they were not blocked at the policy level in DoD or elsewhere.

Indeed, Secretary of Defense Donald Rumsfeld was himself frustrated that the CIA took the lead on much of the initial war effort. In a terse October memorandum (known as a "snowflake") to chairman of the JCS Gen Richard Myers, Rumsfeld asked:

> Does the fact that the Defense Department can't do anything on the ground in Afghanistan until CIA people go in first to prepare the way suggest that the Defense Department is lacking a capability we need? Specifically, given the nature of our world, isn't it conceivable that the Department ought not to be in a position of near total dependence on CIA in situations such as this? After you have reflected on this, please come back to me with a

---

[12] Shultz, 2004.

coordinated proposal as to what we might want to do about it, if anything.[13]

Rumsfeld had been out of government since the 1970s and had thus missed much of the acrimony surrounding SOF in the 1980s and 1990s. His limited exposure to SOF since becoming secretary again had been generally positive. His frustration, combined with a generally positive view of SOF, created a major opportunity for SOF. This opportunity was reinforced by the success of the campaign in Afghanistan, which orchestrated CIA and SOF personnel on the ground with indigenous allies and massive U.S. airpower.

Stakeholder Analysis

Members of the SOF policy community quickly began to fill significant CT-related positions. GEN (ret.) Wayne Downing, a former SOCOM commander, became Deputy National Security Advisor for combating terrorism and requested by name as one of his staff CAPT William McRaven, a Navy SEAL and future SOCOM commander.[14] Other SOF policy community members offered advice to Secretary Rumsfeld.[15] Perhaps most notably, Rumsfeld broke with precedent by making retired Schoomaker, the former SOCOM commander, Chief of Staff of the Army in 2003. This was the first time a career special operations officer had become Chief of Staff, as well as the first time an officer was recalled from retirement to become Chief of Staff.

Key Decisions

These members of the SOF policy community helped Secretary Rumsfeld recognize relatively quickly that the current size of SOF was insufficient to support the demands of a campaign that would stretch far beyond Afghanistan for an indefinite period. One solution, which

---

[13] Donald Rumsfeld, "Subject: Afghanistan," memorandum to Gen Myers, October 17, 2001.

[14] Interview with former senior military officer, March 30, 2016.

[15] Interview with former senior military officer, March 16, 2016.

Rumsfeld requested from chairman of the JCS General Myers in August 2002, was to shift as many roles and missions as possible from SOF to conventional forces to reduce demand on SOF. However, it was clear that only a small number of missions could be transferred, limiting the efficacy of this solution.[16]

Another solution was to draw on a major untapped pool of potential SOF recruits—the U.S. Marine Corps. In early 2005, Rumsfeld, in conjunction with SOCOM commander GEN Doug Brown, concluded that the creation of a service SOF component for the Marines—Marine Special Operations Command (MARSOC)—was worth studying.[17] By November 2005, Rumsfeld, Brown, and Marine Corps Commandant Gen. Michael Hagee had agreed on the formation of MARSOC, which was incorporated into the 2006 QDR.[18] This too was an important but only a partial solution, expected to add a few thousand SOF operators along with such critical enablers as intelligence.[19]

A third solution was to fill out the existing SOF force structure, which, in many cases, had not been manned at 100 percent before 9/11. For example, there were roughly 230 unfilled special forces billets on September 11, 2001.[20] SOCOM, along with the service components, took steps to expand recruitment and selection for SOF. Naval Special Warfare, for example, stood up two new SEAL Teams, 7 and 10, in 2002. Most notably, USASOC invested in the pipeline for the Special Forces Qualification course and opened an "18X" route for direct

---

[16] Donald Rumsfeld, "Subject: Reducing Demands on Special Operations Forces," memorandum to Gen. Myers, September 26, 2002.

[17] Donald Rumsfeld, "Subject Marine Special Operations Command," memorandum to Gen. Doug Brown, February 7, 2005.

[18] The QDR "is a legislatively-mandated review of Department of Defense strategy and priorities. The QDR will set a long-term course for DOD as it assesses the threats and challenges that the nation faces and re-balances DOD's strategies, capabilities, and forces to address today's conflicts and tomorrow's threats." For an overview, see "Quadrennial Defense Review," U.S. Department of Defense website, undated.

[19] Donald Rumsfeld, "Subject: Marine Special Operations Component (MARSOC)," memorandum to Gen. Pete Pace, November 4, 2005; and interview with former senior military officer, April 12, 2016.

[20] Interview with former senior military officer, April 12, 2016.

accession to special forces.[21] The decision to invest in the pipeline rather than immediate force growth would pay dividends, as noted below.[22]

Outcomes

The immediate post-9/11 period decisively ended the obstacles of the 1990s. It also empowered the SOF policy community, which occupied important positions both formally and informally. Combined with the expanding budgets for DoD generally and Rumsfeld's disdain for bureaucratic answers, SOF were able to expand organically during this initial period.[23]

Big Changes: SOF Expansion 2006–2010

Catalyst 2: 2006 QDR

As the wars in Iraq and Afghanistan ground on in 2004 and 2005, the limited organic expansions to SOF size became increasingly unable to maintain SOF readiness. According to one interviewee, there were signs in late 2004 and early 2005 that at least some elements of SOF were actually *smaller* than they had been before 9/11 because of casualties and/or materiel losses.[24] This realization provided the catalyst for a major assessment of the status and size of SOF, directed by Secretary Rumsfeld and chairman of the JCS Gen. Peter Pace.

Stakeholder Analysis

Downing was selected to lead the assessment, with assistance from MG (ret.) William Garrison and Michael Vickers, a former SOF and CIA officer. The policies the three eventually proposed (detailed below) had many supporters, including SOCOM commander GEN Doug

---

[21] Thomas and Dougherty, 2013, pp. 32–33.

[22] Interview with former senior military officer, March 16, 2016.

[23] Many interviewees noted that Rumsfeld was dismissive of even four-star-level bureaucracy and was willing to publicly berate those with weak answers.

[24] Interview with former senior military officer, April 12, 2016.

Brown and his deputy VADM Eric Olson as well as Army Chief of Staff General Schoomaker. Indeed, some interviewees believed the Downing report reflected rather than generated consensus on SOF issues and was more an exercise in "bureaucratic insurance" than original analysis.[25] Regardless, the report helped crystalize the need for SOF force structure expansion.

Olson in particular played a major role advocating for SOF in the 2006 QDR. Brown, realizing how critical the QDR would be for SOF, assigned Olson to lead SOCOM QDR efforts. While this disconnected Olson from the day-to-day functioning of the command to some degree (he spent the bulk of his time in Washington), it meant SOCOM had a very senior and well-respected representative at the table alongside the services.[26]

Proposal Formation

The Downing report first noted the scale of post-9/11 expansion. In particular, Army SOF "increased throughput from 282 new active duty enlisted Special Forces troops in 2001 to 617 new Special Forces troops in 2005—the equivalent of an additional SF Battalion a year—with a further goal of 750 students per year."[27] This was in large part because of the immediate post-9/11 investments in the Special Forces pipeline, including the Special Warfare Center at Fort Bragg. But, despite this success, the report noted several ongoing shortfalls, including those implicit in recommendations to "Increase SOF capabilities and capacities for the GWOT [Global War on Terror] in several areas, most importantly in Special Forces and SMU capacity."[28] For Special Forces, the authors believed two new Special Forces groups (six battal-

---

[25] Interview with former senior military officer, April 12, 2016.

[26] Interview with former senior military officer, March 30, 2016.

[27] Downing, 2005, p. 2.

[28] Downing, 2005, p. 3.

ions) would be required, along with two more Ranger Regiment battalions and a 33 percent increase in SMU squadrons.[29]

These recommendations were not simply the view of Downing and his coauthors. They made an extensive effort to get views from a variety of sources, including

> senior officials in the Office of the Secretary of Defense, the Joint Chiefs of Staff, the Department of State, the Central Intelligence Agency, the National Counterterrorism Center, the Geographic and Functional Combatant Commands, United States Special Operations Command, and the Theater Special Operations Commands [TSOCs]. I also consulted several United States Ambassadors in priority and high priority GWOT countries. . . .[30]

The effort to incorporate a wide variety of stakeholder perspectives ensured that much of the resistance to many of Downing's proposals would be at least partly defused. Thus, even if the Downing report did not generate truly novel policy proposals, it did a great service in ensuring that virtually all important stakeholders felt they had been included in a deliberative policy process.

Downing and Vickers were also members of a Red Cell established to provide an alternative to the emerging consensus within the 2006 QDR process. The QDR consensus appeared to be gravitating toward making incremental rather than substantial changes to force structure, despite the radically changed security environment since the previous QDR. Several observers noted that SOF in particular seemed to be receiving only modestly increased resources relative to the vastly expanded operational activity SOF had been conducting.[31]

As the Red Cell worked to make its recommendations outside the normal QDR process, Olson advocated for SOF inside the process. Perhaps most notable was his effort to ensure SOF would have expanded

---

[29] Wayne Downing, "Special Operations Forces Assessment," memorandum for the Secretary of Defense, Chairman, Joint Chiefs of Staff, November 9, 2005, p. 4.

[30] Downing, 2005, p. 1.

[31] Interview with former senior military officer, March 30, 2016.

intelligence collection capability, including an organic unmanned aerial vehicle unit.

Key Junctures and Outcomes

The outcome of the 2006 QDR was dramatic, adding "13,119 additional billets to USSOCOM's end strength at a cost of $7.5 billion."[32] According to one source, only about 25 percent of this expansion was in frontline SOF operators: The rest were in a variety of enabling and supporting positions.[33] Much of this expansion was derived at least in part from the Red Cell's recommendations, which paralleled those of the Downing report and were ultimately incorporated into the QDR.

It is worth noting some of the differences between the Downing report recommendations and the ultimate shape of the QDR expansion. Downing's recommendation regarding Special Forces, for example, was for two additional groups of three battalions, while the form adopted in the QDR was to add a fourth battalion to each of the five existing groups. While the number of additional battalions was nearly identical, the structures had very different implications. Two additional groups would have added two coveted O6-level commands to Special Forces, each of which could be the nucleus for a deployed special operations task force. However, creating these new groups would also have required resources (including time) over and above those for the additional battalions. The expansion of existing groups was thus likely a policy compromise that achieved much of the effect the Downing report was seeking in terms of supporting a rotation base for Special Forces without requiring the additional resources of new groups.

Similarly, the Downing recommendation on additional Ranger battalions was distributed across then-current units. Rather than two operational battalions, Ranger Regiment received one additional company in each of its three existing battalions. It also got a new special troops battalion, which consolidated and expanded support, intelligence, and maintenance elements for the regiment. While this did not greatly expand the operational capability of the regiment, it very much

---

[32] Thomas and Dougherty, 2013, p. 32.

[33] Interview with former senior military officer, March 30, 2016.

supported the Downing report's objectives of shifting to a "globally persistent presence force" that could "collect low-level intelligence."[34]

The QDR did expand SOF operational capacity for the missions additional Ranger battalions might have undertaken. It did so by adding to each SEAL Team's manning a total of several hundred additional SEALs to a community that, at the time, numbered fewer than 2,000.[35] This decision likely helped defuse any concerns that the Downing report's recommendations were overly Army-centric (Downing, Garrison, and Vickers were all Army veterans), while ensuring SOF were able to draw on as broad a pool of potential applicants as possible for the largest expansion of SOF since Vietnam.

The QDR also mandated expansion not included in the Downing report, including formal endorsement of the creation of MARSOC. Most notable among these was the establishment of the SOF unmanned aerial vehicle squadron Olson had been seeking. The 2006 QDR also directed a one-third increase in civil-affairs and psychological-operations personnel.

While the 2006 QDR on paper looked like a significant policy success for SOF, it nonetheless required significant follow-up in the implementation phase. This was to ensure that, as Congress authorized and appropriated funds, none of the QDR decisions was "undermined by lobbying."[36] The monitoring of implementation was not particularly acrimonious, but it made clear by its presence that no policy success could be taken for granted.

---

[34] Downing, 2005, p. 4.

[35] Thomas and Dougherty, 2013, p. 33; and interview with former senior military officer, March 30, 2016.

[36] Interview with former senior military officer, March 30, 2016.

Fine Tuning: SOF Expansion 2010–2014

Catalyst 3: 2010 QDR

The expansion mandated by the 2006 QDR would take years to actually accomplish. For example, Special Forces added about one battalion (out of the five it was directed to add) a year, completing the build-out in October 2012.[37] Yet, by the time of the 2010 QDR, it was clear SOF expansion had ameliorated many of the readiness and rotation base issues identified in the Downing report. However, more needed to be done to enhance the capacity of SOF for persistent and global engagement.

Stakeholder Analysis

LTG Frank Kearney, deputy commander of SOCOM from 2007 to 2010, played the same role in the 2010 QDR that Olson had in the 2006 QDR. Olson, who had become SOCOM commander, remained sensitive to the importance of senior SOCOM representation for the QDR. Michael Vickers, who had been a part of the Downing review and 2006 QDR Red Cell, had been appointed the ASD/SOLIC in 2007 and likewise remained a proponent for SOF, along with other such key staff members as Garry Reid.[38]

Proposal Formation

The main shortfall identified by the SOF policy community in 2009 was enablers, particularly airlift and intelligence. In a March 2009 testimony to Congress, Robert Martinage noted:[39]

> The high operations tempo of SOF ground units in Iraq and Afghanistan has already overwhelmed the 160th SOAR's [Special

---

[37] Ramon M. Marrero, "4th Battalion, 7th Special Forces Group Activates," *Paraglide*, October 25, 2012.

[38] Interview with former DoD official with responsibility for special operations, Washington, D.C., March 25, 2016.

[39] Martinage was from the Center for Strategic and Budgetary Assessments, the think tank where Michael Vickers had been a senior fellow before becoming ASD/SOLIC.

Operations Aviation Regiment] lift capacity. Over the past several years, conventional Army aviation units have routinely provided lift support for about two thirds of SOF ground units. In Afghanistan, nearly fifty percent of the lift requests to support Joint Special Operations Task Force-Afghanistan operations have been unmet in recent years, owing primarily to competing demand from JSOC's SMUs and conventional ground forces. Given the ongoing expansion of Army SF and SEAL force structure by one third, as well as the standing up of the Marine Special Operations Advisor Group and two Marine Special Operations Battalions under MARSOC, the demand for rotary-wing aviation is certain to expand.[40]

Martinage and other analysts called for a major expansion of SOF aviation, including an additional battalion of MH-47G heavy-lift helicopters as well as an expanded role for the Navy in providing rotary-wing support to SOCOM. In addition to expanding rotary-wing aviation, many called for additional investment in Air Force Special Operations Command fixed-wing aviation (i.e., the transport and gunship fleets). The average age of those fleets was more than 35 years, driving maintenance costs up. Given demand increases, both fleets were almost literally in danger of falling to pieces.

At the same time, others in the SOF policy community identified a continuing need for additional SOF intelligence assets. In 2008, Michael Flynn, Rich Juergens, and Thomas Cantrell published a widely read article, "Employing ISR: SOF Best Practices." The article was based on the authors' extensive experience supporting a special operations task force in Iraq. In addition to calling for additional airborne intelligence, surveillance, and reconnaissance (ISR), the article highlighted that "[a] critical enabler in employing ISR was having forward processing, exploitation, and dissemination (PED)."[41]

---

[40] Robert Martinage, *Special Operations Forces: Challenges and Opportunities*, testimony before the U.S. House of Representatives House Armed Services Committee, Subcommittee on Terrorism, Unconventional Threats and Capabilities, Washington, D.C., March 3, 2009, p. 17.

[41] Michael T. Flynn, Rich Juergens, and Thomas L. Cantrell, "Employing ISR: SOF Best Practices," *Joint Forces Quarterly*, Vol. 50, 2008, p. 59.

Key Junctures and Outcomes

The 2010 QDR ultimately mandated SOF expansion that was smaller than some of the more ambitious proposals noted above. For example, instead of an entire MH-47G battalion, the 2010 QDR mandated an additional company. The expansion and recapitalization of fixed aircraft was nonetheless extensive, with the Air Force directed to create 16 new gunships and allowed to retire older models while still expanding the fleet from 25 to 33. It also directed additional expansion in intelligence support for forward operations.[42] In total, the 2010 QDR added almost 3,600 new billets to SOCOM.[43]

Summary of Lessons

The experience of SOF before and after 9/11 underscores the crucial importance of policy windows. In the 1990s, the newly established SOCOM was able to build its credibility and capability by exploiting, to the extent possible, a policy window for CP activity that opened with the collapse of the Soviet Union. Yet little progress was possible on CT, as there was no window, despite the efforts of such policy entrepreneurs as Richard Clarke, to open one. Then, after 9/11, SOCOM was able to exploit the opening of a CT policy window to expand further. In both periods, senior SOF leaders had to navigate the policy world successfully though personal relationships and engagement with both formal and informal policy processes. This suggests the following lessons.

Do not try to force a policy window. Although, in hindsight, the efforts of many in the SOF policy community to promote the use of SOF against al Qaeda and other terrorists were correct, the policy window for such action was not open. Attempts to force a window by such advocates as NSC Director Clarke were counterproductive, as these advocates were branded as "pariah cowboys" and became less effective as a result. Those planning future efforts to advocate the use

---

[42] DoD, *Quadrennial Defense Review Report*, Washington, D.C., February 2010, pp. 21–23.

[43] Thomas and Dougherty, 2013, p. 34.

of special warfare should carefully evaluate whether a policy window exists before committing significant resources to advocacy.

Exploit opportunities to develop capability and credibility. The CP mission, which had not really been a SOCOM mission in 1990, had become central to SOCOM by 1998. In contrast to CT, the policy window for CP had been wide open, and the command's embrace of the mission had allowed it to gain resources even in an era of post–Cold War military drawdown. This allowed a command still in the process of establishing itself to gain credibility with the broader defense policy establishment. Similarly, special warfare advocates should scan the horizon for opportunities to build capability and credibility, even if the opportunity is not directly related to the core of special warfare.

Cultivate personal relationships. Many of the most effective advocates for SOF expansion had opportunities to cultivate personal ties to senior policymakers. Downing knew most of the George W. Bush administration's senior leadership from his time on the NSC. Likewise, Schoomaker had developed a relationship of trust with Rumsfeld that was sufficient to lead the secretary to overturn precedent and appoint a retired special operations officer Chief of Staff of the Army. Special warfare advocates should likewise seek to build personal relationships with the civilian policy world.

Generate stakeholder consensus to the extent possible. While some doubt the novelty of the recommendations in the Downing report, it was nonetheless important because it canvassed stakeholders both inside and outside DoD. This meant the recommendations had already been socialized before being translated into the QDR, reducing the likelihood of strong negative reaction.

Do not rely exclusively on formal process, but do not ignore it either. The success of SOF expansion in the 2006 QDR was a result of disciplined engagement with the formal process of the QDR supplemented by the external interventions of the Downing report and the Red Cell. Without the focus on the QDR that Brown and Olson maintained, including implementation, many elements of SOF expansion might have been watered down. At the same time, the external prodding by the Downing report and Red Cell was an important catalyst for an almost unprecedented change.

CHAPTER NINE
Special Operations Capabilities: Special Mission Unit Expansion

Overview

One of the major aspects of the post-9/11 SOF expansion was the increase in size, scope, and authority of special operations task forces focused on CT. These task forces, built around such elite special-mission units as the 75th Ranger Regiment, began to evolve in the period before 9/11. Post-9/11, they became central to the GWOT, requiring very significant changes in organization and authority.

For clarity, the short-hand term *SMU community* will be used here to refer to the overarching construct that governed these units. When deployed, the SMU community is part of a task force typically referred to by a number.

Early Transformation: The 1990s

In the 1980s, the formative period for the special operations command and units most associated with the SMU community, operations were almost exclusively discrete missions, deploying directly from the continental United States. For example, units associated with the SMU community supported or conducted operations globally during this period but seldom spent long periods away from home station. These discrete operations required exquisite planning and execution but in many cases did not require the SMU community–associated units to develop their own intelligence. Likewise, they did not require the management of geographically dispersed units deployed for weeks or months.[1]

The nature of operations conducted by SOF units began to change in the 1990s. One of the most widely noted of these was the deployment of Task Force Ranger to Somalia in August 1993. The task force was ordered to capture Somali warlord Mohamed Farah Aideed and other members of his Habr Gidr clan militia.[2]

Task Force Ranger marked one of the first times such a task force operated on a sustained basis, conducting six missions against Aideed's militia in August and September 1993. This sustained deployment required the development of a command and control relationship to higher headquarters. As an Army history notes:

> The command and control structure of TF [Task Force] Ranger evolved during its time in theater. It eventually was a carefully worked out arrangement that ensured coordination of American elements on the ground without compromising its security or U.S. national interests. In accord with the Goldwater-Nichols Defense Reorganization Act, the unified commander (in this case, [Central Command commander] General Hoar) had command and control over all U.S. military resources in theater, including the units supporting UNOSOM [United Nations Operations Somalia] II and TF Ranger. However, TF Ranger did not report to General Montgomery, the U.S. commander on the ground in Somalia who was dual-hatted as the UNOSOM II deputy commander. Instead, General Hoar had the TF Ranger commander, Maj. Gen. William F. Garrison, report to him directly. Thus, TF Ranger, as a strategic U.S. asset, did not fall under the UNOSOM II commander but rather remained strictly under American operational command and control. For his part, after an initial misstep during a poorly coordinated mission that hit a UN compound, General Garrison worked to ensure that he coordinated all TF Ranger operations with General Montgom-

---

[1] Interview with former senior military officer, April 12, 2016.

[2] Richard W. Stewart, *The United States Army in Somalia, 1992–1994*, Washington, D.C.: Center of Military History, CMH Pub 70–81–1, 2002, pp. 17–18.

ery. He also closely tied in his force to the U.S. QRF by exchanging liaison officers.[3]

While the experience of Task Force Ranger set a certain precedent, the issue of command and control relationships between a deployed SOF task force, higher headquarters, and other U.S. and coalition units would persist as an issue for much of the following decade. Task Force Ranger's mission ended after an intense battle during and after the task force's seventh mission in Somalia on October 3–4.[4]

Following the Dayton Peace Accord ending the civil war in the former Yugoslavia, SOF began participating in a second mission requiring longer-duration deployment. As part of the North Atlantic Treaty Organization (NATO)–led stabilization force (SFOR), SOF participated in operations to capture persons indicted for war crimes (PIFWCs). As President Bill Clinton described in a communication to Congress in 1997,

> The SFOR has contributed to efforts to bring persons indicted for war crimes into custody in The Hague. . . . United States force contribution to SFOR in Bosnia remains approximately 8,500. United States forces participating in SFOR are U.S. Army forces that were stationed in Germany and the United States. Other participating U.S. forces include special operations forces.[5]

This mission was lower profile in some ways than Task Force Ranger but was similarly focused on manhunting. As an aviation sergeant major noted in an official unclassified recounting of his unit's mission in Bosnia for the U.S. Army's Sergeants Major Academy: "Our mission was to move quickly and safely as possible inserting special operations soldiers and infantry soldiers into the prescribed sector

---

[3] Stewart, 2002, p. 18.

[4] Stewart, 2002, pp. 18–25.

[5] William J. Clinton, "Communication from the President of the United States: A Report on Continued U.S. Contributions in Support of Peacekeeping Efforts in the Former Yugoslavia," December 17, 1997.

to snatch PIFWCs under the cover of night operations using NVGs [night-vision goggles]."[6]

One of the major elements of the PIFWC mission for SOF units was the collection of intelligence. This had been part of the Task Force Ranger mission as well, but the PIFWC mission lasted substantially longer (at least 1997–2006) and was thus more significant. The mission was absorbing a sufficiently large element of SOF that post-9/11 chairman of the JCS Gen Richard Myers, tasked by Secretary of Defense Rumsfeld to find missions that could be shifted from SOF to conventional units, listed one as "Intelligence support related to PIFWCs in Bosnia-Herzegovina and Kosovo."[7]

By the time of the 9/11 attacks, SMU community–associated units had begun to adjust to two of the major challenges they would face in the GWOT. The first was command and control of persistently deployed, geographically dispersed units. The second was the need to generate and disseminate actionable intelligence for manhunting. Yet, the scale of post-9/11 operations was massive compared with the operations of the 1990s, requiring significant further evolution in structure and authorities.

Initial Expansion and Change: 2001–2005

Catalyst 1: Afghanistan

SMU community–associated units were a major component of the war in Afghanistan almost from the beginning. One was "a key SOF unit for advanced force operations, such as reconnaissance and strikes against high value targets," that is, those central to the campaign.[8] While the

---

[6] Greg Springer, *The Element of Surprise*, Ft. Bliss, Tex.: U.S. Army Sergeants Major Academy, p. 4.

[7] Richard Myers, "Reducing Demands on Special Operations Forces," memorandum to Secretary of Defense, September 26, 2002.

[8] Richard Kugler, *Operation Anaconda in Afghanistan: A Case Study of Adaptation in Battle* (Case Studies in Defense Transformation, Number 5), Washington, D.C.: National Defense University, Center for Technology and National Security Policy, 2007, p. 8.

overall campaign in Afghanistan was extraordinarily successful, operations in the Shah-i-Kot Valley in 2002 highlighted some of the same command and control challenges seen in Mogadishu almost a decade earlier.[9]

The SMU community also became a major element of the war in Iraq a year later. After the initial invasion, elements of the task force "were tasked with capturing or killing the high value former Baathist leaders."[10] In addition to command and control challenges, by late 2003, the task force commander, then–Major General McChrystal, and his subordinates identified exploitation, analysis, and dissemination of intelligence for targeting as well as links between forward SOF units and rear-echelon headquarters as serious deficiencies in the task force construct.[11] These challenges would catalyze substantial transformation of the SMU community in a short period.

Stakeholder Analysis
McChrystal was, without question, the central advocate for change and expansion of the SMU community, but he had substantial support from both his seniors and subordinates. U.S. Central Command (CENTCOM) commander GEN John Abizaid was a major advocate. He convened a conference at his headquarters in Tampa in January 2004 to press for greater interagency cooperation, yielding positive responses from senior intelligence community leaders. This created an opportunity for McChrystal to expand interagency collaboration. Abizaid agreed to McChrystal's request to be the single interface between the CENTCOM leader and his task force, regardless of his physical location.[12] He also received support from SOCOM commander GEN Doug Brown.

---

[9] Kugler, 2007.

[10] McChrystal, 2014, p. 100.

[11] McChrystal, 2014, pp. 105–107; and Christopher J. Lamb and Evan Munsing, *Secret Weapon: High-Value Target Teams as an Organizational Innovation*, Washington, D.C.: National Defense University Press, March 2011, pp. 16–17.

[12] McChrystal, 2014, pp. 95 and 116.

McChrystal's subordinates were equally important in helping develop and implement his vision. These subordinates included his deputy, then–RADM William McRaven, as well as COLs Tony Thomas, Scott Miller, Michael Flynn, and Bennet Sacolick.[13] McChrystal also carefully chose junior SOF officers for key positions to ensure his vision of interagency cooperation was appropriately executed.[14]

Key Decisions

The first key decision followed Abizaid's January 2004 conference in Tampa. McChrystal used this opportunity to call for the establishment of a Joint Interagency Task Force (JIATF) at Bagram Air Base in Afghanistan. It would subsequently be complemented by a JIATF based at Balad Air Base in Iraq.[15]

In describing JIATF development in Iraq, Christopher Lamb and Evan Munsing note the importance of McChrystal's efforts to persuade and encourage rather than dictate to the interagency:

> He wanted constant, seamless tracking of clandestine enemies, which was impossible without all-source intelligence working in direct cooperation with his operators. He also knew he could not command such assets and would have to woo them instead. . . . He asked senior officials from other departments and agencies to join his headquarters staff. He attracted support from the Intelligence Community through personal contacts and made a point of demonstrating how much they were valued as members of the team. Eventually, he was able to bring in a senior Intelligence Community official as his deputy for interagency operations, which raised the angst of Pentagon lawyers who worried about violating the statutory basis of the military chain of command. . . . He made sure everyone from every agency felt that they were part of the team. He was assiduous in recognizing contributions from interagency partners, often calling out individuals by name in

---

[13] McChrystal, 2014.

[14] Lamb and Munsing, 2011, p. 17.

[15] McChrystal, 2014.

meetings and video teleconferences, which could be held as often as four or five times a week.[16]

In parallel to the establishment of the JIATF, McChrystal and his subordinates developed a methodology known as F3EA—find, fix, finish, exploit, analyze. While "find, fix, finish" were not new concepts, the emphasis increasingly shifted to "exploit and analyze." This required significant internal change within the task force, enhancing the importance of sharing and connectivity.[17] For example, McChrystal highlights expanded connectivity with the Defense Intelligence Agency's National Media Exploitation Center as crucial to improving the exploitation of captured documents and other records:

> To pump terabytes of images and video to them, we augmented the thicket of antennae on our hangar roof with a grove of huge satellite dishes. We learned to feed their linguists intelligence about raided targets, so they had valuable context to help them parse the material. The operators, seeing greater value arise from captured documents, became more focused and effective in retrieving them . . . .[18]

In addition to leveraging interagency partners, the SMU community grew organically in its ability to exploit and analyze intelligence. While this process had begun in the 1990s, the expansion following 9/11 was much more significant. The SMU community had its own interrogation facilities and accumulated "a brigade sized force of intelligence people" during McChrystal's tenure.[19]

---

[16] Lamb and Munsing, 2011, p. 17.

[17] McChrystal, 2014; Lamb and Munsing, 2011; Flynn, Juergens, and Cantrell, 2008; and Jeffrey A. Builta and Eric N. Heller, "Reflections on 10 Years of Counterterrorism Analysis," *Studies in Intelligence*, Vol. 55, No. 3 (unclassified extracts), September 2011.

[18] McChrystal, 2014, p. 155.

[19] McChrystal, 2014, p. 156.

Outcomes

By the end of 2005, the efforts of McChrystal and his team had substantially changed the nature of the SMU community. The efforts begun in the 1990s to develop persistence and intelligence collection had finally been fully realized. The SMU community had transformed from "a collection of niche strike forces into a network able to integrate diverse elements of the U.S. government into a unified effort."[20]

Catalyst 2: Global Expansion, 2006–Present

While McChrystal and his team had been successful in changing the nature of the SMU community, command and control issues remained, along with resource constraints. The SMU community had increasingly global responsibilities, with Iraq and Afghanistan the major theaters of operations but not the only ones. These global responsibilities, coupled with the expanded size of the SMU community, began to raise concerns about command and control. At the same time, McChrystal himself was seen by many as integral to the success of the SMU community; yet, after more than two years in command, he was nearing the point at which he would normally be promoted to lieutenant general and move on. These two factors catalyzed a reevaluation of the status of the SMU commuinty and its command and control in late 2005.

Stakeholder Analysis and Proposal Formation

One of the major advocates for enhancing the status of the SMU community generally and McChrystal specifically was Secretary of Defense Donald Rumsfeld. By no later than mid-2005, McChrystal's operational success, combined with his careful attention to the Washington policy realm, had caught Rumsfeld's attention. In a note from July

---

[20] McChrystal, 2014, p. 119.

2005, Rumsfeld praised McChrystal's performance at a short-notice NSC meeting, adding a handwritten "[y]ou did a superb job!"[21]

In September 2005, Rumsfeld wrote a note to VADM (ret.) M. Staser Holcomb, his adviser on senior personnel matters:

> Please find out when Stan McChrystal's rotation is due. I think we ought to keep him right where he is. We can't afford to move him. We also might want to give some thought to a promotion, but don't spread that around.[22]

Rumsfeld's consideration of promoting McChrystal in place was reinforced by advocacy from the assessment of SOF led by GEN (ret.) Wayne Downing in fall 2005. This assessment, from November, concluded that the leadership of the SMU community should become a three-star command, with multiple two- and one-star subordinates. This would allow up to five simultaneous task forces to be deployed under the broader SMU community construct.[23]

Key Junctures

By January 2006 (if not sooner), Rumsfeld was convinced McChrystal needed to stay in place with a third star and greater resources and authorities. He forwarded a chart from McChrystal titled "What Is Needed to Win" to chairman of the JCS Gen. Peter Pace and Under Secretary of Defense for Policy Eric Edelman with the covering note to "[p]lease take a look at it, and if you don't understand what he is talking about, get in touch with him and find out. Then let's have a meeting to discuss what we can do to help him." The chart included expanding ISR access, operational capability, and CIA partnerships.[24]

---

[21] Donald Rumsfeld, "Your Attendance at the NSC Meeting," note to MG Stan McChrystal, July 1, 2005.

[22] Donald Rumsfeld, "Stan McChrystal," note to VADM Staser Holcomb, September 29, 2005.

[23] Downing, 2005, p. 4.

[24] Donald Rumsfeld, "Stan McChrystal's Chart," note to Gen. Peter Pace and Eric Edelman, January 5, 2006.

Rumsfeld spoke with SOCOM commander Brown about promoting McChrystal to three stars. Brown readily agreed to promote McChrystal, but there were questions about the long-term position of the SMU community commander. This had implications across the SOF community, as the TSOCs would remain lower-ranking commands.[25] A permanent increase in the rank of the SMU community commander would shift the balance of power in the community.

The promotion also had command and control implications. The SMU community was increasingly dual hatted, with theater responsibilities for the regional combatant commander and global responsibilities for SOCOM, which was now the global synchronizer for CT.[26] This was further complicated by the existence of a four-star commander for both Iraq and Afghanistan.

Decision and Outcome Analysis

In February 2006, despite the complications, McChrystal was promoted to lieutenant general, and several other SOF senior billets were also "bumped up" to higher rank. If General Brown faced any resistance in making these promotions, Secretary Rumsfeld's strong endorsement seems to have quashed it. He was willing to tell even very senior officers "to sit down and shut up."[27]

McChrystal's promotion was based on the forward deployment of the SMU community, which cemented the dual-hatted nature of the command, reporting as it does to both geographic and functional combatant commanders. The SMU community at this point also generated requests for forces through both CENTCOM and SOCOM, further complicating the command and control. However, this dual arrangement, combined with the promotion of the SMU community leadership, brought substantial resources. McChrystal noted, "I had the additional influence that came with my third star, and we had resources, from ISR aircraft to interrogators, that I'd only dreamed of

---

[25] Interview with former senior military officer, April 12, 2016.

[26] Interview with former senior military officer, March 30, 2016.

[27] Interview with former senior military officer, March 30, 2016.

in 2004."[28] It is unclear at the unclassified level if the SMU community received everything requested in the "What Is Needed to Win" slide, but it seems it received a substantial portion. McChrystal would command the SMU community for another two years, giving him time to cement the changes he had made.

Summary of Lessons

The development of the SMU community mirrors, to some degree, the previous chapter on the expansion of SOF. From modest experiments with sustained operations in the 1990s, the SMU community developed the foundations for its post-9/11 expansion. As with SOCOM generally, the SMU community was able to exploit the policy window for CT in large part because of the cultivation of strong ties with Washington policy communities and the interagency. This suggests three lessons.

Revolution requires evolution. McChrystal and his team were able to make rapid revolutionary change in the SMU community. Yet much of the groundwork for this change took place much earlier, in Somalia, the Balkans, and the early days of Afghanistan. Many of McChrystal's key subordinates were veterans of these earlier efforts and could draw on lessons (from both successes and failures) from them as they changed the SMU community.

Engage stakeholders as full partners. The successful transformation of the SMU community hinged on full interagency participation, which required giving stakeholders a reason to participate. McChrystal's investment in cultivating relationships and ensuring stakeholders saw benefit in participating was vital to policy change. Most notably, he was willing to make an intelligence community representative one of his deputies, a level of commitment that helped cement a vital (if sometimes contentious) relationship. In addition, McChrystal set the stage for an information-sharing relationship by opening task force files to the intelligence community.

---

[28] McChrystal, 2014, p. 237.

Leverage success with senior leaders. The transformation of the SMU community was the result of McChrystal and his subordinates' focus on internal changes in SOF's own organizational culture and practices, including a special emphasis on the need to build partnerships. However, the expansion in resources and authorities required leveraging success from that transformation with senior leaders, most notably Secretary Rumsfeld. CENTCOM commander General Abizaid also supported McChrystal's career, his operational objectives, and the changes required to achieve them.

CHAPTER TEN
Operational Authorities and Employment of SOF: Section 1208

Overview

Section 1208 of the FY 2005 Ronald Reagan NDAA created an authority to "provide support to foreign forces, irregular forces, groups, or individuals engaged in supporting or facilitating ongoing military operations by United States special operations forces to combat terrorism."[1] This authority is commonly called "Section 1208" instead of its official title, "Support of Special Operations to Combat Terrorism." Section 1208 differs in scope from USASOC's original proposal for a UW-specific authority to support only irregular forces, groups, and individuals. Nonetheless, USSOCOM today considers the authority one of its most critical tools in combating terrorism, and consistently advocates for additional support for it from Congress.

Accessible only by SOF, Section 1208 programs are active in multiple areas of the world. They are used as a tool to leverage both organized national forces and irregular groups and individuals to conduct operations in support of U.S. efforts.[2] While Section 1208's existence and authorizing language are unclassified, the specific locations and operations supported by Section 1208 are classified. Nevertheless, Section 1208 is specifically prohibited from support of covert operations; neither is it characterized as a security assistance authority because pro-

---

[1] Public Law 108–375, 2004.

[2] Interview with DoD official with responsibility for special operations, Arlington, Va., April 29, 2016.

vision of training and equipment is intended to be incidental to the overall operational purpose of the authority.

Section 1208 legislation has been reauthorized and expanded with only minor modifications several times since its creation, reflecting the Geographic Combatant Command's (GCC)'s use of the authority and the support that it has from Congress. Originally limited to $25 million in FY 2005, Section 1208 has increased incrementally as USSOCOM and its units have demonstrated the authority's utility, and will be increased to $85 million as of FY 2017.

Catalyst

The war in Afghanistan revealed a deficit in authorities for SOF to support indigenous partners, a critical part of SOF capabilities. Section 1208 was created out of a concept originally designed to better support U.S. Army Special Forces in Afghanistan in executing their UW mission.[3] Beginning in 2001, Special Forces and the CIA closely collaborated to support the Northern Alliance militia and conduct operations in Afghanistan against al Qaeda and the Taliban. Although Special Forces were trained to use funds to solicit cooperation from foreign forces, they lacked UW authority to enable them to directly pay foreign individuals to conduct or support U.S. operations. Instead, the CIA funded the efforts, while Special Forces led the training, equipping, and advising of the Northern Alliance to fight al Qaeda.[4] This relationship was functional but unsustainable given that the arrangement could last only as long as CIA and Special Forces efforts were aligned in prioritization, time, and location. DoD wanted to avoid a situation in which it was unable to pay individuals who were conducting operations supporting the U.S. military if the CIA were unable or unwilling. Further, Special Forces wanted to use the funds for clandes-

---

[3] Interview with USASOC official, Washington, D.C., June 23, 2016.

[4] Interview with former military officer with responsibility for special operations, Arlington, Va., April 12, 2016; and interview with former DoD official with responsibility for special operations, Washington, D.C., March 10, 2016.

tine support of military operations, rather than intelligence operations, creating a natural divide between CIA and Special Forces objectives.[5] Without the CIA's assistance, DoD was unable to financially support the Northern Alliance's conduct of UW and could not provide lethal aid.[6]

By 2002, Special Forces teams determined that, to most efficiently and effectively solicit support for critical military operations in Afghanistan, they would need to be able to quickly provide discretionary cash to their Northern Alliance partners. Additionally, as al Qaeda was moving into Pakistan and diverting CIA attention away from Afghanistan, USASOC concluded that leveraging CIA funding to support DoD operations would no longer be feasible.[7]

Proposal Formation

In response to this situation, USASOC, led by LTG Bryan D. Brown, drafted a legislative proposal (LP) in spring 2002 requesting authority to provide small amounts of discretionary funds to Special Forces in Afghanistan.[8] USASOC intended that the funds be used to support the Northern Alliance resistance efforts by leveraging individuals to conduct such simple but critical tasks that would support Special Forces operations as fixing a damaged runway or to conduct other UW operations that required lethal aid.[9] The proposal was designed to be a flexible means to support only the conduct of UW, enabling Special Forces the ability to provide assistance to irregular forces, groups, and

---

[5] Interview with former DoD official with responsibility for special operations, Washington, D.C., March 10, 2016.

[6] Interview with USASOC official, Washington, D.C., June 23, 2016.

[7] Interview with former DoD official with responsibility for special operations #2, Washington, D.C., March 10, 2016.

[8] Interview with USASOC official, Washington, D.C., June 23, 2016.

[9] Interview with former military officer with responsibility for special operations, Arlington, Va., April 12, 2016; and interview with USASOC official, Washington, D.C., June 23, 2016.

individuals engaged in clandestine support to military operations. It was not intended for intelligence collection.[10] Further, it was meant to support local irregular forces in conducting UW, rather than to aid in developing direct surrogates for local forces.[11]

Using the annual DoD LP process, USASOC submitted the LP to USSOCOM for consideration. There, without strong support for UW initiatives, it stagnated through 2002. In 2003, however, when the proposal was submitted for a second time, Brown had been promoted to four-star general and commanded USSOCOM. Brown, who was an advocate for expanding UW authorities, made the proposal a top legislative priority, and it was pushed through the LP process up to the Pentagon.[12]

Stakeholder Analysis and Key Junctures

To develop momentum in DoD for the proposal, Brown worked closely with then–ASD/SOLIC Thomas W. O'Connell to solicit support throughout the Pentagon. O'Connell and Brown conferred on a daily basis and coordinated closely on SOF initiatives. O'Connell strongly supported USSOCOM's proposal, as he did for most of the initiatives that Brown put forward during his tenure.[13]

Some officials in the Pentagon and other government agencies were concerned that USSOCOM would use the authority to develop and operate local militias without oversight. However, because of their high-level advocacy within DoD and with other key U.S. government

---

[10] Interview with former DoD official with responsibility for special operations, Washington, D.C., March 10, 2016.

[11] Interview with USASOC official, Washington, D.C., June 23, 2016.

[12] Interview with former DoD official with responsibility for special operations, Washington, D.C., March 10, 2016.

[13] Interview with former military officer with responsibility for special operations, Arlington, Va., April 12, 2016.

leaders, Brown and O'Connell were able to develop the necessary support to bring the proposal to Capitol Hill.[14]

As the proposal moved through the extensive coordination process for LPs, the language was edited to satisfy multiple equities, and the purpose and scope of the original USASOC proposal changed. During the coordination process, language was added from other Executive Branch agencies requiring concurrence for each program under the authority from both the Secretary of State and the Director of Central Intelligence (DCI). Further, the proposal was no longer specific to UW but focused on "combating terrorism." *Combating terrorism*, a phrase that encompasses both CT and defensive antiterrorism, was specifically chosen to link Section 1208 to support the GWOT.[15] While the original proposal was intended to provide operational funds to Army SOF for the conduct of UW, USSOCOM leadership still felt that the proposal would provide badly needed flexibility to its deployed forces, albeit in a different manner than originally envisioned. OSD agreed and supported the proposal in its revised form.[16]

Decision and Outcome Analysis

At the time, Congress was generally supportive of efforts to better enable effective combat operations, particularly in areas where success was perceived to be likely.[17] Further, some defense committee staff members were more receptive to USSOCOM proposals, both because SOCOM had developed relationships with them and because some staff had prior military experience working with special operations.[18]

---

[14] Interview with former military officer with responsibility for special operations, Arlington, Va., April 12, 2016.

[15] Interview with USASOC official, Washington, D.C., June 23, 2016.

[16] Interview with former special operations official, March 10, 2016.

[17] Interview with former military officer with responsibility for special operations, Arlington, Va., April 12, 2016.

[18] Interview with former USSOCOM official, Springfield, Va., May 16, 2016; and interview with former congressional official, May 19, 2016.

However, when congressional staff initially reviewed the proposal, many questioned how the program would work and whether DoD was moving too aggressively to undertake efforts traditionally executed by other government agencies.[19] USSOCOM responded by engaging those staff members to answer their questions with what defense committee staff considered to be sufficient detail, while emphasizing the urgent operational need for the authority.[20]

The central theme USSOCOM emphasized in its interactions with Congress was that the authority requirement was derived directly from accounts of operational experience from deployed SOF who were repeatedly frustrated that, because of the lack of authorities, they were unable to work with groups they encountered that could assist in supporting U.S. operations to combat terrorism.[21] This message of operational urgency, combined with the beliefs on the part of key congressional staff that their concerns had been adequately addressed by USSOCOM, helped secure support for the proposal. To ensure that Congress could retain sufficient oversight of the program, SASC staff added a provision to the language requiring periodic reporting, directed that DoD would need to seek reauthorization after FY 2007, and capped the authority at $25 million.[22]

Following on their staffs' efforts to engage with Congress to support the proposal, Brown and Secretary Rumsfeld advocated directly with key lawmakers, a practice usually reserved for initiatives of the highest priority. In 2004, before House and Senate conference negotiations on the NDAA were complete, Brown and Rumsfeld met with nearly a dozen key members of Congress in a single day to underscore the urgent need for such an authority.[23] The proposal was able to command such high-level engagement from the Pentagon because

---

[19] Interview with former congressional official, May 19, 2016.

[20] Interview with former congressional official, May 19, 2016.

[21] Interview with former DoD official with responsibility for special operations, Washington, D.C., March 10, 2016.

[22] Interview with former congressional official, May 19, 2016.

[23] Interview with former military officer with responsibility for special operations, Arlington, Va., April 12, 2016.

it was USSOCOM's top legislative priority and because Rumsfeld had become an advocate for SOF support since the 9/11 attacks.[24]

The measure was added as Section 1208 of the FY 2005 NDAA and passed into law on October 28, 2004. Section 1208 authorized the expenditure of $25 million per fiscal year through FY 2007 "to provide support to foreign forces, irregular forces, groups, or individuals engaged in supporting or facilitating ongoing military operations by United States special operations forces to combat terrorism."[25] Funding was to come from the operations and maintenance funds of USSOCOM's budget. The measure specifically prohibited DoD from using the authority to conduct covert operations. The Secretary of State and DCI concurrence provisions did not remain in the final language.[26] However, the addition of "foreign forces" to the measure meant that Section 1208 could be used to support national forces, as opposed to irregular forces as originally intended.

How Section 1208 Has Grown

Since its passage in 2004, Section 1208 has been reauthorized, increased, or modified several times (see Table 10.1), but the overall purpose of the authority has not changed. The amount authorized has increased from $25 million in FY 2005 to $85 million in FY 2017, and oversight has increased in the form of more clearly defined congressional reporting and required Chief of Mission signature for each program. A summary of those changes is detailed in Table 10.1.

---

[24] Interview with former military officer with responsibility for special operations, Arlington, Va., April 12, 2016.

[25] Public Law 108-375, Ronald W. Reagan National Defense Authorization Act for Fiscal Year 2005, October 28, 2004.

[26] Interview with former DoD official with responsibility for special operations, Washington, D.C., March 10, 2016.

Table 10.1
Changes as a Result of Section 1208 Legislation

FY	Substantive Changes	Extension	Total Authority	Legislation
2005	Initial authorization	Initial Sunset 2007	$25 M	Sec. 1208 of FY 2005 NDAA; P.L. 108-375
2008	Detailed annual congressional reporting requirements	2010	$25 M	Sec. 1202 of FY 2008 NDAA; P.L. 110-181[a]
2009	Required concurrence of "relevant Chief of Mission"; title changed to Special Operations	2013	$35 M	Section 1208 of FY 2009 NDAA; P.L. 110-417[b]
2010	Congressional notification of scope or funding level changes; amended congressional reporting requirements	N/A	$40 M	Section 1202 of FY 2010 NDAA; P.L. 111-84[c]
2011	N/A	N/A	$45 M	Section 1201 of FY 2011 NDAA; P.L. 111-383[d]
2012	N/A	2015	$50 M	Section 1203 of FY 2012 NDAA; P.L. 112-81[e]
2015	N/A	2017	$75 M	Section 1208 of FY 2015 NDAA, P.L. 113-291[f]
2016	15-day advance notification unless in extraordinary circumstances; biannual reporting requirement	N/A	$85 M, starting in FY 2017	Section 1274 of FY 2016 NDAA, P.L. 114-92[g]

[a] Public Law 110-181, National Defense Authorization Act for Fiscal Year 2008, Sec. 1202, Authority for Support of Military Operations to Combat Terrorism, January 28, 2008.

[b] Public Law 110-417, Duncan Hunter National Defense Authorization Act for Fiscal Year 2009, Sec. 1208, Extension and Expansion of Authority for Support of Special Operations to Combat Terrorism, October 14, 2008.

[c] Public Law 111-84, National Defense Authorization Act for Fiscal Year 2010, Sec. 1202, Expansion of Authority and Modification of Notification and Reporting

Requirements for Use of Authority for Support of Special Operations to Combat Terrorism, October 28, 2009.

ᵈ Public Law 111-383, Ike Skelton National Defense Authorization Act for Fiscal Year 2011, Sec. 1201, Expansion of Authority for Support of Special Operations to Combat Terrorism, January 7, 2011.

ᵉ Public Law 112-81, National Defense Authorization Act for Fiscal Year 2012, Sec. 1203, Extension and Expansion of Authority for Support of Special Operations to Combat Terrorism, December 31, 2011.

ᶠ Public Law 113-291, Carl Levin and Howard P. "Buck" McKeon National Defense Authorization Act for Fiscal Year 2015, Sec. 1208, Extension and Modification of Authority for Support of Special Operations to Combat Terrorism, January 3, 2014.

ᵍ Public Law 114-92, National Defense Authorization Act for Fiscal Year 2016, Sec. 1274, Modification of Authority for Support of Special Operations to Combat Terrorism, January 6, 2015.

Today, Section 1208 is considered a critical authority to USSOCOM and across DoD.[27] While it faces increasing scrutiny as the authority level grows, DoD has successfully managed the program in Congress's view.[28] Several factors likely contributed to the initial passage and ongoing support for Section 1208.

Addressing Congressional Issues

In the FY 2009 NDAA, Congress added the requirement that Section 1208 programs obtain the concurrence of the U.S. Chief of Mission in the country where the activities are to take place. In the FY 2010 NDAA, Congress added more specific reporting requirements for these programs, details of which are classified. These two revisions were made to address concerns raised by some in Congress. The requirement for Chief of Mission concurrence addressed concerns over the proliferation of DoD authorities that did not give the U.S. Department of State a

---

[27] Interview with congressional official, Arlington, Va., March 22, 2016; interview with former DoD official with responsibility for special operations, Washington, D.C., March 25, 2016; interview with DoD official with responsibility for special operations, Arlington, Va., April 29, 2016; and William H. McRaven, "Purple Note," in *USSOCOM, Global Special Operations Forces Network Operational Planning Team: A History*, 2011.

[28] Interview with congressional official, Arlington, Va., March 22, 2016; and interview with DoD official with responsibility for special operations, Arlington, Va., April 29, 2016.

role in their oversight.[29] The requirement for more detailed information about the classified programs provided Congress with a greater ability to evaluate the programs' value and effectiveness. Because Section 1208 programs have clear near-term goals to support specific SOF operations, they have the potential to create effects in a shorter time frame compared with security assistance programs.

Although the specific programs authorized under Section 1208 are classified, USSOCOM commander GEN Joseph Votel characterized the utility and effectiveness of the programs in this prepared statement to Congress in March 2016:

> Section 1208 remains a critical tool in our combating terrorism efforts. It allows small-footprint SOF elements to take advantage of the skills and unique attributes of indigenous regular and irregular forces—local area knowledge, access, ethnicity, and language skills to achieve effects that are critical to our mission objectives, especially in remote or denied areas where U.S. formations are infeasible. Our ability to quickly provide enabling support to willing partners under Section 1208 has resulted in hundreds of successful tactical operations. These operations have disrupted terrorist networks and their activities and denied them operating space across a wide range of operating environments, at a fraction of the cost of other programs.[30]

Small Size, Low Cost

The small size (and relatively low cost) of Section 1208's programs makes them relatively agile and responsive. That key attribute allows the programs to start quickly, since USSOCOM can quickly purchase required equipment and mobilize SOF teams. Further, the small footprint and relatively inexpensive program cost mean that Section 1208

---

[29] Nina M. Serafino, *Security Assistance Reform: "Section 1206" Background and Issues for Congress*, Washington, D.C.: Congressional Research Service, 7-7500, RS22855, April 4, 2014.

[30] Joseph L. Votel, "Advanced Policy Questions Delivered to the 114th Congress, Senate Armed Services Committee," Washington, D.C., March 9, 2016.

programs do not draw the same attention and scrutiny that security assistance programs sometimes do and can be easier to coordinate within the Pentagon and State Department.[31]

Interagency Support and Coordination

Extensive interagency coordination contributes to the ongoing support that Section 1208 has enjoyed. Several U.S. government agencies, as well as the NSC, coordinate on Section 1208 programs as they move through the approval process; that is in addition to the Chief of Mission concurrence required by law. DoD officials involved with Section 1208 administration and policy also routinely interact with the congressional defense committees through briefings and reports to update lawmakers on program progress and challenges. While certain members and staffs in Congress disagree about which committees should have jurisdiction over Section 1208, the congressional defense committee staffs have historically supported USSOCOM's Section 1208 efforts and have resisted attempts by others to change the legislation substantially.

Further, some on Capitol Hill feel that DoD has exercised prudent program management by terminating or modifying programs at the USSOCOM level if they are not meeting performance expectations.[32] DoD also undergoes routine evaluations of its programs and reviews each Section 1208 proposal carefully to ensure each program's primary goal is to support critical SOF operations to combat terrorism, efforts that are critical to demonstrating to Congress that DoD is using Section 1208 appropriately.

In FY 2017, per a measure in the FY 2015 NDAA, Section 1208 funding will increase to $85 million. As this report is being written, a measure to permanently codify Section 1208 authority is under consideration in Congress but has not been passed into law. Supporters of Section 1208 seek to make the authority permanent to increase DoD's

---

[31] Interview with DoD official with responsibility for special operations, Arlington, Va., April 29, 2016.

[32] Interview with congressional official, Arlington, Va., March 22, 2016; and interview with DoD official with responsibility for special operations, Arlington, Va., April 29, 2016.

ability to plan several years out for its programs. Further, they believe codification is warranted because of Section 1208's record of transparency with Capitol Hill, its operational results, and the fact that multiple COCOMs consider it an enduring requirement.[33] Also, as authorities that require periodic NDAA reauthorization are at risk of lapsing if the bill is not passed on an annual basis, codifying Section 1208 would help to protect its programs and ensure continuity.

Summary of Lessons

The case study on Section 1208 authority demonstrates SOCOM's ability to not only secure a critical and unprecedented authority but also sustain support for it over time from DoD, Congress, and other government agencies. Specifically, the case of Section 1208 highlights that DoD grasped the importance of advocacy during a period of policy opportunity, of continuous and open congressional staff engagement, and of messaging urgency and gravity to decisionmakers. Also, the case of Section 1208 displays that DoD has been effective in enlisting support from throughout the Pentagon and the federal government, which has been critical in both the adoption and sustainment of the program. Finally, this case highlights the benefits that can sometimes be gained by embracing what is perceived to be an imperfect solution.

Through this case study of Section 1208 authority, several lessons can be derived. The following lessons are those elements over which DoD personnel have the most control and are most clearly linked to change or maintenance of support for Section 1208.

Partial gains are still gains. DoD opted to move forward with the LP even after it was modified during the Executive Branch coordination process. Although Section 1208 became restricted to support U.S. operations to combat terrorism, the provision still addressed an authority gap that USSOCOM saw utility in filling. Additionally, Congress was an ally to DoD in removing the language that would have required the Secretary of State and the DCI to approve each Section 1208

---

[33] Interview with congressional official, Arlington, Va., June 9, 2016.

program, which would have reduced the speed of program commencement. Subsequent changes to the authorities to require enhanced reporting and Chief of Mission concurrence were embraced to the overall benefit of the program and its long-term support by Congress.

Timing matters. The proposal gained traction in Congress in large part because staff and members recognized the near-term need to better enable U.S. forces to achieve success in Afghanistan. The SOF leadership moved quickly to exploit the gap revealed in those operations to press for legislative remedy.

Engage congressional staff. USSOCOM effectively engaged key congressional staff and leveraged standing relationships, providing anecdotes and other information to defense committee staff who are relied on heavily by senators and representatives to provide advice. While USSOCOM and OSD engaged at senior levels as well, the consistent communication between USSOCOM staff and congressional staff members was critical to gaining support for Section 1208.

Develop a clear and consistent message. An important part of gaining the requisite support for Section 1208 was DoD's consistent message that highlighted urgency and operational need for the authority. Using powerful anecdotes from SOF deployed in theater, and frequent communication between USSOCOM and Congress, DoD's message successfully persuaded Congress to support its request.

CHAPTER ELEVEN
Operational Authorities and Employment: The Global SOF Network Initiative

Overview

The GSN, a conceptual framework that USSOCOM advocated starting in 2011, was designed to strengthen USSOCOM's ability to respond to global contingencies and to develop a collaborative network among U.S. SOF and interagency and international partners. Led by then–USSOCOM commander ADM William McRaven, the GSN comprised several initiatives that ranged in scope and ambition, some of which required agreement across the GCCs and changes to legislation and presidential-level documents. Ultimately, the GSN was an ambitious effort that sought to provide USSOCOM expanded operational authorities, enable the USSOCOM commander to direct forces across geographic COCOM boundaries, increase SOF forward presence and security force assistance (SFA) activities, elevate USSOCOM's presence and strategic-level reach in Washington, lead certain international partnership efforts, and expand the support and role of TSOCs. Approval and institutionalization of the GSN efforts required significant DoD, State Department, and congressional interaction to gain approval for each major line of effort.

USSOCOM generally focused on four main lines of effort intended to expand the GSN: to empower the TSOCs, establish Regional SOF Coordination Centers (RSCCs), strengthen USSOCOM's relationships among interagency partners in Washington and beyond, and gain broad and flexible authorities to conduct SFA more effectively.[1]

These objectives have since evolved, with some elements finding success and some facing significant challenges. While McRaven held significant political capital within Washington when he assumed command of USSOCOM, the GSN initiatives that he advocated—and the approach that USSOCOM took to implement the initiatives—were often met with resistance among key decisionmakers in Congress, the State Department, and DoD. Other initiatives, such as the effort to assign the TSOCs to USSOCOM, received enough support to be adopted. What differentiated these successful efforts, in policy circumstances and in USSOCOM's approach, is documented in this case.

To address the complexity of the various lines of effort that composed the GSN, this chapter is divided into two sections and seven subsections. The first section looks at the overall GSN framework and major factors affecting the GSN's eventual outcome. The GSN concept was consistently promoted by USSOCOM as a set of interdependent and comprehensive initiatives, each of which was thereby affected by similar stakeholder perspectives and critical junctures in the policymaking process.

The first section is divided into seven subsections, each analyzing the trajectory of the major GSN initiatives. USSOCOM pursued many of these initiatives concurrently, so the subsections are not intended to be chronological. The second section summarizes key lessons from this case on pursuing policy change. The chapter concludes with a summary of lessons detailed throughout the GSN case study.

The Global SOF Network Framework

Catalyst and Proposal Formation

In May 2011, McRaven successfully led JSOC to plan and execute the operation to kill Osama bin Laden in Pakistan. As the most public face of that mission, McRaven earned significant political capital and was

---

[1] U.S. Special Operations Command, 2012a.

held in high regard as a military leader within both civilian and uniformed circles. This created the visibility and opportunity for him to press for changes that he had come to believe were needed based on his career experience including his tour in Europe as commander of Special Operations Command–Europe and his earlier tour at the White House, where he served as director of CT on the NSC staff.

In August 2011, McRaven assumed command of USSOCOM and established priorities for his tenure. These priorities included the expansion of the GSN, which was intended to increase USSOCOM's support to the GCCs, enable stronger relationships between USSOCOM and its interagency and international partners, and allow USSOCOM to better respond to emerging crises. McRaven established operational planning teams (OPTs) in September 2011 to focus exclusively on those priorities.[2] The GSN team was tasked via a "Purple Note" memo from McRaven to develop initiatives to empower the TSOCs, to strengthen coordination with partner-nation SOF via the establishment of regional centers modeled after NATO SOF Headquarters (NSHQ), and to improve on relationships with USSOCOM's interagency partners.[3]

In response, the GSN OPT developed key tasks that GSN believed would be integral to successfully expand the GSN. Over several months, the tasks and how they were messaged evolved, ultimately converging in efforts in the following categories:[4]

- **Empower the TSOCs** to optimize to make them the "force of choice"[5] for GCCs and senior policymakers.
- **Establish RSCCs** to create regional SOF training, education, and coordination hubs throughout the world in the mold of NSHQ.

---

[2] U.S. Special Operations Command, "Global Special Operations Forces Network Operational Planning Team: A History," 2014.

[3] McRaven, 2011.

[4] This summary description is drawn from numerous briefing decks and draft papers created by USSOCOM.

[5] U.S. Special Operations Command, 2014, p. 1.

- **Create USSOCOM–National Capital Region (NCR)** to establish a USSOCOM entity in Washington to serve as a central node for all USSOCOM activities in the NCR and coordinate more effectively with interagency personnel.
- **Gain SOF SFA authority** to obtain a congressional authority that enables predictable funding for USSOCOM to develop partner-nation SOF capabilities and establish persistent engagement in critical areas before crises arise. While USSOCOM also sought to gain authorities to employ U.S. SOF globally, those initiatives are analyzed in this chapter with other efforts to empower the TSOCs.

In support of the GSN vision, and, in particular, to more easily connect to trusted multinational SOF partners, USSOCOM also aimed to implement communications systems known as U.S. Battlefield Information Collection and Exploitation Systems/International Intelligence Programs (US BICES/IIP). However, as efforts to implement BICES were largely internal and did not require extensive congressional or interagency coordination at the time, they are not covered extensively in this report.

In December 2011, after validating the GSN team's initial estimate of key initiatives required to expand the GSN, McRaven presented his vision to TSOC commanders and component commanders and began a series of working groups to identify each GCC's SOF requirements.[6] At the time, these working groups were only internal to DoD and the GSN ideas had not been presented publicly.

Nonetheless, and despite the predecisional nature of these initiatives at the time, the USSOCOM efforts were quickly drawn into the public eye through news reporting starting in January 2012, before entities outside of USSOCOM and the GCCs had been formally briefed.[7] These surprised entities included OSD, which is responsible for providing policy and budget oversight of USSOCOM; the State Department,

---

[6] U.S. Special Operations Command, 2014.

[7] Kimberly Dozier, "Bin Laden Raid Commander Seeks Global Expansion," Associated Press, January 26, 2012.

which manages diplomatic relationships that the GSN could affect; and Congress. Despite McRaven's popularity in Washington, this premature disclosure caused many to be suspicious of the GSN's purpose and overall cost, and discontent that they had not been consulted in the initial stages of GSN development.[8] This order of engagement—public first, then key government actors—invited widespread scrutiny of the GSN initiatives that would hinder McRaven's ability to control USSOCOM's messaging about the GSN throughout its life cycle.

Decision and Outcome Analysis
The GSN can be characterized as a partial success. Important components of the endeavor received the support McRaven sought and transformed the way that USSOCOM provides support to the GCCs. In March 2016, DoD's Joint Requirements Oversight Council (JROC) approved USSOCOM's request to change doctrine so as to formalize two important USSOCOM ambitions: its vision for SOF support of the GCCs and its goal of embedding the GSN changes in DoD structure. Further, although quite different from McRaven's original vision for the RSCCs, USSOCOM has incorporated foreign liaison officers in its headquarters to facilitate stronger transnational communication and partnerships.

However, several other GSN initiatives did not gain necessary levels of support, and the GSN effort overall was burdened by negative perceptions. DoD and congressional officials named several key reasons why USSOCOM was unable to gain support for the entire GSN package: disjointed messaging, approval process violations, and inopportune timing given the budget climate.[9] While USSOCOM is still pursuing initiatives intended to grow interagency relationships and expand globally distributed SOF presence to enhance GCC efforts, the command uses the term *transregional synchronization*, suggesting that

---

[8] RAND summary of interview findings with DoD, U.S. Department of State, and USAID officials, January 29, 2013.

[9] Interview with former DoD official with responsibility for special operations, Washington, D.C., March 25, 2016; interview with former OSD official, Washington, D.C., March 2, 2016; and interview with congressional staff, Washington, D.C., January 29, 2016.

USSOCOM is attempting to distance itself from the original *Global SOF Network* term.[10]

The links between those initiatives that received widespread support are evident: They were coordinated along established processes; their nature and purpose were clearly conveyed and backed by validated requirements; they included rehearsals, conferences, and open forums to discuss changes; and the manner in which the changes would fit into an existing chain of command structure was effectively specified. The trajectory and outcome of each of the major initiatives are covered in detail in subsequent sections of this case study.

Stakeholder Analysis and Key Junctures
By February 2012, the GSN had stimulated significant interest in Washington, and USSOCOM's GSN team began executing McRaven's direction to move as quickly and as deeply into DoD structure and doctrine as possible to create changes that would last beyond his tenure as commander.[11]

While USSOCOM frequently presented the GSN expansion effort as a complementary set of proposals, each initiative required a specific approach to gaining support and approval, which will be analyzed in later sections of this case study. In general, USSOCOM proceeded within established DoD systems to gain approval for its initiatives to empower the TSOCs. This included holding a series of inclusive DoD-wide planning sessions to identify GCC requirements for SOF capabilities, which ultimately supported USSOCOM's request to modify DoD's existing "Forces For" tables; working within the biannual Unified Command Plan (UCP) update process to propose changes there; and navigating DoD's notoriously slow and bureaucratic Joint Capabilities and Integration Development System (JCIDS) to formalize U.S. SOF requirements. In each of those cases, USSOCOM was successful in gaining the requisite support for its initiatives. However, this deliberate method of leveraging established, familiar processes to effect policy

---

[10] Interview with SOCOM official, March 21, 2016.

[11] Interview with SOCOM official, March 21, 2016.

change was not used as heavily for the remaining GSN objectives, a decision that may have contributed to the outcome of those initiatives.

Both McRaven and the GSN team began engaging stakeholders within the broader DoD (including the military service departments, the GCCs, the TSOCs, OSD, and the Joint Staff), the State Department, and Congress, particularly the defense authorization and appropriation committees. These engagements included formal and informal briefings, educational events with national security officials, public events, white papers, phone calls, and office visits at the staff and senior levels. USSOCOM also sought to engage experts in think tanks, academic institutions, and the broader interested public.[12]

USSOCOM's messaging of the GSN was intended to convey that it would provide the GCCs greater global forward presence and persistent engagement, increased coordination among interagency and international partners, and increased flexibility. In an early iteration of a briefing paper, USSOCOM argued,

> The Global SOF Network represents a way to empower and enable a global effort with capable allies and partners, allocate burdens effectively, and assure access to and use of the global commons through maintaining and improving relevant and interoperable special operations capabilities.[13]

Throughout their engagements with DoD, the State Department, and Congress, McRaven and his staff often referred to the 2012 Defense Strategic Guidance (DSG) as a mandate for the GSN proposals and attempted to tie each GSN line of effort to DSG principles.[14] Understanding that linking major initiatives to strategic-level guidance often resonates in Washington, USSOCOM presentation materials and briefings frequently emphasized that the GSN initiatives would directly support the DSG by enabling USSOCOM, via the GCCs,

---

[12] U.S. Special Operations Command, 2014.

[13] U.S. Special Operations Command, "The Global SOF Network," predecisional draft paper, March 2, 2012c, pp. 3–4.

[14] McRaven, 2013.

to "be agile, flexible and ready for the full range of contingencies."[15] USSOCOM also frequently cited the DSG's direction that, "whenever possible, we will develop innovative, low-cost, and small-footprint approaches to achieve our security objectives."[16]

However, USSOCOM's messaging was frequently perceived as inconsistent and, while impressive in presentation, lacking in substantive details.[17] The inconsistency was driven in part by USSOCOM's distribution of evolving draft briefing materials while the concepts were still in development; the inconsistency also occurred because, at times, the USSOCOM plans and policy division, the budget division, and the GSN team were simultaneously preparing presentation materials on GSN-related efforts.[18] Others felt that USSOCOM's messaging reflected its desire to gain policy approvals for the concept before providing adequate details.[19]

While some viewed the concept as forward-leaning and aligned with sequestration-imposed budget constraints, many felt that USSOCOM would not allow other agencies to help shape the initiatives given how aggressively they were moving forward. Further, USSOCOM's selective outreach created the perception throughout various agencies that officials were chosen for engagement and feedback based on USSOCOM's assessment of that individual's likelihood to support the GSN.[20]

---

[15] U.S. Special Operations Command, "Enabling the Global SOF Network," briefing slides, March 13, 2012b, p. 3.

[16] DoD, Sec. 308 Special Operations Security Force Assistance, draft legislative proposal, 2012a, pp. 3–4; U.S. Special Operations Command, 2012b.

[17] RAND summary of interview findings with DoD, U.S. Department of State, and USAID officials, January 29, 2013; interview with congressional staff, Washington, D.C., January 29, 2016; and interview with OSD official, January 11, 2013.

[18] Interview with SOCOM official, March 21, 2016; and interview with OSD officials familiar with special operations policy, Washington, D.C., February 9, 2016.

[19] Interview with congressional staff, Washington, D.C., January 29, 2016; and interview with congressional staff, Washington, D.C., January 21, 2016.

[20] RAND summary of interview findings with DoD, U.S. Department of State, and USAID officials, January 29, 2013.

The State Department and the congressional foreign relations committees were particularly concerned about the RSCC line of effort being duplicative and potentially infringing on diplomatic relationships with partner nations, which the State Department formally oversees.[21] Some felt that McRaven appeared to be open to coordination on specific missions that would be part of the GSN (as is common practice between USSOCOM and the State Department's in-country ambassadors), but not on the overall strategy.[22]

Even within DoD, support for McRaven's efforts was uneven. While certain initiatives had support after USSOCOM deliberately involved relevant stakeholders in the planning process, some felt that the Joint Staff and the GCCs harbored significant, if often quiet, discontent with the way in which USSOCOM was attempting to gain support for its initiatives. OSD officials were also dissatisfied with USSOCOM's manner of unveiling and seeking approval for certain GSN initiatives without working through traditional Pentagon coordination mechanisms. This was widely perceived as a disregard of established processes.[23]

Many within the Pentagon felt that McRaven's efforts, born at a time when budget cuts were pervading all of DoD, would be costly and would pull directly from the shrinking shared defense budget.[24] In March 2013, budget sequestration officially began, initiating a period of automatic cuts that included mandatory military and civilian billet reductions. While USSOCOM viewed the resource constraints as a compelling reason to invest in the GSN initiatives, it was difficult for many throughout conventional military organizations to justify additional resources for USSOCOM when their own budgets were being cut in a way that many, including Secretary of Defense Leon Panetta,

---

[21] Interview with congressional staff, Washington, D.C., January 29, 2016.

[22] Email communication from RAND researchers, summarizing SOCOM GSN presentation, January 31, 2013.

[23] Interview with former OSD official, Washington, D.C., March 2, 2016.

[24] Interview with former DoD official with responsibility for special operations, Washington, D.C., March 25, 2016.

believed would have the effect of degrading military readiness.[25] Further, there was concern that funding USSOCOM's initiatives such as TSOC empowerment, the RSCCs, and USSOCOM-NCR, would not be feasible given personnel and other resource reductions throughout the armed services.[26]

USSOCOM's hesitance to take advantage of its oversight entity in the Pentagon, the office of the ASD/SOLIC, had implications within the Executive Branch and also in Congress. ASD/SOLIC had (and continues to have) deep networks in and understanding of policy mechanisms in OSD, the White House–led interagency NSC process, and Congress. Officials from ASD/SOLIC met frequently with their counterparts in those organizations to provide policy context and details on USSOCOM-related issues. When possible, ASD/SOLIC attempted to assist USSOCOM on certain initiatives by advising on strategic outreach. It also sought to help with proposal structure by attempting to break down the GSN concept into its component parts to increase likelihood of approval.[27]

However, wanting to gain approval for the GSN initiatives quickly, USSOCOM often engaged policy stakeholders without consulting with OSD representatives.[28] This resulted in uncoordinated messaging, which cast more suspicion on the GSN.[29] This occurred at both staff and senior levels: In the latter case, McRaven's interaction

---

[25] Interview with former DoD official with responsibility for special operations, Washington, D.C., March 25, 2016; Jonathan Greenert, "House Appropriations Subcommittee on Defense: Hearing on President Obama's Fiscal 2016 Budget Request for the Navy," February 26, 2015; and Elisabeth Bumiller, "Panetta Warns of Dire Consequences to Military from Budget Cuts," *New York Times*, February 6, 2013.

[26] Andrew Feickert, *U.S. Special Operations Forces (SOF): Background and Issues for Congress*, Congressional Research Service, 7-7500, RS21048, September 18, 2013.

[27] Interview with former DoD official with responsibility for special operations, Washington, D.C., March 25, 2016.

[28] Interview with SOCOM official, March 21, 2016.

[29] Interview with congressional staff, Washington, D.C., January 29, 2016.

with Congress on GSN initiatives before DoD had approved them put Pentagon leadership in a difficult position.[30]

By 2013, certain Congress members had turned from strong advocacy for USSOCOM-related issues to open skepticism about the GSN initiatives.[31] Congressional staff felt that, although McRaven spoke about transparency often in GSN-related presentations with U.S. government officials, the communication was one-way and directive; USSOCOM was briefing the initiatives they were pursuing without asking for help in shaping them. Further, many in Congress shared DoD's and the State Department's concerns that certain GSN initiatives would be too costly, were not adequately explained nor coordinated within the interagency, and were duplicative or unnecessary.[32]

Congress was particularly skeptical of three proposals: the RSCCs, USSOCOM-NCR, and the SOF SFA LP. Congressional staff viewed the RSCCs as duplicative, given that training centers already existed in the geographic areas where USSOCOM wanted to establish them, and also as inexplicably expensive given that the concept was to increase partner-nation burden sharing.[33] USSOCOM-NCR was also viewed as a redundant organization whose unique purpose Congress did not feel was adequately explained despite USSOCOM's budget request for it.[34] Further, although the initial SOF SFA proposal was never formally submitted to Congress, USSOCOM introduced the effort to congressional staff during GSN briefs and sent drafts of the proposal to defense committee staff without formal DoD or Executive Branch approval. This violation of standard process contributed to perspectives in Congress that the SOF SFA proposal did not have adequate analysis or DoD support.[35]

---

[30] Interview with former OSD official, Washington, D.C., March 2, 2016.

[31] Interview with senior OSD official, January 30, 2013.

[32] Interview with congressional staff, Washington, D.C., January 29, 2016.

[33] Interview with congressional staff, Washington, D.C., January 29, 2016.

[34] Interview with congressional staff, Washington, D.C., January 29, 2016.

[35] Interview with congressional staff, Washington, D.C., January 21, 2016.

Across the broader security-oriented Executive and Legislative Branch community, concerns that aspects of the GSN initiatives were overreaching or insufficiently developed were fairly consistent.[36] As the GSN effort progressed, many throughout Washington and in the COCOMs were increasingly suspicious that USSOCOM was seeking to gain sweeping policy changes and operate without oversight by circumventing traditional decisionmaking processes and forcing decisions without proper socialization. Despite widespread admiration for McRaven and significant effort by USSOCOM to convince policy stakeholders otherwise, USSOCOM was unable to fully shed that perception throughout the duration of the GSN effort.[37]

Initiative 1: Theater Special Operations Command Empowerment

The TSOC empowerment line of effort was intended to enable SOF to more effectively support the GCCs by clarifying the relationship between USSOCOM and the TSOCs, providing greater resources to the TSOCs, or increasing the USSOCOM commander's ability to move forces rapidly. The TSOC empowerment effort consisted primarily of four distinct but related initiatives: (1) for USSOCOM to gain command and control of the TSOCs using the "Forces For" memorandum and assignment tables; (2) to formalize USSOCOM support to the GCCs in a GSN concept of operations (CONOPS) using the joint capabilities integration process; (3) to expand the USSOCOM commander's role beyond synchronization of global CT efforts in the Unified Command Plan; and (4) to capture the preceding three initiatives in a broad campaign plan.

---

[36] RAND summary of interview findings with DoD, U.S. Department of State, and USAID officials, January 29, 2013.

[37] Interview with OSD official, January 11, 2013.

Gaining Combatant Command Authority over the TSOCs ("Forces For" Changes)

The USSOCOM commander is tasked with "ensuring the combat readiness of forces assigned to the special operations command."[38] However, as the GSN effort was getting underway in 2011, TSOCs were assigned to their respective GCCs, meaning that the GCCs held servicelike responsibilities to man, train, and equip their respective TSOC forces in addition to maintaining operational control of TSOC forces when they were deployed in theater. This command and control relationship meant that, while USSOCOM oversaw readiness of U.S.-based forces, the command was unable to move resources and personnel to better support the TSOCs and other forward-deployed forces directly. Another issue was relative seniority in budget negotiations: TSOCs, commanded by either one- or two-star officers, were subunified commands partially funded by the GCCs. TSOC commanders were continually challenged with obtaining appropriate resources from the four-star geographic combatant commander, and, without direct resourcing responsibility to the TSOCs, the USSOCOM commander could only petition the GCCs to support the TSOCs' requirements rather than resource them in full.[39]

In response to these challenges, McRaven directed USSOCOM to seek ways to "improve USSOCOM's ability to laterally synchronize, manage and resource its forces to support the GCCs to meet future, unforeseen demands in multiple theaters."[40] This was an effort to both better support the TSOCs—resource and man them to most effectively support the GCC's mission—but also to change the relationship between USSOCOM on the TSOCs so that TSOC growth could be possible.

To analyze the need for SOF support globally, USSOCOM initiated a series of conferences called rehearsal of concept (ROC) drills starting in April 2012. The ROC drills focused participants on specific

---

[38] United States Code, Title 10, Section 167, Unified Combatant Command for Special Operations Forces, December 19, 2014.

[39] Interview with OSD staff, April 1, 2016.

[40] U.S. Special Operations Command, 2012c, p. 4.

areas in which SOF could be optimally employed and what requirements would be necessary.[41] In these drills, representatives from the military departments, OSD, the GCCs, and the TSOCs attended to provide input into each GCC's SOF requirements. The drills started at the staff level and ended with four-star commander participation. To gain an understanding of what the GCCs' true need for SOF support would be if each did not have to compete with another for resources, the ROC SOF requirements were determined without notional budget constraints.[42] USSOCOM used this information to highlight where USSOCOM could resolve the gap between each GCC's requirements and existing resourcing and personnel levels at the TSOCs.

From design to validation, representatives throughout the DoD community were included in the process, which was critical in ultimately gaining GCC approval of USSOCOM's proposal to assign the TSOCs to USSOCOM.[43] Through this deliberate process, USSOCOM generated a demand signal that not only made the case for providing additional resources to each TSOC according to its needs and priorities, but also bolstered USSOCOM's argument in the budgeting process to increase overall SOF end strength.[44] USSOCOM also used this process to identify manpower requirements within each of the TSOCs that could be addressed quickly by transferring USSOCOM personnel to the TSOCs without additional funding requirements, which displayed goodwill toward the GCCs.[45] An additional consequence of the ROC drill process was the approval of Special Operations Command North in 2012, whose foundation was based in part on U.S. Northern Command's participation in the requirement validation process.[46]

---

[41] Interview with SOCOM official, March 21, 2016.

[42] Dave Ahearn, "Team Leaders Q&A: Improving SOF Support to Geographic Combatant Commands, Col. Stuart W. Bradin Chief Global SOF Network Operational Planning Team SOCOM," *Special Operations Technology*, Vol. 11, No. 2, March 2013.

[43] Interview with SOCOM official, March 21, 2016.

[44] U.S. Special Operations Command, 2014.

[45] Interview with SOCOM official, March 21, 2016.

[46] U.S. Special Operations Command, 2014.

Supported by the ROC drill process, USSOCOM pursued command and control of the TSOCs so it could directly provide them personnel and resources. Reassignment of TSOCs to USSOCOM required a change to the Forces For Unified Commands Memorandum and assignment tables, governed by an established DoD revision proposal process. USSOCOM had recently been exposed to the Forces For process when reassigning forces from the disestablished U.S. Joint Forces Command to USSOCOM and used that experience as a template for the proposal.[47]

Using the validated requirements derived from the ROC drills as a basis for demonstrating need for the COCOM changes, USSOCOM secured approval for the Forces For changes from the GCCs and military service chiefs in September 2012, and then from Secretary Panetta in February 2013.[48] While congressional approval was not directly required to gain approval of the proposed Forces For revisions, staffers were largely supportive of the initiative to empower the TSOCs because it was messaged effectively and was geared toward amplifying the GCCs' ability to operate rather than strengthening USSOCOM.[49] Additionally, USSOCOM's proposal to shift some of its personnel to operational commands was in line with the headquarters reductions proposals that sequestration required, garnering further support from Congress.[50]

Approval of these substantive changes can be attributed to several key factors: USSOCOM successfully explained that the command relationship change would directly support the GCCs and would not infringe on their operational control of the TSOCs;[51] USSOCOM was addressing a resourcing gap that the GCCs wanted to be filled; USSOCOM had included a wide DoD audience in the process to iden-

---

[47] Interview with SOCOM official, March 21, 2016.

[48] U.S. Special Operations Command, 2014.

[49] William H. McRaven, "Posture Statement of Admiral William H. McRaven, USN Commander, United States Special Operations Command, Before the 113th Congress, House Arms Service Committee, Washington, D.C., March 6, 2013.

[50] Interview with congressional staff, Washington, D.C., January 29, 2016.

[51] Interview with OSD staff, April 1, 2016.

tify TSOC requirements from the beginning stages, creating goodwill among those consulted in the ROC drills; and SOCOM took advantage of an existing procedure and worked deliberately through that process to gain approval.[52] Using these strategies, USSOCOM was able to overcome skepticism of its intent in empowering the TSOCs and was ultimately successful in its goal of gaining command and control of the TSOCs. While the GCCs retain operational control of SOF in theater, the TSOCs are now USSOCOM's subordinate unified commands to man, train, and equip regardless of geographical disposition. While some still express concern that the original intent of the TSOC empowerment line of effort was only partially filled, the gains USSOCOM made toward robust support of and clarity in relationship to the TSOCs are noteworthy.[53]

Global SOF Network Concept of Operations

Following the ROC drills, the GSN team identified that doctrinal changes would be required to ensure the longevity of USSOCOM's efforts. Changes in DoD doctrine require formal proposals submitted to JROC, which feeds into JCIDS. USSOCOM intended the changes in doctrine to be pursued in parallel with the rest of the GSN initiatives, understanding that the JCIDS process is deliberately slow and formal changes can take years to approve.[54]

To initiate this process, the GSN team drafted the "Global SOF Network 2020 Concept of Operations" (GSN 2020 CONOPS) to serve three purposes: to explain USSOCOM's vision for SOF to operate in a networked configuration, to serve as a foundation for subsequent reviews of doctrinal changes, and to gain JROC validation that those concepts had joint implications.[55] USSOCOM submitted

---

[52] Interview with SOCOM official, March 21, 2016; and interview with OSD staff, April 1, 2016.

[53] Interview with former SOCOM official, April 18, 2016.

[54] Interview with SOCOM official, March 21, 2016.

[55] Interview with SOCOM official, March 21, 2016; and Office of the Vice Commander, U.S. Special Operations Command, "Global Special Operations Forces Network Concept of Operations," memorandum to Directors for Force Structure, Resources, and Assessments, May 1, 2013.

the GSN 2020 CONOPS to the JROC in May 2013 and received initial approval that October.[56] Initial approval formalized the term *Global SOF Network*, enabled USSOCOM to institutionalize GSN initiatives in its future budget requests, and entered into JCIDS the initial capabilities document (ICD), which detailed TSOC capability requirements.[57] The ICD was approved by the vice chairman of the JCS in December 2015.[58]

USSOCOM then submitted a formal request to change joint DOTMLPF-P to further outline USSOCOM's command and control of and support to the TSOCs and to provide options for resolving TSOC resourcing gaps identified in the ICD.[59] After coordinating that proposal through JCIDS, USSOCOM gained approval in March 2016, fundamentally changing doctrine to formalize the USSOCOM-TSOC relationship and to ensure that the TSOCs are enabled to command operations in support of the GCC.[60]

Although the process was lengthy and required significant coordination, it was necessary for USSOCOM to pursue achieving the doctrinal changes required to institutionalize TSOC empowerment. According to an official involved in the doctrine change request, USSOCOM faced opposition from senior levels in the JROC throughout the process, which may have been mitigated if USSOCOM had more carefully involved the ASD/SOLIC and the Army organizations that provide the majority of joint manpower to the TSOCs as coadvocates.[61]

---

[56] James A. Winnefeld, Jr., "Global SOF Network 2020 Concept of Operations," memorandum for the Under Secretaries of Defense, Military Service Vice Chiefs, and Combatant Commanders, Washington, D.C.: U.S. Department of Defense, October 16, 2013.

[57] U.S. Special Operations Command, 2014; U.S. Special Operations Command, Joint DOTMLPF-P Change Recommendation for Theater Special Operations Command Headquarters Command and Control, September 2015.

[58] U.S. Special Operations Command, 2014.

[59] U.S. Special Operations Command, 2015.

[60] Paul J. Selva, "Theater Special Operations Command and Control Doctrine, Organization, Training, Material, Leadership and Education, Personnel, Facilities, and Policy (DOTMLPF-P) Change Recommendation," Washington, D.C.: U.S. Department of Defense, March 11, 2016; and U.S. Special Operations Command, 2015.

[61] Interview with SOCOM official, March 21, 2016.

Expanding USSOCOM Responsibility Beyond Synchronization (UCP Changes)

The Forces For effort only focused on gaining command and control of the TSOCs and forward-deployed SOF. USSOCOM believed that the commander also needed the authority to move forces rapidly between theaters to support the 2012 DSG's direction to be adequately agile.[62] USSOCOM focused on the UCP, a document required in federal code that establishes the missions, responsibilities, and forces assigned to each combatant command and that is approved by the President of the United States.[63] According to the UCP, the USSOCOM commander is responsible for synchronizing planning for global CT operations. This means that USSOCOM only had authority to "conduct activities designed to deter emerging threats, build relationships with foreign militaries, and potentially develop greater access to foreign militaries."[64] McRaven viewed this scope of responsibility as too narrow to adequately respond to contingencies worldwide and directed his staff to seek revisions to the UCP.

In early 2012, USSOCOM began socializing its rationale for the proposed UCP changes as a way to help the GCCs respond more quickly to emerging crises around the globe. The proposal was to expand the USSOCOM commander's responsibilities beyond synchronization of planning CT operations to include the coordination, deployment and, in certain cases, the employment of SOF, with the approval of the GCCs and other relevant agencies as appropriate, and to increase the purview of USSOCOM's activities beyond CT. These efforts to expand the USSOCOM commander's role initially caused concern throughout DoD, and particularly from the GCCs, who voiced their concerns to other policymakers that the changes could result in a shift

---

[62] U.S. Special Operations Command, 2014.

[63] United States Code, Title 10, Section 161, Combatant Commands: Establishment, October 1, 1986.

[64] Andrew Feickert, *U.S. Special Operations Forces (SOF): Background and Issues for Congress*, Congressional Research Service, November 2015, summary.

in the operational control of theater SOF to McRaven.[65] ADM (ret.) Timothy Keating, former commander of U.S. Northern Command and USPACOM, addressed the issue at an April 2012 Center for International and Strategic Studies forum on the changes McRaven sought. Speaking from the GCC perspective, Keating stated, "I'm not so sure that the proposal, as I understand it, will fix anything because I don't fundamentally understand what needs fixing."[66]

In response, USSOCOM worked closely with OSD to engage the GCCs, the service chiefs, and Joint Staff officials about the intent and the limits of the proposed UCP changes, established a consistent message about why the changes were necessary, and built on the goodwill generated through the ROC drill process. As a result, in August 2012, the GCCs and the service chiefs approved USSOCOM's proposed revisions to the UCP.[67] In the end, USSOCOM was able to gain support for the UCP changes despite initial high-level resistance. By involving the GCCs, the Joint Staff, and OSD in the planning process and developing a clear and supportable message, USSOCOM eventually convinced key stakeholders that expanding the USSOCOM commander's responsibilities would ultimately strengthen the GCCs' ability to respond effectively to crises using SOF.

Campaign Plan
Initially, USSOCOM attempted to gain flexibility in the commander's ability to move forces globally by pursuing a "Global SOF Employment Order." This was an initiative without procedural precedent that prompted concern throughout DoD that McRaven was attempting to circumvent normal processes and civilian oversight. As a result, USSOCOM shifted its efforts in late 2012 to the campaign plan process.[68]

---

[65] Interview with former DoD official with responsibility for special operations, Washington, D.C., March 25, 2016.

[66] "The Future of Special Operations: Proposed Changes in the Unified Command Plan," *Global Security Forum 2012, Conference Proceedings,* Washington, D.C.: Center for Strategic and International Studies, April 2012.

[67] U.S. Special Operations Command, 2014.

[68] U.S. Special Operations Command, 2014.

Understanding that to avoid suspicion and gain necessary support USSOCOM needed to staff the campaign plan effort through traditional Pentagon processes, the GSN team drafted a planning order for the chairman of the JCS to formally task USSOCOM to compose such a plan. Called the *Global Campaign Plan for Special Operations* (GCP-SO), it was intended to formalize the GCC requirements identified in the ROC drill process. Working closely with the Joint Staff, USSOCOM gained GCC validation of its SOF requirements via a memorandum to McRaven and was officially tasked to compose the campaign plan in April 2013. McRaven and the GSN team conducted multiple senior-level meetings and events throughout DoD to develop support for the campaign plan as it was developed. USSOCOM submitted the 800-page GCP-SO to the Joint Staff for formal coordination in October 2013.[69]

The GCP-SO described USSOCOM's strategy for enabling the GSN: by supporting the GCCs through its TSOCs, reorganizing internally, improving its coordination throughout DoD and other U.S. government agencies, and increasing information sharing with partner nations. Ultimately, the GCP-SO was more of a resourcing and implementation document than a traditional campaign plan that guides military planning for warfighting, which caused the effort to stagnate in DoD.[70] GEN Joseph Votel, who succeeded McRaven as the commander of USSOCOM, eventually signed the campaign plan at his level after the GCP-SO had remained in Pentagon staffing for two years. Votel's signature meant that the GCP-SO, now finally approved, was limited to providing guidance internally within SOCOM rather than to the broader DoD community.

Initiative 2: Regional SOF Coordination Centers

During his tenure as commander of Special Operations Command–Europe, McRaven oversaw the establishment of NSHQ, an organization to coordinate SOF training and activities among NATO allies.

---

[69] U.S. Special Operations Command, 2014.

[70] Interview with OSD officials familiar with special operations policy, Washington, D.C., February 9, 2016.

With NSHQ as his model, McRaven viewed international partnerships and alliances as integral to the success of the GSN. As part of the Purple Note that established the GSN OPT, McRaven indicated his desire to "establish a NSHQ-like institution in each region where we think we can establish buy-in."[71] Noting that not every region would be hospitable to such a structure, McRaven further directed his staff to focus on how to augment bilateral relationships in regions that would not be suitable hosts to an NSHQ-like structure.

The OPT quickly responded to McRaven's directive, developing notional structures called RSCCs in the USPACOM and U.S. Southern Command (USSOUTHCOM). The RSCCs, as the international element of the GSN, were intended to empower partners to improve their SOF competency and capability to a level at which they could contribute most effectively to coalition operations (such as in Afghanistan) or other multinational SOF operations.[72]

USSOCOM envisioned RSCCs as hubs for interoperability and sustained engagement throughout each region. They were to be hosted by a foreign government but supported by U.S. SOF and interagency personnel and open by invitation to multiple partner countries. According to USSOCOM, the RSCCs would enable persistent presence in a region; serve as a node to coordinate SOF education, training, and operations throughout the region; and increase information sharing among partners. USSOCOM also advocated the RSCCs' ability to shift responsibility—and associated cost—for regional security onto the shoulders of local nations.[73]

USSOCOM's central tenet in advocating for the RSCCs—and, to an extent, the broader GSN—was that "you can't surge trust," a sentiment USSOCOM repeated frequently in support of the GSN.[74]

---

[71] McRaven, 2011.

[72] Interview with SOCOM official, March 21, 2016.

[73] Interview with SOCOM official, March 21, 2016; and U.S. Special Operations Command, 2012b.

[74] U.S. Special Operations Command, Special Operations Forces 2020: Enhancing the Global SOF Network, 2013a; and U.S. Special Operations Command, "Special Operations Forces 2020: You Can't Surge Trust," briefing slides, 2013b.

McRaven and the OPT believed that relationships with key partners need to be formed and sustained prior to a crisis: Trust must be gained before it was to be leveraged.[75]

As early as March 2012, the GSN team began informally discussing the RSCCs with interested parties in DoD, other U.S. government agencies, and Congress. In an attempt to gain buy-in and ascertain potential challenges early in the approval process, USSOCOM conducted many of these discussions before the RSCC concept had been fully developed. The OPT, without a comptroller staff element at the time, provided rough budget estimates that did not have detailed analysis behind them.[76] Further, the GSN OPT tailored its briefs and white papers to various USG entities, often with different levels of detail and messaging about the RSCCs, which contributed to confusion about the purpose and operational details of the RSCCs among policy stakeholders.[77] Many within DoD and on Capitol Hill questioned why the RSCCs, which USSOCOM described as training and education centers, were needed in USPACOM and USSOUTHCOM, since the COCOMs already operated training and education centers for partner nations. USSOCOM was moving out quickly on the RSCCs, per McRaven's guidance, but that speed combined with the lack of a clear purpose for the RSCCs attracted significant scrutiny. The estimated cost of the RSCCs, which many on Capitol Hill felt was unjustified, only added to the resistance against the RSCCs in particular and the GSN in general.[78]

In May 2012, during an international SOF conference hosted by USSOCOM, McRaven discussed RSCCs with global SOF partners in attendance before either DoD or Congress had approved the concept or its funding. Colombia informed McRaven that it was interested in hosting an RSCC, and planning began. While the U.S. ambassador to Colombia reportedly gave a verbal endorsement for the effort in

---

[75] Ahearn, 2013.

[76] Interview with SOCOM official, March 21, 2016.

[77] Interview with SOCOM official, March 21, 2016.

[78] Interview with congressional staff, Washington, D.C., January 29, 2016.

January 2013, formal approval from State Department headquarters or other relevant coordinating offices had not been obtained.[79] While USSOCOM eventually gained formal endorsement of the RSCCs by the USSOUTHCOM and USPACOM commanders in 2013, the early outreach to foreign nations created friction with the State Department and its oversight committees on Capitol Hill.[80]

Further, congressional staff noted that USSOCOM staff at times appeared to give the impression that stated that Congress's approval for the RSCCs' had already been secured, despite significant interagency opposition and congressional questions that remained.[81] At a February 2013 briefing attended by congressional staff and DoD personnel, USSOCOM representatives claimed that the RSCC in USPACOM was finalized and ready to be implemented, since they had gained approval from ADM Samuel Locklear, the USPACOM commander. These assertions further contributed to the impression that USSOCOM was not interested in seeking collaboration on its GSN initiatives, and animosity toward SOCOM's efforts throughout Washington continued to grow.[82] USSOCOM's assumption that it no longer needed to socialize the RSCC concept once the GCC commander's approval was secured effectively alienated other government stakeholders that may have otherwise been supportive.

Congress formally indicated its opposition to USSOCOM's RSCC proposal through legislation in 2013, although the opposition was reportedly less about the concept and more about the high price tag and what congressional staff saw as a lack of rigorous analysis on the part of USSOCOM to support its request.[83] Both the Senate and House versions of the FY 2014 NDAA included language to prohibit funds from being expended to support the RSCCs and required a joint

---

[79] U.S. Special Operations Command, 2014.

[80] U.S. Special Operations Command, 2014; and interview with congressional staff, Washington, D.C., January 29, 2016.

[81] Interview with congressional staff, Washington, D.C., January 29, 2016.

[82] Email communication from RAND researchers summarizing interagency concerns, February 1, 2013.

[83] Interview with congressional staff, Washington, D.C., January 29, 2016.

DoD–State Department report on their purpose, budget, and planned activities.[84]

In response, USSOCOM, through OSD, submitted a paper in April 2014 that covered the intent, purpose, and cost of the RSCCs, steps USSOCOM would take to deconflict RSCC efforts with existing State Department initiatives, and what legislative authorities would be required to implement the organizations.[85] However, without funding or widespread interagency support, which would be critical for the RSCCs, USSOCOM decided to formally end the RSCC line of effort.

Portions of the RSCC initiative had some success. The RSCC in Colombia as originally envisioned was never created, but Colombia established a similar military institution that focuses on education and training.[86] In line with USSOCOM's original vision to empower partner nations to share more burden for global security, Colombia hosts and runs the center with multinational participation and support.[87]

Further, during the development of the RSCC concept and while McRaven was still commander, USSOCOM initiated an effort to increase the number of embedded foreign SOF personnel at its Tampa, Florida, headquarters. Despite challenges posed by classified office space, USSOCOM initially brought on board liaison officers from countries such as the United Kingdom, Canada, France, Italy, and Spain.[88] That coordination element, now called the International SOF

---

[84] Andrew Feickert, *U.S. Special Operations Forces (SOF): Background and Issues for Congress*, Congressional Research Service, 7-7500, RS21048, September 18, 2013; U.S. Senate, 113th Cong., 1st Sess., Limitation on Funding for Regional Special Operations Coordination Centers, Sec. 342 of National Defense Authorization Act for Fiscal Year 2014, Washington, D.C., S. 1197, June 20, 2013; U.S. House of Representatives, Limitation on Establishment of Regional Special Operations Forces Coordination Centers, Sec. 1245 of National Defense Authorization Act for Fiscal Year 2014, Washington, D.C., H.R. 1960, July 8, 2013.

[85] Office of the Secretary of Defense, U.S. Department of Defense, *Establishment of Regional Special Operations Coordination Centers*, April 16, 2014.

[86] Interview with SOCOM official, March 21, 2016; and Escuela Superior de Guerra [Superior School of War], *Centro Regional de Estudios Estrategicos en Seguridad* [regional center for strategic security studies], undated.

[87] Interview with SOCOM official, March 21, 2016.

[88] Ahearn, 2013.

Coordination Center, has grown to 18 foreign liaisons, who sit side by side and share information in person and through the BICES system.[89]

Initiative 3: SOCOM National Capital Region

When McRaven took command of USSOCOM, approximately 350 personnel assigned to USSOCOM were based in Washington, D.C., working throughout DoD and in other such government offices as the State Department and the FBI. As USSOCOM believed their challenges required an increasingly collaborative approach with interagency actors to gain support for SOF missions throughout the world, McRaven had directed the GSN OPT to determine how to strengthen relationships among decisionmakers.

USSOCOM placed heavy emphasis on the importance of proximity: Since most critical interagency partners were located in Washington, USSOCOM wanted its primary coordination base to be there as well. Accordingly, in early 2012, the GSN OPT began to pursue the establishment of USSOCOM-NCR, an organizational hub for fostering collaboration (or "thickening" relationships, as SOCOM put it) among USSOCOM personnel within the Washington area.[90]

In June 2012, USSOCOM formally initiated the process to establish USSOCOM-NCR by placing USSOCOM's vice commander, Lt Gen Eric Heithold, in charge of the effort based out of USSOCOM's Washington office in the Pentagon. In addition to consolidating various organizations under its jurisdiction in Washington into USSOCOM-NCR, it sought to transfer its interagency coordination activities from Tampa.[91] The proposed functions of SOCOM NCR were to coordinate whole-of-government approaches to national security challenges; to "shape, coordinate and support the synchronization of global SOF activities" throughout the interagency and in the private

---

[89] Interview with SOCOM official, March 21, 2016.

[90] U.S. Special Operations Command, 2012b; and U.S. Special Operations Command, 2013b.

[91] U.S. Special Operations Command, 2014.

sector; and to bring multiple USSOCOM elements together in one organization.⁹²

Elements of the GSN OPT began to set up infrastructure for the entity even before the proposal was approved. They set about searching for suitable office space, establishing an initial liaison element in Washington, and designating personnel for transfer from Tampa to Washington. However, while skepticism was high throughout Washington about USSOCOM-NCR's utility, the central purposes of the organization—to better coordinate USSOCOM activities with interagency actors and to oversee USSOCOM entities in Washington in one node—were not particularly objectionable.⁹³

In fact, the concept of promoting strong interagency relationships was generally supported throughout the broader national security community, given that such USSOCOM coordination organizations as the USSOCOM Washington office and JIATF NCR already existed. There was even some support in Congress for the consolidation of USSOCOM's Washington organizations and for placing Heithold in Washington, as the proximity could foster a closer alliance with ASD/SOLIC.⁹⁴

Instead, it was the process by which USSOCOM sought to gain funding and approval for the effort, and the lack of rigorous analysis in defending the proposal, that created opposition to it.⁹⁵ Similar to other GSN initiatives, USSOCOM's messaging of USSOCOM-NCR was often conflicting and unclear, with emphasis on expediency and not enough explanation of the purpose, proposed functions, and rationale for funding requests.

These functions appeared to some in Washington to be redundant with existing organizations, including the ASD/SOLIC's office.⁹⁶ Although USSOCOM framed USSOCOM-NCR as a reorganization

---

⁹² U.S. Special Operations Command, 2014, p. 8.

⁹³ Interview with congressional staff, Washington, D.C., January 29, 2016.

⁹⁴ Interview with congressional staff, Washington, D.C., January 29, 2016.

⁹⁵ Interview with congressional staff, Washington, D.C., January 29, 2016.

⁹⁶ Interview with congressional staff, Washington, D.C., January 29, 2016.

of existing personnel and organizations in Washington, it was still unclear why a new structure—instead of expanding the activities of the USSOCOM Washington office—would be required.[97] Combined with other simultaneous GSN efforts, USSOCOM-NCR contributed to the widespread perception, extending to Capitol Hill, that McRaven was endeavoring to build an empire.[98]

Many in Congress did not feel that USSOCOM had made a compelling argument about why a new office space outfitted with expensive, cutting-edge technology was required for the entity when they already had substantial space throughout the NCR. Further, some in Congress felt that how they initially learned of the USSOCOM-NCR initiative—by finding it deep within DoD's annual budget justification books sent to Congress, with no forewarning or explanation—raised suspicions that the effort was poorly conceived.[99]

In report language accompanying the House of Representatives' FY 2014 Defense Appropriations Act, the House Committee on Appropriations explained why they opted not to fund the $10 million request for USSOCOM-NCR and directed that USSOCOM not obligate or expend funds toward USSOCOM-NCR until specific information that the defense committees requested about the organization had been provided. The report language also addressed the committee's dissatisfaction with USSOCOM's justification for its funding request for USSOCOM-NCR, stating:

> The Committee remains unclear about the function, purpose, and costs associated with the operations, infrastructure, and facilities for this entity both in the interim phase and the final end-state. Further, the Committee has received conflicting information over the course of the last year as to the purpose of this entity. At times it has been described as an efficiency mechanism to relo-

---

[97] Email communication from RAND researchers summarizing USSOCOM interview, February 6, 2013.

[98] Eric Schmitt and Thom Shanker, "A Commander Seeks to Chart a New Path for Special Operations," *New York Times*, May 1, 2013; and interview with congressional staff, Washington, D.C., January 29, 2016.

[99] Interview with congressional staff, Washington, D.C., January 29, 2016.

cate over 300 SOCOM personnel to one consolidated location within the NCR. The Committee is confused by this explanation given that the vast majority of SOCOM personnel assigned to the NCR function as liaison officers and Special Operations Support Teams to other federal agencies and as such should remain resident at such agencies. At other times, some functions of the new SOCOM-NCR appear to duplicate functions already resident at SOCOM headquarters.[100]

The final NDAA for FY 2014 included similar language requiring that no funds be spent on USSOCOM-NCR until a detailed report on its purpose, intended activities, and anticipated funding requirements was delivered to the congressional defense committees.[101] These congressional provisions functionally ended USSOCOM's bid to establish USSOCOM-NCR while simultaneously sending a strong message about USSOCOM's GSN initiatives more broadly.

In February 2014, USSOCOM officially terminated its efforts to establish SOCOM NCR and redirected its efforts inside the Interagency Partnership Program (IAPP).[102] The IAPP, functionally a streamlined version of the originally envisioned USSOCOM-NCR, serves as a hub to coordinate the more than 300 USSOCOM personnel activities in the NCR. The IAPP leverages existing USSOCOM funds and personnel to operate its NCR office, which was created from space USSOCOM had already leased instead of through an additional contract. Given its small footprint and narrow functional scope, the IAPP has not energized significant opposition in Congress, further suggesting that the opposition to USSOCOM-NCR can be attributed, at least in part, to its proposed budget and possibly the relocation of personnel from Tampa to Washington. In addition, some interviewees

---

[100] U.S. House of Representatives, 113th Cong., 1st Sess., Department of Defense Appropriations Act, Washington, D.C., H.R. 2397, July 30, 2013.

[101] Public Law 113-66, National Defense Authorization Act for Fiscal Year 2014, Sec. 343, Limitation on funding for United States Special Operations Command National Capital Region, December 26, 2013.

[102] U.S. Special Operations Command, 2014.

believed that SOCOM had not provided rigorous analysis supporting a well-defined case for another bureaucratic structure.

Initiative 4: SOF Security Force Assistance Authority

Another initiative pursued as part of the GSN was USSOCOM's attempt to gain an SOF-specific SFA legislative authority. At the outset of the GSN initiative, USSOCOM believed existing legislative authorities were not sufficient to adequately develop foreign partners' SOF capabilities and to develop trusting relationships that could be leveraged during crises. Starting in early 2012, USSOCOM frequently stressed during its discussions regarding GSN the need for U.S. SOF to have an authority that enabled persistent engagement with a wide range of foreign partners. At the time, many existing security-assistance authorities restricted the types of support that could be provided and forces that DoD could partner with. Furthermore, traditional SFA authorities have a reputation for being slow because of lengthy procurement processes and the time and coordination required to gain signatures from both the Secretary of Defense and the Secretary of State.

To address the perceived authority gap, USSOCOM submitted an LP to DoD in spring 2012, LP 308.[103] The Pentagon's LP submission deadlines had passed months earlier, so USSOCOM's late submission required significant coordination in a short time frame to approve the proposal and pass it through the required Office of Management and Budget (OMB) interagency adjudication process in time for Congress to consider the language in its annual defense authorization bill, usually crafted in May each year. LP 308 was the earliest major GSN initiative to gain significant attention in Congress and throughout the U.S. government, and the manner in which USSOCOM attempted to push LP 308 to Congress contributed significantly to the overall negative tenor of the subsequent GSN rollout.[104]

---

[103] DoD, *Sustaining U.S. Global Leadership: Priorities for 21st Century Defense*, Washington, D.C., January 2012b.

[104] Interview with congressional staff, Washington, D.C., January 21, 2016.

If approved, the draft of LP 308 provided to the RAND research team stated that it would have furnished $25 million

> to provide support for the rapid development and long term development of special operations capacities and capabilities of the national security forces of a partner nation to conduct special operations missions or to participate in or support military, stability, or peace support operations consistent with United States foreign policy and national security interests.

Through LP 308, SOCOM also sought to expand SOF authorities to train a range of foreign forces beyond those that belong to a Ministry of Defense, to address non-CT threats, to provide logistic support and fund minor military construction, to provide refresher training or replacement equipment, and to assess partners' absorptive capacity and tailor assistance accordingly.[105] These were perceived needs that such security assistance authorities as Section 1206 Global Train and Equip did not address.

Congress learned of LP 308 during various budget and GSN briefings, before it was approved by DoD. USSOCOM also actively engaged congressional staff about the proposal before it was formally approved by DoD, a tactic considered to be a violation of the traditional LP procedures. SOCOM may have hoped that its early engagement with Capitol Hill would create support there for LP 308, but congressional staff viewed the command's direct engagement as an attempt to circumvent the OMB approval process. In particular, some staff felt that the proposed language suggested that USSOCOM was simply seeking a "workaround" of existing authorities and their associated approval processes. Further, SOCOM's aggressive approach created the perception that the command believed that it was no longer required to work within the traditional policy approval systems, since they had earned sufficient "credit" through operational successes.[106]

---

[105] USSOCOM, 2012a.

[106] Interview with congressional staff, Washington, D.C., January 21, 2016.

USSOCOM made attempts to justify its proposal, adding a five-page analysis to the LP explaining its necessity and why existing authorities were insufficient.[107] However, congressional staff and other U.S. government officials felt that USSOCOM could not adequately explain why a specific SOF SFA measure was needed when other authorities appeared to be sufficient.[108] Officials were also concerned about the purpose of the authority and questioned how USSOCOM could justify bolstering security capabilities in countries whose governance structures were not adequate to support them.[109]

Further, since LP 308 did not require Secretary of State approval, many questioned whether McRaven was purposefully seeking to cut the State Department out of the process. This perception surfaced frequently throughout the duration of the LP 308 effort and also the overall GSN effort, requiring McRaven to state during a May 2012 press conference: "We're not recommending anything that goes around the State Department."[110] McRaven further emphasized this point repeatedly during his USSOCOM Posture Statement to HASC in March 2013.[111]

On May 7, 2012, an NSC-led Deputies Committee attended by Under Secretary–level representatives from a range of government agencies discussed LP 308.[112] In addition to the concerns about process violations and perceived lack of State Department oversight, some officials felt that USSOCOM was overstating the constraints of the existing authorities and believed that all the activities McRaven envisioned SOF conducting could occur if existing authorities were adequately used.[113] Accordingly, the deputies determined that, rather than send-

---

[107] U.S. Department of Defense, 2012b.

[108] Interview with congressional staff, Washington, D.C., January 29, 2016.

[109] Interview with congressional staff, Washington, D.C., January 29, 2016.

[110] Eric Schmitt, "Elite Military Forces Are Denied in Bid for Expansion," *New York Times*, June 4, 2012.

[111] McRaven, 2013.

[112] Schmitt, 2012.

[113] Interview with senior OSD official, January 30, 2013.

ing the proposal to Congress as a stand-alone request, they would set aside $25 million from the existing Global Security Contingency Fund (GSCF) for SOF-specific programs.[114] The GSCF, a joint DoD–State Department authority, is intended to provide authority and funding for a wide range of government programs, including the ability to work with forces outside of the Ministry of Defense.

The Senate Armed Services Committee echoed these concerns, stating in NDAA report language in June 2012 that, while supportive of McRaven's concept to remain persistently engaged with partner forces,

> the committee notes that Congress has made efforts in recent years to provide more flexible and responsive authorities to conduct security force assistance activities. The committee encourages DoD to make more effective use of existing authorities, including the Global Security Contingency Fund, "section 1206" global train and equip authority, and DoD counternarcotics authorities, to better support the security force assistance activities of special operations forces under the command of the theater special operations commands.[115]

USSOCOM responded to the deputies' direction by submitting dozens of SFA proposals to the Joint Staff and OSD. Possibly because of the tight deadline—less than two weeks—that USSOCOM had to draft and submit the proposals, most of them did not meet the requirements of the authority in some cases because they had been previously submitted (but not approved) under other authorities. The high number of unsupportable proposals suggested to some within the government that USSOCOM could not demonstrate a need for the type of authority it was requesting, timeline pressure notwithstanding.[116] However, OSD and the State Department selected three USSOCOM-specific

---

[114] Interview with OSD staff, September 28, 2012; and Schmitt, 2012.

[115] U.S. Senate, 112th Cong., 2nd Sess., National Defense Authorization Act for Fiscal Year 2013, Washington, D.C., S. 3254, June 4, 2012.

[116] Interview with OSD staff, April 14, 2016.

programs (in Bangladesh, Libya, and a combined program for Hungary, Romania, and Slovakia) to submit to Congress for approval.[117]

In September 2012, after multiple engagements with senior DoD leadership, Congress approved the three GSCF SOF carve-out programs just days before the end of the fiscal year.[118] However, despite the programs' approval, the process had caused "unnecessary confusion and friction" and raised serious questions throughout the federal government about the real intent and value of the SOF SFA proposal; it also evoked skepticism about related GSN initiatives.[119] The handling of LP 308 overall, and specifically the opposition and negative perceptions that it created, contrasts with the adept way in which support was garnered within DoD bureaucracy and Congress for what became Section 1208. USSOCOM followed a year later with the same LP under a different number (171), but once again faced opposition and rescinded it.

Summary of Lessons

The uneven success of the GSN initiatives yields several key lessons regarding pursuit of policy change. The GSN case illustrates the importance of correctly identifying a policy window and timing action to take advantage of such opportunities. GSN objectives that were formulated and advanced with clear objectives and systematic inclusion of stakeholder input through established processes were more successful than those that were not. In several instances, USSOCOM did not fully engage the network of potential supporters nor assuage the concerns of skeptical policymakers. Further, the GSN analysis demonstrates that, where USSOCOM was open to adapting its approach and ultimate aims, the command was more successful in achieving a measure of success.

Several specific lessons are identified through analyzing the GSN initiatives. The lessons below are those from the GSN case that most

---

[117] Serafino, 2014b.

[118] Interview with OSD staff, September 28, 2012.

[119] Schmitt, 2012.

directly affected the ultimate policy outcome of each initiative and those over which USSOCOM had the most direct control.

Understand and operate within established processes. Notwithstanding an application's importance or the application's reputation, Washington relies heavily on established processes. Developing and exploiting networks to understand stakeholder concerns and assist in working through those processes (e.g., Forces For, JCIDS, OMB's LPs, the NSC Interagency Policy Committees process) systematically will likely yield greater and faster results than attempting to circumvent or hasten the process. Further, existing processes and programs should be thoroughly analyzed to first build the case that what currently exists—in process, funding, or authorities—is not adequate for current needs. In the RSCC, USSOCOM-NCR, and LP 308 cases, USSOCOM was unable to explain why existing organizations and authorities were unable to meet their stated requirements, contributing to their failure.

Conduct rigorous analysis to defend the case. In the case of the GSN, the initiatives (such as USSOCOM's gaining command and control of the TSOCs) that relied heavily on broad stakeholder input and were justified by rigorous, often exhaustive processes, were more successful. DoD and congressional officials remained unconvinced of the need for RSCCs and USSOCOM-NCR.

Engage the full range of stakeholders for input and enlist support where needed. In the GSN effort, USSOCOM attempted to engage stakeholders, but the message often fell flat: The broader government audience felt like they were being briefed on what USSOCOM had already decided, rather than consulted as a collaborative party to initiative development. Further, USSOCOM officials noted that the GSN efforts may have been more effective if they had more closely involved ASD/SOLIC and other key DoD offices.

Timing matters. Although the GSN initiatives may have met resistance regardless of financial climate, USSOCOM faced even more pushback on its proposals because they were requesting additional funds when the military departments were faced with painful budget and personnel cuts.

Show how the proposal benefits relevant stakeholders. A pertinent example is how the USSOCOM eventually gained the support of GCCs to change the UCP and assume authority over the TSOCs. It is critical to frame efforts appropriately so that key stakeholders understand how a proposal benefits them.

Engage congressional staff. Productive engagements with congressional staff are critical. Although not the elected members of Congress, congressional aides are heavily relied on by the members and the committees they work for and can be a significant asset if they support a proposal.

Develop a clear and consistent message. USSOCOM was unable to develop a clear message about why some of the GSN initiatives were necessary and would not harm existing relationships or processes. Divergent messages contributed to confusion among stakeholders and ultimately bred distrust. But interviewees both inside and outside SOCOM agreed that the command generated concern among many stakeholders that it aimed to extend its reach beyond its established areas of responsibility. A clearer picture of SOF activities would help. A SOCOM interviewee noted that most U.S. officials understand basic train and equip missions and direct-action missions, but do not have a clear grasp of the full range of special operations. Developing a consistent and readily understandable explanation of what SOF do in support of national security objectives would be particularly helpful.

Partial gains are still gains, but a long-term vision is also needed. USSOCOM was not satisfied with the TSOC empowerment line of effort since more support to the TSOCs is still required, and some of the efforts had to be watered down to gain approval. However, the UCP and Forces For changes were initial steps that could be built on to demonstrate success and argue for additional changes to produce more effective use of SOF. A long-term vision and plan for optimizing SOF would need to be developed and embraced by successive USSOCOM commanders as implementation would exceed the term of any one commander.

CHAPTER TWELVE

Operational Authorities and Employment: Irregular Warfare Directive

Overview

The U.S. military's experiences in Afghanistan and Iraq after 9/11, and particularly its difficulties in grappling with insurgencies, led some U.S. officials to believe that institutional adaptations were required to enable the force to cope with the irregular aspects of warfare. The ASD/SOLIC, Michael Vickers, led the effort to create DoD Directive 3000.07, which was signed on December 1, 2008, by the Deputy Secretary of Defense.[1]

Catalyst

The United States was not prepared for the resurgence of the Taliban in Afghanistan or the Sunni insurgency that developed in Iraq after the initial intervention to remove Saddam Hussein from power. The U.S. military and its coalition partners made numerous adaptations in the course of their operations, including surges of troops and adoption of various counterinsurgency methods and new formations. However, these were largely temporary operational adjustments rather than permanent changes to the way in which U.S. forces were trained, organized, and equipped. One notable exception was the sustained effort

---

[1] Department of Defense Directive, "Irregular Warfare (IW)," Washington, D.C.: U.S. Department of Defense, number 3000.07, December 1, 2008.

to revise (or produce, where necessary) doctrine on counterinsurgency and stability operations.

Vickers came to the belief that a policy-level initiative was required to galvanize permanent changes to ensure that the United States prioritized IW in a manner comparable to that for CW. He drew this conclusion from the outcome of the 2006 QDR effort to develop roadmaps for implementation of key initiatives, including IW and building partner capacity. These roadmaps were developed under the purview of the Under Secretary of Defense for Policy and signed by the Deputy Secretary of Defense. The IW roadmap required DoD components to produce an implementation plan but not to execute it. The roadmap exercise thus did not produce the desired institutional commitment to adequate IW resourcing.

Additional impetus for undertaking this initiative came from Congress. The FY 2008 NDAA included a reporting requirement on DoD's plans to address IW requirements, and language was included in the subsequent NDAA draft calling for the Secretary of State to designate a departmental lead for IW. In addition, HASC requested that Vickers testify in February 2008 on the progress made in developing capabilities and capacity for IW.

Proposal Formation

Vickers's staff informed him that the best mechanism for achieving the objective of developing IW capabilities would be a DoD directive, which establishes policy or organizations, defines missions, assigns responsibilities, or delegates authority to those working in and with the military. Particularly if signed by the Deputy Secretary of Defense, a directive would carry sufficient weight to effect budgetary, programmatic, and institutional change. The IW initiative was led by Garry Reid, then–principal director for special operations capabilities and later Deputy Assistant Secretary for Special Operations and CT. Leslie Hunter served as the principal official supporting Reid.

Vickers reached out to USSOCOM to solicit its partnership in the IW initiative. Enlisting the support of USSOCOM as a partner was intended to aid the process within the building as well as ensure USSOCOM input, as it would be one of the major beneficiaries of increased IW capability within the U.S. military as a whole. Vickers's ASD/SOLIC position is somewhat anomalous in that, by law, it is charged with oversight for policy and resources of USSOCOM, but it is only as effective in overseeing a four-star functional combatant command as its superior civilian officials want it to be. The four-star commander has often reached over the ASD to interact directly with the Secretary of Defense or the Under Secretary for Policy. However, the Vickers-Reid team possessed significant experience in special operations and, over time, wielded significant influence within DoD. In this case, USSOCOM and ASD/SOLIC formed a strong partnership to pursue the IW directive. The USSOCOM commander, ADM Eric Olson, supported the initiative and agreed to partner to develop the directive, and USSOCOM created a directorate (J-10) on IW.

Stakeholder Analysis

The ASD/SOLIC team decided that the directive should be crafted with the participation of all stakeholders to gain as much consensus as possible through the process of writing the directive rather than seeking to enlist support in the coordination and signature phase at the end of the process. The principal stakeholders invited to join the tiger team were the Office of the Under Secretary of Defense for Personnel and Readiness, the OSD Cost Assessment and PEO, the Joint Staff's Directorate for Force Structure, Resources and Assessment (J-8), the Joint Forces Command, and USSOCOM, as well as service representatives. The participants were selected for their specific responsibilities and authority to drive needed changes. For example, the Office of the Under Secretary of Defense for Personnel and Readiness could assign skill identifiers to ensure that personnel with needed skills could be developed and tracked, the Cost Assessment and PEO could drive the program budget review process, and J-8 could develop force structure requirements and oversee the JROC and the Joint Capabilities Board.

Perhaps the most important stakeholder other than the special operations community and OSD was the U.S. Army, the principal force provider in IW operations. All the services participated in the wars in Afghanistan and Iraq, but the Army was the most heavily engaged. During the 2006 QDR process, a conceptual framework was developed to assess the demands of the current and future operational environment and the implications for force sizing, posture, and capabilities. The "Michelin Man" drawing represented the homeland defense, CW, and IW in steady-state and surge phases. The graphic of overlapping circles was used to illustrate that the Army and general-purpose forces played a role in all of these circumstances and that its capabilities should therefore be appropriately developed and maintained.

A basic difference of viewpoint drove much of the stakeholder interaction. In SOLIC's perspective, the Army did not treat IW as equal to CW and was generally unwilling to make the needed investments and adaptations to conduct it.[2] On various occasions, a joint staff official related, the Army argued either that it had the needed capabilities or that it viewed IW as a mission for special operations forces. He said, "Vickers did not want them to walk away like they did after Vietnam and lose the capability that they had gained."[3]

The SOLIC IW group teamed with the office next door, Stability Operations, directed by Celeste Ward, who was working to ensure that the Army could conduct stability operations. Her office included Army officer John DeJarnette, who believed that Army doctrine inadequately described the challenges of IW and the means needed to confront it. The Army doctrine defined its basic functions as offense, defense, and stability, and its basic position was that the Army as currently configured could fulfill these functions in the appropriate mixture as circumstances warranted. The service believed that any of its forces could perform advisory functions, for example, and that such specialties as military police existed in adequate numbers.[4]

---

[2] Interview with DoD official, Arlington, Va., May 24, 2016.

[3] Interview with Joint Staff official, Arlington, Va., January 20, 2016.

[4] Interview with DoD official, Arlington, Va., May 24, 2016.

Key Junctures

As the effort progressed, another issue in addition to the Army-SOLIC differences arose. This issue revolved around the definition of IW. The definition proposed by ASD/SOLIC employed the term as an umbrella for UW, CT, foreign internal defense, and counterinsurgency and stability operations. The SOLIC position was that this umbrella term served a critical purpose. As one official described it: "We argued that it was needed because they all include common capabilities required for these mission sets—and it puts the focus on the need to develop capabilities on a par with conventional warfare."[5] Those capabilities include linguists, cultural expertise, population-centric skills, military police, training and advising, and information and messaging. In SOLIC's view, were IW to draw its share of resources, a broad-spectrum, collective effort was needed to win over those who preferred to emphasize CW capabilities.

The objections to this umbrella term came from various quarters for various reasons. The stability operations directorate had succeeded in developing DoD Directive 3000.05, Military Support for Stability, Security, Transition, and Reconstruction (SSTR) Operations, signed in 2005. This directive gained a similar stature for stability operations as the current effort hoped to achieve for IW, in getting them named a "core U.S. military mission that the U.S. Department of Defense shall be prepared to conduct and support" and that should receive a "priority similar to combat missions."[6] The SSTR proponent did not want to see directive 3000.05 subordinated or subsumed by the IW directive, as might be the case if IW were defined to include stability operations.

A number of stakeholders pointed out that the term *irregular warfare* did not apply to postconflict stability operations or other operations in the stabilization phase of military operations (Phase IV) or the subsequent Phase V, enabling civil authority. In addition, it was argued

---

[5] Interview with DoD official, Arlington, Va., May 24, 2016.

[6] For text of the original directive, see Department of Defense Directive, "Military Support for Stability, Security, Transition, and Reconstruction (SSTR) Operations," Washington, D.C.: U.S. Department of Defense, number 3000.05, November 28, 2005.

that the IW term would make it more difficult to bring in U.S. government civilian departments and agencies as well as allies or coalition partners.

The draft directive was circulated for coordination and comment at the O-6 level. It elicited thousands of comments. In addition to the views outlined above, doctrine representatives objected that the proposed definition was inconsistent with current joint doctrine. The Army response indicated that it felt stability was an adequate umbrella term for its activities.

To take the discussion to a more senior level, Vickers formed a Counterterrorism Coordinating Council (CTCC) with Director of the Joint Staff LTG Stanley McChrystal, whose background was in SOF, joining him as cochair. Reid and Hunter served as secretariat for the council. Meanwhile, the tiger team incorporated language regarding stability operations to address some of the concerns and worked through the voluminous comments.

The tiger team also received significant data to bolster its overarching case for development of capabilities and sufficient capacity from J-8. Its capacity analyses in particular provided clear evidence of shortfalls in Afghanistan and Iraq.

Vickers decided to seek a July 2008 final decision meeting by general and flag officers (GOFOs), given that the Barack Obama administration would be taking office the following January. He wanted the directive to be signed before the end of the George W. Bush administration so it could help drive changes in the new one. Initiatives that do not reach completion by the end of an administration risk being sidelined, revised, or redirected. He called for the CTCC to adjudicate the GOFO round of comments on the revised draft directive.

The three primary issues that were raised by the GOFOs and that the CTCC met to adjudicate were (1) concerns over the *irregular warfare* term, (2) the Army's resistance to adopting skill identifiers for IW and its desire to maintain full spectrum capability, and (3) proponency for IW. The stability operations issue was finessed by incorporating language that indicated that the ability to conduct special operations outside of warfare would be enhanced by the overall increase in IW proficiency. The reply to the Army was to acknowledge that some capabilities are fungible between IW and CW. Instead of naming a joint

IW proponent, the responsibilities were assigned to various parties. All the Joint Staff, OSD, and service representatives in the room essentially deferred to the Director of the Joint Staff (McChrystal). The meeting was adjourned with the agreement to move the directive forward for signature, and DoD 3000.07 was signed on December 1, 2008.

An official interviewed for this report emphasized that having an SOF three-star general in such a key decisionmaking position made a significant, if not pivotal, difference in obtaining the concurrence necessary for the directive's approval. As a special operations general, McChrystal thoroughly understood the rationale and need for enshrining IW as a key requirement for the entire U.S. military, as SOF does not perform their missions without support from the conventional forces. As the Director of the Joint Staff, he had the clout necessary to make this case and persuade other bureaucratic stakeholders. Vickers and his team possessed the expertise and the standing within the special operations community. The team did the necessary work, supported by USSOCOM, but successfully surmounting the DoD processes clearly benefited from this additional bureaucratic clout within the building.

Decision and Outcome Analysis

DoD Directive 3000.07 established that it is DoD policy to "recognize that IW is as strategically important as traditional warfare" and to "improve DoD proficiency for IW." It requires DoD to "maintain capabilities and capacity so that the Department of Defense is as effective in IW as it is in traditional warfare" and enumerates six specific capability areas.[7]

The signing of DoD Directive 3000.07 set in motion a series of processes to drive institutional change. As it turned out, Vickers remained in office in the incoming administration, and this continuity of personnel led to energetic efforts to implement the directive. The Reid-Hunter team led the IW issues in the 2008 QDR, and again they

---

[7] For text of the original 2008 directive, see Department of Defense Directive, 2008.

relied on the data and operational availability assessments of the J-8 to provide evidence of capacity gaps. The team argued that development of capabilities was essential for the implementation of directive 3000.07. The QDR and subsequent program budget review resulted in additional capacity development: The Navy added riverine capacity, the Army added more military police and an advisory-training element at Fort Polk's Joint Readiness Training Center, and the planned growth in SOF continued.

Among the follow-on steps set in motion through the JCIDS process were regular IW capability assessments, an IW joint-operating concept, and the reissuing of a revised directive in 2014.[8] While recent budget cuts have resulted in rollbacks of some of the capabilities and capacity gained, there is an institutionalized process now housed in the Joint Staff's Joint Force Development (J-7) directorate.

Despite the budget constraints, the demand signal for IW capabilities continues to be sent by the operational environment, with the rise and spread of the Islamic State and the creeping subversion and coercion tactics employed by China, Russia, and Iran. While the primary gaps identified are in the conventional forces, one interviewee suggested that SOF should be equally concerned about IW capability development in the services because SOF are extremely reliant on supporting conventional capabilities and because the demand signal for IW in multiple countries or theaters can easily outpace SOF capacity.[9] In addition, service-common capabilities are provided by services to be used or modified by SOF. For example, both SOF and conventional forces are being deployed to Iraq and elsewhere in smaller but similar missions to earlier periods to conduct CT, training, and advisory operations.

---

[8] For the DoD 3000.07 revision signed on August 28, 2014, see Department of Defense Directive, "Irregular Warfare (IW)," Washington, D.C.: U.S. Department of Defense, number 3000.07, August 28, 2014.

[9] Interview with Joint Staff official, January 20, 2016.

Summary of Lessons

In this case, the catalyst for action was the failure of the previous attempts to develop and institutionalize sufficient IW capability. SOLIC as the primary proponent of the initiative wielded authorities at its disposal and enlisted key support from USSOCOM. It included a wide array of stakeholders in the process and employed an ingenious stratagem to overcome opposition that threatened to derail the outcome. The ultimate outcome required persistent effort by the proponent to ensure implementation of the directive and the necessary SOF-conventional force collaboration. The specific lessons derived are summarized below.

Leverage established processes to achieve objective. When the QDR roadmap did not produce the desired change—an institutionalized commitment to develop and maintain IW capabilities as an equal priority to conventional warfare capabilities—Vickers asked his staff what other mechanisms existed to pursue this objective. A DoD directive signed by the Deputy Secretary of Defense constituted a high-level commitment with numerous explicit follow-on requirements for specific stakeholders to include assessment and implementation processes.

Incorporate stakeholders from the outset to solicit input and encourage buy-in. The tiger team included all relevant stakeholders from both OSD and the services, with a clear understanding of their equities and roles in implementing the desired changes and thus enhancing the prospect that the directive would result in the intended outcome. For example, OSD would need to take personnel, budget, and force structure decisions pursuant to the directive, and the services would need to make the necessary changes in doctrine, organization, training, materiel, leadership development and education, personnel, and/or facilities to produce and maintain capabilities for IW. The stability operations office was a valuable ally even if it also wanted to protect the gains achieved in the directive that was already signed.[10]

Recruit and employ a high-level official to break through resistance. Perhaps the most controversial element of this case was Vickers's enlistment of McChrystal and the CTCC as arbiters of dis-

---

[10] Department of Defense Directive, 2005.

agreements that the established process could not resolve. By placing a high-level official who supported his objectives in the position of adjudicator, Vickers created a decisionmaking mechanism to override the objections and lingering reservations of key stakeholders, in particular the Army, which believed it had adequate IW capability. At the same time this tactic was employed, compromises were offered to resolve other areas of disagreement. For example, language acknowledging the stability-operations equities was included, and the issue of joint proponency was finessed.

To institutionalize change, push for continuity of effort when possible. The signing of the directive created a mechanism for pursuing needed changes; follow-on decisions and implementation would be required to achieve the intended objectives. The fact that Vickers remained in office after the transition in the White House administration increased the odds that momentum would be maintained. In addition, key deputies such as Garry Reid remained in SOLIC and served as the primary point of continuity. The SOLIC office, together with USSOCOM and the Joint Forces Command, oversaw the writing of joint operating concepts for IW and the joint capabilities assessment. The Joint Staff's J-7 directorate assumed an institutional function as chair of the IW Working Group.

CHAPTER THIRTEEN
Operational Authorities and Employment: SOF and Plan Colombia

Overview

The U.S. government engaged in a long-term effort to support the Colombian government's counternarcotics and counterinsurgency campaign against the Fuerzas Armadas Revolucionarias de Colombia (FARC), designated a foreign terrorist organization by the U.S. Department of State. This multifaceted effort involved many U.S. departments and agencies, including a substantial role by U.S. SOF, who provided extensive training, advice, and assistance to the Colombian military and in particular its special police and special operations units. As it would later do in Afghanistan and Iraq, U.S. SOF provided assistance to Colombian SOF at battalion, brigade, division, and high command levels, as well as support to create a training cadre, selection and training procedures, and other institutional development. U.S. SOF also participated in providing intelligence and operational advice to the high command and defense ministry, including an in-depth assessment requested through USSOUTHCOM. The initiative began in 1998 with the formation of Plan Colombia and the initiation of substantial U.S. funding and continued through 2010.

This case focuses on the key policy decisions and factors that led the U.S. government to undertake and sustain a long-term effort that included a persistent U.S. SOF presence in Colombia. Despite public concerns and congressional criticism, the U.S. government managed to sustain funding for this program and successfully address or quell the opposition to it. While funding and force levels represented the primary focus of policy debate (in addition to recurring concerns about human rights abuses), operational issues were not central since the program did not involve combat activity by U.S. SOF. Nonetheless, any prolonged presence of U.S. forces in the pre-9/11 era, and particularly in Latin America, with its history of U.S. interventions, aroused sensitivities and heightened attention. Operational issues did come to the fore after three U.S. defense contractors were kidnapped by the FARC in 2003; their rescue in Operation Jaque ("Checkmate") in July 2008 required some operational-level support from U.S. forces, including intelligence and contingency plans for quick reaction forces. However, the Colombian military's successful execution of this operation, which rescued a total of 15 hostages including a former presidential candidate, became worldwide news and a talking point for those highlighting the overall achievements of Colombia's own professionalization efforts as well as sustained advisory assistance from U.S. special operations forces and other U.S. agencies. The case study represents a notable example of how long-term U.S. support assisted a government in eventually reducing an intractable, decades-long conflict.[1]

Catalyst

The catalyst for increased and sustained U.S. assistance to Colombia, including the U.S. SOF advisory presence, was the growth of counternarcotics trafficking and the increased involvement of the FARC in the drug trade. The United States had for years supplied counternarcotics assistance to the Colombian police and law enforcement authorities, underwriting aerial and manual coca eradication and crop substitution program. Despite this, substantial battlefield defeats of the Colombian military by the FARC in the late 1990s led to proposals for military assistance. These concerns combined to create sufficient interest in the U.S. government for a newly ambitious approach to address the multiple vectors of conflict, violence, and corruption. The result was Plan

---

[1] Carlos Ospina and Thomas A. Marks, "Changing Strategy Amidst the Struggle," *Small Wars and Insurgencies*, Vol. 25, No. 2, 2014, pp. 354–371.

Colombia, which provided training and assistance, as well as the provision of Blackhawk and Huey II helicopters, in a multifaceted program carried out by DoD, the State Department's Bureau of International Narcotics and Law Enforcement, and the U.S. Agency for International Development (USAID). Beginning in 2001, the U.S. government expanded the U.S. military training to the Colombian military beyond the counternarcotics brigade. U.S. SOF helped establish and train Colombia's Commando Brigade, its Rapid Deployment Force, and its Urban Counterterrorism Special Forces Group. U.S. civil-affairs and psychological-operations troops were also deployed.

Proposal Formation

The initial focus of U.S. counternarcotics assistance under Plan Colombia included U.S. SOF training and assistance to a counternarcotics army brigade and assistance to its counternarcotics paramilitary police known as the Junglas. The largest portion of the $8 billion in U.S. assistance from 1999 to 2012 paid for helicopters and maintenance as well as a massive aerial fumigation program and development aid, including crop-substitution programs. The FARC's placement on the Foreign Terrorist Organization list and a subsequent decision by the Bush administration permitted the liberal use of counternarcotics funding to support Colombia's counterinsurgency, in what became known as a counternarcoterrorism campaign. As the effort progressed, U.S. SOF broadened their training, advice, and assistance to a wide variety of conventional and special operations units.

U.S. SOF assigned to Special Operations Command South (SOCSOUTH) expanded their training to Colombian units in a variety of locations. SOF units advised a Colombian military unit charged with protection of a critical oil pipeline in the northern province of Arauca, accompanied by civil affairs and military information support operations units. At the same time, Special Forces Operational Detachments Alpha began intensive training, advising, and assistance to build Colombian special operations units, first at Tolemaida base and then at the Tres Esquinas base in the heavily conflicted south.

Navy SEALs provided maritime and riverine training and advice to Colombian marines and naval units, and U.S. Air Force special operations conducted aviation foreign internal defense. Planning and assistance training teams were placed at brigade and other command echelons around the country as the Colombian military sought to wrest significant swaths of territory from the FARC, which numbered at more than 20,000 full-time armed combatants.[2] As in the Philippines, U.S. forces were barred from engaging in combat but were permitted to accompany Colombian units in the field on certain occasions.

Stakeholder Analysis

Many key stakeholders across the U.S. government aligned in their analysis that Colombia in the 1990s was in dire straits, and that the situation merited increased support from the United States. Those stakeholders in the administration found both supporters and opponents in Congress. One of the critical factors in overcoming opposition was the close working relationship that developed both within the U.S. government and with the government of Colombia. This included a willingness to address concerns and comply with congressional restrictions and reporting requirements. The aid to Colombia built on a U.S. consensus for counternarcotics programs and later came to include counterinsurgency assistance as well.

In the wake of the Cold War, DoD gradually became more focused on counternarcotics as a mission area. Beginning in 1989, Congress granted DoD a number of authorities and roles in counternarcotics activities abroad. The decline of traditional military threats was matched by a rising concern over the power and reach of Latin American drug cartels, and the burgeoning coca cultivation and cocaine production centered in Colombia in the 1980s and 1990s. The FARC became enmeshed in the drug trade during the 1990s, and the proceeds allowed it to amass arms and recruits, which, in turn, fueled an expansion of its de facto control of much of Colombia's rural terri-

---

[2] In addition, estimates of part-time militias run as high as 20,000.

tory. The rising violence and rampant corruption made this a central issue as President Andrés Pastrana assumed office in 1998. Pastrana and the Clinton administration joined together to fashion Plan Colombia, which was envisioned as a three-year, $7.5-billion effort to be funded by the United States, Colombia, and other countries.[3]

In addition to DoD, retired General Barry R. McCaffrey was a key stakeholder and proponent of increased assistance to Colombia. McCaffrey became intimately familiar with Colombia during his tenure as commanding general of the USSOUTHCOM. He subsequently served as the head of the Office of National Drug Control Policy at the White House. He personally took part in fashioning Plan Colombia and lobbying for it to Congress. The USSOUTHCOM and SOLIC, particularly its counternarcotics office, oversaw the military assistance.

The State Department played a significant role in marshaling support for action at the policy level. Senior State Department officials recognized the deepening crisis in Colombia in part because they were intimately involved in El Salvador's raging insurgency in the 1980s and early 1990s. Under Secretary of State for Political Affairs Tom Pickering was the senior State Department official involved in crafting and overseeing civilian elements of Plan Colombia, including initiation of a free-trade pact and other measures to help the Colombian economy. As ambassador in El Salvador, he oversaw civilian support to Salvadoran counterinsurgency forces and later assisted with peace overtures there. Phil Chicola, Peter Romero, James Mack, Rand Beers, and other diplomats, including a succession of strong ambassadors, coordinated civilian and military programs that were run out of the country team in Bogota and an interagency Plan Colombia Task Force in Washington.

These efforts by the U.S. government would not likely have succeeded without the personal relationship that developed between President Clinton and President Pastrana, who initiated peace talks with the FARC to see whether they were amenable to striking a deal within constitutional bounds. Moreover, Colombia benefited from an extremely

---

[3] Gabriel Marcella, *Plan Colombia: Strategic and Operational Imperatives*, Carlisle, Pa.: Strategic Studies Institute, U.S. Army War College, April 2001.

active and astute ambassador, Luis Alberto Moreno, in Washington. Moreno tirelessly engaged with U.S. Congress members, critics, and supporters, to build what would turn out to be an enduring coalition of supporters for assistance to Colombia. After renewed peace talks in 2012, the Colombia government of President Juan Manuel Santos (who had served as defense minister from 2006 to 2009) concluded an agreement with the FARC in 2016 that, if implemented, will end the 48-year-long war.

Key Junctures

The initial advisory effort was staffed by some 100 U.S. SOF, but the size of the mission gradually expanded along with the congressionally mandated cap, which permitted 500 DoD personnel and 300 contractors in 2002 and, after 2004, up to 800 DoD personnel and 600 contractors in Colombia at any given time. The U.S. SOF component was initially managed by an O-5 Special Forces officer, with advanced operational bases located in the south and north of the country. The U.S. Military Group commander at the U.S. Embassy oversaw the U.S. military effort in the early years, with the narcotics assistance section of the embassy overseeing the counternarcotics program.

After three U.S. military contractors were taken hostage by the FARC in 2003 when their surveillance plane crashed in the southern jungle, a U.S. SOF general officer was sent to Colombia to oversee U.S. assistance in hostage recovery efforts. As the campaign to locate and rescue them and the large number of hostages held by the FARC gathered steam, SOCSOUTH established a SOC Forward O-6 position, which was permanently staffed. The SOCSOUTH commander, a one-star general, frequently visited Colombia to monitor U.S. support to Colombia's counterinsurgency.

With the election of Álvaro Uribe as president in 2003, the momentum of the Colombian counterinsurgency effort increased dramatically. The president personally led the framing of a national plan, which he called the Democratic Security Plan, and the supporting military plan, Plan Patriota, which was infused by a new tax on Colombians to improve the equipment and pay for the increased operational tempo of the Colombian military. The Uribe government abandoned its successor's efforts to negotiate a peace accord with the FARC and launched a full-court press to retake ungoverned space and to capture or kill the FARC leadership. Because of the rampant kidnapping, bombings, and other abuses, along with the well-documented drug trafficking activities by the FARC, Colombian public opinion overwhelmingly backed Uribe's approach.

Human rights groups increased their scrutiny and lobbying for congressional action as documented accounts of Colombian military ties to right-wing paramilitary groups emerged.[4] The Leahy amendment of 1997 provided that U.S. security assistance be withheld from units credibly accused of abuses. Starting in 2002, Congress made funding to the Colombian military contingent on an annual certification by the State Department that the military was severing links to paramilitary groups and investigating and prosecuting charges. This issue became a subject of ongoing contention as human rights groups alleged that the U.S. administration was insufficiently strict in applying the standards and that Colombian judicial processes had proceeded too slowly.[5]

In September 2005, the U.S. military was provided an execution order to conduct Operation Willing Spirit in support of the U.S. hostage rescue. The SOCSOUTH commander, then–BG Charles Cleveland, oversaw increased operational training, combined hostage rescue rehearsals, and reconnaissance missions.[6] Despite the great desire to recover U.S. hostages, Cleveland understood that a unilateral U.S. operation would damage the years of cooperation with the Colombians and would be perceived in country as a violation of sovereignty.

Moreover, any appearance that Colombia could not handle threats inside its borders would undermine the years of hard-won progress the

---

[4] See, for example, "Colombia: The Ties That Bind: Colombia and Military-Paramilitary Links," *Human Rights Watch*, Vol. 12., No. 1 (B), February 2000.

[5] June S. Beittel, "Colombia: Background, U.S. Relations, and Congressional Interest," Washington, D.C.: Congressional Research Service, 7-5700, RL32250, November 28, 2012.

[6] Interview with senior SOF officer, October 29, 2012.

Colombian military had made. Competent military leaders such as General Carlos Ospina Ovalle and General Alberto Mora Mora developed strategy and achieved numerous successes employing counterinsurgency techniques, including a local defense program called "Soldados de mi pueblo."[7] Threats to judges were addressed by special courts that protected judges' identities while allowing the rule of law; these efforts were supported by U.S. Department of Justice programs. One of the most successful initiatives was a reintegration campaign, supported by U.S. military information support operations units, that persuaded thousands of former insurgents to lay down their arms and aided their reintegration through counseling, housing, jobs, and education.

A cross-border strike into Ecuador by the Colombian military killed a major FARC leader in March 2008; a massive trove of intelligence was captured at the camp. A few months later, the Colombian military launched the daring rescue of the U.S. and Colombian hostages. Uribe was reelected, and the series of successes continued as other senior FARC leaders were captured or killed, and the FARC returned to guerrilla-style warfare after years of massing frontal attacks. Colombian civilian government programs began to reach the conflict areas and rural police were supported with fortified police stations.

In 2010 Santos was elected president and announced a new effort to negotiate a peace accord with the FARC while continuing to prosecute the war. A major land reform and other initiatives were passed by the legislature. Although the FARC's ranks had dwindled to some 8,000, the group reconsolidated in a major province and began to increase attacks. The situation was compounded by a series of scandals that beset the Colombian military. The president replaced his civilian and military leadership team to reenergize the war effort. The national plan, "Consolidation," and the new military plan, "The Sword of Honor," were accompanied by a thorough review ordered by the new minister and chief of defense and led by a Colombian officer with

---

[7] Interview with senior SOF officer, October 29, 2012.

degrees from the U.S. Advanced Military Studies Program and the Naval Postgraduate School.[8]

While the Colombian military largely developed its own strategies and plans and conducted its own institutional reform, the close bilateral relationship also led it to seek input from its long-time partner. For example, USSOUTHCOM was invited to send a consultative team, which SOCSOUTH organized and supplied in the summer of 2012.[9] Staffed by U.S. officers with extensive experience in the U.S. counterinsurgency campaigns of the previous decade, the team conducted a wide-ranging evaluation of the Colombian military organization, its campaign plan, and the latter's execution. Among their findings were that the Colombian plan had become overly focused on decapitation and had lapsed in the areas of asserting state control, gaining popular support, and securing the population. It recommended, among other steps, increased emphasis on rural police, an established training cycle, a dedicated training cadre, and development of noncommissioned officers.[10]

Part of the Colombian military had been organized into regional joint task forces assigned to pursue the FARC fronts, but these offensive formations had fewer intelligence resources and ability to develop intelligence than the territorial brigades. Insufficient intelligence-sharing between the military and the police also limited their effectiveness. In 2012 the Colombian military began to build a civil-affairs capability aided by U.S. civil-affairs units. By 2013, guerrilla activity, kidnapping, and other crimes were on the decline again, and cocaine seizures reached a new record.[11] The defense ministry also undertook a

---

[8] David Spencer, "The Sword of Honor Campaign in the Cauca Valley: 2011–2013 Colombian Conflict Focus of Effort," *Small Wars Journal*, May 31, 2013.

[9] Interview with Andean Regional Engagement Branch chief and former forward commander, July 3, 2013.

[10] Headquarters, Department of the Army, U.S. Army South, U.S. Military Group Colombia, "Colombia Joint Task Force Consultative Team Report," September 17, 2012.

[11] Data supplied by the Colombian ministry of defense show a 14.9 percent decrease in kidnapping, 28.8 percent decline in "subversive activity," and a seizure of 207 tons of cocaine. See, also, U.S. Government Accountability Office, *Plan Colombia: Drug Reduction Goals*

series of reforms to improve efficiency and personnel management and prepare for the shift to a postwar structure when the FARC was defeated on the battlefield or the war terminated by a negotiated settlement.

While continuing to tackle the internal threats of insurgency and narcotics trafficking, the Colombian military and police also became exporters of security. Colombia's professionalism was welcomed in both bilateral and multilateral training and peacekeeping endeavors. The government began to offer training and cooperation with other countries in the region. More than 9,200 military and police in Central and South America and Mexico were trained by the Colombians in 2010 to 2012. SOCSOUTH supported these efforts as the scope of advisory activities began to wind down by rotating SOCSOUTH personnel from its Andean Regional Engagement Branch to forward positions in Colombia.[12] This model ensured continuity of understanding among the SOCSOUTH staff.

The U.S. effort to support Colombia evolved into a full-scale integrated Foreign Internal Defense effort in support of the Colombian government's next national plan, called the National Consolidation Plan. The U.S. interagency effort coordinated by the State Department, the Colombia Strategic Development Initiative, provided support at the national level and in priority geographic locations in a range of sectors, including drug eradication and interdiction; building the capacity of the military, national police, and prosecutor units; employment options in the licit economy, particularly in the agricultural sector; support for reforms in land restitution; reparations for victims and vulnerable populations; demobilization and reintegration of ex-combatants; promoting respect for human rights and the rule of law and protection of vulnerable citizens (such as human rights and labor activists); and addressing global climate change and environmental issues in one of the most ecologically diverse countries in the world.[13]

Were Not Fully Met, but Security Has Improved, U.S. Agencies Need More Detailed Plans for Reducing Assistance, Washington, D.C., GAO-09-07, October 2008.

[12] Interview #52, June 10, 2013.

[13] Bureau of Western Hemisphere Affairs, "Fact Sheet: U.S. Relations with Colombia," Washington, D.C.: U.S. Department of State, November 19, 2013.

Decision and Outcome Analysis

The policy success of Plan Colombia lay in sustained support for a continuous effort for more than a decade, and the results have greatly dampened violence and brought an end to the war through a peace accord within reach. Various academic observers have deemed the assistance that U.S. SOF provided to Colombia as generally successful at increasing that country's counterinsurgency capabilities.[14] The war on drugs has been less successful, and a large body of literature suggests that effective approaches to stemming the drug trade and the demand for illegal drugs remain elusive.[15] However, the nexus of narcotrafficking and terrorist insurgency has begun to unwind as the FARC has lost ground. Rates of criminality may spike, however, if the former combatants are not successfully integrated into the formal economy and political life.

The success that U.S. SOF achieved in carrying out long-term training, advice, and assistance to Colombian security forces may be attributed to numerous factors, including the steady commitment of the 7th Special Forces Group and Naval Special Warfare East Coast teams to the enduring mission. The factors that contributed to a sustained effort included the fact that the activities carried out were relatively low in cost; the major expenditures, as noted, were to provide helicopters and equipment maintenance and to construct or upgrade bases in Colombia's jungles. Moreover, the fact that the mission did not involve combat made it less controversial, although Congress instituted U.S. manning caps and kept a close watch to ensure that they were not exceeded. The most painful issues were recurrent allegations of human rights abuses in the Colombian military, including a damaging 2008 scandal in which civilians were killed to inflate body counts, which led to the dismissal of the Army chief. The great majority of abuses in the war, nonetheless, was committed by the paramilitary and rebel forces,

---

[14] Michael Shifter, "Plan Colombia: A Retrospective," *Americas Quarterly*, Summer 2012.

[15] Daniel Mejía, *Plan Colombia: An Analysis of Effectiveness and Costs*, Washington, D.C.: Brookings Institution, 2016.

and the Colombian military retained a highly favorable public opinion rating.

Poor performance or misbehavior by U.S. SOF could have jeopardized the policy consensus behind the long-running program. However, no blatant incidents occurred and the consensus was maintained. U.S. SOF benefited from a significant and cohesive policy framed by the interagency community. As such, SOF did not play a major role in creating or maintaining the policy consensus, although its activities were reported to Congress and the administration, primarily by USSOUTHCOM. SOF had only to carry out its roles in planning and execution competently, and in concert with its U.S. and Colombian partners. US SOF did fulfill its responsibility to work closely with its higher command, USSOUTHCOM, and to obtain the necessary approvals for operational authorities, particularly in Operation Willing Spirit, to support the recovery of the U.S. hostages. Since this steady and low-visibility effort over more than a decade contributed to the overall success that Colombia experienced, SOF can rightly claim their share of credit. In recent years, this "success story" has gained more attention, although the wider policy implications for applying the approach elsewhere have not been studied or adopted.[16]

Summary of Lessons

U.S. SOF—in support of the Colombian security forces—were the major proponents and implementers of the military aspects of Plan Colombia. This policy initiative was promoted and supported by a wide and diverse array of stakeholders in the White House, State Department, and Congress. As such, it may be the premier case in which an SOF-related initiative was largely carried forward by others at a time when insertion of U.S. military forces for such missions was not nearly as common as it was after 9/11. This case yields important lessons for seeking, creating, and maintaining this type of "large tent" approach

---

[16] See, for example, David Petraeus and Michael E. O'Hanlon, "The Success Story in Colombia," Brookings Institution website, September 24, 2013.

in future cases. The diverse coalition provided answers to critics and conceded to restrictions and oversight to implement the program over more than a decade.

Use existing policy consensus and proponents to develop consensus for expanded and/or revised approach. The policy consensus for combating narcotrafficking crossed party lines and enjoyed support in multiple administrations and Congress. The FARC's deep and growing involvement in the drug trade provided the needed connection for military officials and policymakers to argue for increased attention to the threat that the FARC posed. Empowered by drug money, the FARC made significant military progress in controlling territory, overrunning military installations, and staging urban attacks, kidnappings, and other terrorist activity. The resulting policy and legislative decisions permitted U.S. SOF to support Colombia's counterinsurgency, given this link to the drug trade by an officially designated foreign terrorist organization.

Use existing authorities and funding sources to accomplish objectives. Counternarcotics authorities and funds were primary sources of funding for U.S. SOF activities, which were overseen by a Deputy Assistant Secretary of Defense in SOLIC. These authorities were particularly flexible funding authorities, allowing transfers among accounts as circumstances warranted, with appropriate notification to Congress. The SOLIC Deputy Assistant Secretary of Defense maintained a close and productive working relationship with the State Department's assistant secretary for INCLE, whose bureau oversaw much of the programming and in-country implementation. This working relationship extended to the INCLE's Narcotics Assistance Section at the U.S. Embassy in Colombia, which coordinated closely with the deployed U.S. SOF personnel.

Policy-level leadership and support is indispensable to long-term SOF operations. The White House drug czar and senior State Department personnel provided consistent support for Plan Colombia across administrations. Senior Colombian leaders, including Presidents Pastrana and Uribe, defense ministers, and the Colombian ambassador in Washington, developed and maintained active networks of supporters at senior levels of the administration and in Congress. This active engagement strategy also included professional technocratic advice from highly skilled, U.S.-educated vice ministers of defense.

The U.S. military and U.S. country team established a track record of compliance, transparency, and results. The U.S. military scrupulously complied with conditions imposed by Congress, including force caps, Leahy vetting requirements, and active scrutiny through congressional visits and engagement in Colombia and at USSOUTHCOM. A succession of USSOUTHCOM commanders provided detailed testimony to Congress, and the U.S. country team provided briefings to visiting delegations. While a low-visibility approach was taken to avoid inflaming anti-Americanism in a region that historically was subject to U.S. military interventions, the intragovernmental flow of information was maintained. The progressive results were not widely known publicly, but as Colombia stabilized, it gained international credibility for successes it rightly deserved, including the 2008 hostage rescue. However, the lack of public knowledge represents a missed opportunity for wider understanding of the utility of SOF when applied in this low-visibility, long-term, noncombat way.

CHAPTER FOURTEEN
Operational Authorities and Employment: SOF Support to Syrian Fighters

Overview

This case study of the Syrian conflict focuses on those policy deliberations related to potential use of special operations forces at various junctures to determine whether different proposals or approaches might have been advanced for more effective results in earlier stages of the conflict. The administration opted for three different programs over 2013–2015, in addition to nonlethal assistance to civilian opposition groups beginning in 2012.

The Syrian conflict, which began in March 2011 as an Arab Spring protest against President Bashir al-Assad's rule, bedeviled the Obama administration as it morphed into a complex struggle involving a fractured resistance, rising jihadist groups, and a wide variety of actors supplying arms to one side or another. The administration's early attempts, in concert with the United Nations (UN), to pursue negotiations to achieve a political transition did not bear fruit. The Assad regime's intransigence and the rise of extremist groups prompted Senator John McCain in March 2012 to introduce a resolution calling for support to military and materiel support for the opposition.[1]

In late summer 2012, senior figures within the Obama administration endorsed a plan proposed by CIA Director David H. Petraeus to arm Syrian rebels. The President declined to approve the plan right

---

[1] For the text of the resolution, see "Senators Unveil Congressional Resolution on Syria," Senator John McCain website, March 28, 2012.

away, but endorsed a version of it in April 2013.[2] In September 2014, Congress approved an administration proposal for the U.S. military to arm and train Syrian rebels to fight the Islamic State. In 2015, the administration revised the program based on poor results from its initial efforts. In addition, in late 2014, the United States began providing air support to Syrian Kurdish rebels fighting the Islamic State in the north and east of Syria.

Catalyst

A protracted policy debate occurred in 2011–2012 as the administration evaluated the risks and benefits of possible options. It declined to pursue military options in this period, but supplied nonlethal assistance, imposed sanctions, and pursued diplomatic negotiations. In 2013–2016, as the conflict worsened, the administration pursued a variety of military options to varying effect. Derek Chollet, the ASD ISA at the time, wrote,

> Once the administration decided to provide direct military assistance to the armed Syrian opposition in 2013, it proved not to be enough, leading us to embark on a large-scale, Pentagon-led effort a year later. And when that failed in 2015, the U.S. returned to a more modest, small-scale effort, providing weapons and guidance from special operations forces.[3]

Key Junctures

To understand the consideration of military—and specifically special operations options—and to determine the factors influencing the timing, content, and fate of the proposals, it is necessary to first provide

---

[2] Derek Chollet, "Inside Obama's Syria Choices (A Guide for Dissenting Diplomats)," DefenseOne.com, June 16, 2016; and White House, "Statement by Deputy National Security Advisor for Strategic Communications Ben Rhodes on Syrian Chemical Weapons Use," Washington, D.C., June 13, 2013.

[3] Chollet, 2016.

a summary of the conflict's trajectory and the successive measures considered and undertaken by the United States.

After the Assad regime brutally cracked down on peaceful opposition protests that began in March 2011, the United States, the UN, and the European Union levied an array of sanctions against the state and individual members of the regime. In summer 2011, the Free Officers Movement became the Free Syrian Army, and the expatriate Syrian National Council was formed. President Obama called on President Assad to "step aside" in August. Russia and China vetoed a UN Security Council resolution to that effect, but the Arab League imposed its own sanctions. In January 2012, al-Nusra Front (renamed Jabhat Fateh al Sham in 2016) was formed and declared its allegiance to al Qaeda. This, plus the foundering UN efforts at a negotiated solution, led Senator McCain to call for arming the Syrian resistance. Multiple countries in the region, including Qatar, Turkey, and Saudi Arabia, began sending small arms and antitank weapons to various resistance factions. The rebels made some headway in northwest Syria, and defections from the Syrian army continued. However, the Assad regime was sustained by an ongoing pipeline of materiel and aid from both Russia and Iran, including aircraft, tanks, artillery, and arms.

In March 2012, the administration, which had requested that the Pentagon formulate military "contingency" options, signaled that it did not foresee a resort to military means at that time, and Gen. James Mattis, commander of USCENTCOM, testified about the various pitfalls military action would encounter.[4] Chairman of the JCS GEN Martin Dempsey said in June that the use of U.S. military force was "hypothetical in the extreme."[5] Shortly after, CIA Director Petraeus put forward his proposal for arming Syrian rebels, a plan that was endorsed at the time by Secretary of State Hillary Clinton, Secretary of Defense Leon Panetta, and Chairman Dempsey, but not approved by the White House.

---

[4] Matthew Schofield, "Few Military Options for U.S. in Syria, General Says," *McClatchy Newspapers*, March 6, 2012.

[5] Eric Scmitt, "C.I.A. Said to Aid in Steering Arms to Syrian Opposition," *New York Times*, June 21, 2012.

In addition to sending humanitarian aid, the State Department in 2012 provided approximately $50 million in nonlethal assistance to the civilian opposition and other civil-society groups, including local councils and grassroots organizations in a bottom-up effort to promote a democratic transition. The assistance included support for independent media, efforts to document regime abuses, and transition planning, according to a December 10, 2012, fact sheet released by the department. The effort, run by the Conflict and Stabilization Operations bureau, brought opposition out of Syria to Turkey for training and contacts with donors. The program fielded four satellite television stations and nine radio stations and supplied nonlethal aid to 500 policemen providing services in opposition-controlled areas of Aleppo. At the time, there was no companion U.S. military effort, as the administration hoped to promote a nonviolent transition, but information was shared. According to a State Department official, the program aimed to promote unity among the opposition groups and increase U.S. access to, influence on, and understanding of these groups.[6] Also in December 2012, the administration formally recognized the Syrian National Council, the political umbrella group for the opposition, as did Britain, Turkey, France, and the Gulf states. The nonlethal aid increased substantially over the coming months.

In April 2013, in an attempt to assert leadership over al-Nusra Front, the Islamic State declared its existence. At the same time, reports of the regime's use of chemical weapons began surfacing. The Senate Foreign Relations Committee passed the Syria Transition Act, which included arms and training for the Syrian opposition, but the measure was not approved by the full Congress. On June 13, 2013, the White House announced that it had, after an extended intelligence review, confirmed the regime's use of chemical weapons, and decided to increase its aid to the Syrian opposition by providing direct support. Deputy National Security Advisor Ben Rhodes stated, "Put simply, the Assad regime should know that its actions have led us to increase the scope and scale of assistance that we provide to the opposition, including direct support to the SMC [Supreme Military Council of

---

[6] Interview 41, April 12, 2016.

the Syrian Opposition Coalition]. These efforts will increase going forward."[7] Rhodes said no decision had been made about other military options. "We are prepared for all contingencies, and we will make decisions on our own timeline," he said.

The cautions evident in the President's statements were mirrored in public statements by Chairman Dempsey. On July 19, 2013, at the request of the SASC, Chairman Dempsey provided a letter that described in unclassified terms the five military options presented to the President, including stand-off strikes, the establishment of no-fly and buffer zones, measures to control chemical weapons and training, and advice and assistance to the opposition. Dempsey voiced several cautions in this letter, describing the options as "no less than an act of war."[8] Some options, he wrote,

> may not be feasible in time or cost without compromising our security elsewhere. Once we take action, we should be prepared for what comes next. Deeper involvement is hard to avoid. We should also act in accordance with the law, and to the extent possible, in concert with our allies and partners to share the burden and solidify the outcome.

Dempsey described the option of training the opposition, would involve U.S. special operations forces:

> **Train, Advise, and Assist the Opposition.** This option uses nonlethal forces to train and advise the opposition on tasks ranging from weapons employment to tactical planning. We could also offer assistance in the form of intelligence and logistics. The scale could range from several hundred to several thousand troops with the costs varying accordingly, but estimated at $500 million per year initially. The option requires safe areas outside Syria as well as support from our regional partners. Over time, the impact would be the improvement in opposition capabilities.

---

[7] White House, 2013.

[8] Luis Martinez, "Gen. Martin Dempsey Lays Out U.S. Military Options for Syria," ABC News, July 22, 2013.

Risks include extremists gaining access to additional capabilities, retaliatory crossborder attacks, and insider attacks or inadvertent association with war crimes due to vetting difficulties.[9]

The administration debate about the scale and uses (and prospects for success) was not public, but numerous interviewees reported the development of numerous narrow, small-scale proposals for military train, advise, and assist programs. Attention then shifted dramatically to the other military options after the regime launched chemical attacks in the Damascus area and elsewhere in August 2013. After the regime's attacks in Ghouta, which killed hundreds of Syrians, the United States planned to conduct airstrikes on Syria. The British Parliament voted against joining in the planned strikes, and backing from the U.S. Congress also appeared in doubt. The President then reconsidered his inclination to strike militarily and opted for the diplomatic track. The President asked Russian President Vladimir Putin if he would press for removal of Assad's chemical weapons.[10] The ensuing agreement and effort to remove chemical weapons from Syria moved to the fore until the country was declared free of such weapons in June 2014.

A U.S. military official involved in Syria who was interviewed for this study said that the U.S. failure to launch strikes after the Ghouta attack severely demoralized the Syrian moderate opposition, which had expected U.S. airstrikes and a consequent boost to its military campaign against the regime.[11] Various published accounts reported that Syrian fighters began moving toward the extremist factions in ever greater numbers.[12] An extended public debate began over what effects U.S. airstrikes might have achieved at this juncture.[13] A U.S. official

---

[9] Martinez, 2013. The article reprints Dempsey's letter in full.

[10] Jeffrey Goldberg, "The Obama Doctrine," *The Atlantic*, April 2016.

[11] Interview, April 1, 2016.

[12] Charles R. Lister, *The Syrian Jihad: Al-Qaeda, the Islamic State and the Evolution of an Insurgency*, Oxford: Oxford University Press, 2016.

[13] William G. Young, David Stebbins, Bryan Frederick, and Omar Al-Shahery, *Spillover from the Conflict in Syria: An Assessment of the Factors That Aid and Impede the Spread of Violence*, Santa Monica, Calif.: RAND Corporation, RR-609-OSD, 2014; and Chollet, 2016.

interviewed for this report believed that the strikes alone, if carried out as planned, would have gravely weakened, and perhaps unseated, the Syrian regime by taking out key military units and aircraft.[14]

As will be discussed at greater length below, the President differed with that judgment, pointing to the superior firepower of Assad's patrons Iran and Russia. He told an interviewer, "The notion that we could have—in a clean way that didn't commit U.S. military forces—changed the equation on the ground was never true."[15]

At any rate, the fortunes of the Syrian moderate opposition declined thereafter. A particular low point for the Free Syrian Army occurred in December 2013, when extremists overran one of its bases and seized its equipment. The Free Syrian Army's leader, Salim Idris, was replaced in February 2014, and, in May 2014, the city of Homs was retaken by the regime. Aid to some groups was suspended in 2014 because their weapons were found in the hands of extremists, and al-Nusra Front took most of Idlib province. These setbacks were capped in June by the Islamic State's dramatic conquest of territory in Iraq and Syria and its declaration of a caliphate headquartered in Raqqa. The Islamic State's beheading of Americans shifted the focus of U.S. attention to the group, and the United States launched airstrikes against it beginning in August 2014.

As part of this airstrike campaign, the United States began providing air support to Syrian Kurds organized in the People's Protection Units (also known as YPG, the acronym for their Kurdish name, *Yekîneyên Parastina Gel*). The YPG is the armed wing of the Democratic Union Party, which is affiliated with the Kurdistan Workers' Party, a Turkish resistance group that is on the U.S. list of foreign terrorist organizations. As the campaign moved forward, U.S. support for the YPG would greatly complicate U.S. relations with Turkey and perhaps more importantly with the Arab groups that the United States sought to support in Syria.[16] However, the YPG proved to be America's

---

[14] Interview with DoD official, June 10, 2016. See also Chollet, 2016.

[15] Goldberg, 2016.

[16] Linda Robinson, *Assessment of the Politico-Military Campaign to Counter ISIL and Options for Adaptation*, Santa Monica, Calif.: RAND Corporation, RR-1290-OSD, 2016.

most-effective military ally in Syria against the Islamic State, eventually taking back control of much of the northeastern border region of Syria from the group.

In September 2014, Congress approved a $500 million administration request for U.S. SOF to train and equip the Syrian opposition to counter the Islamic State. As the proposal made its way through the process, it became restricted to the objective of countering the Islamic State rather than waging war against the Syrian regime.[17] Numerous restrictions were imposed on the program to address the long-standing concerns that policymakers, senior military leaders, and legislators had expressed, including requirements to exclude extremists, keep weapons out of extremists' hands, and to ensure that arms recipients would not use them against Assad. Further decisions were made to build new training camps outside Syria and require that fighters make their way to the camps.

All of these factors produced enormous delays and a small trickle of vetted fighters, who were then prematurely inserted into the highly complex battlefield of northern Syria in September 2015, with perhaps predictable results. Al-Nusra fighters kidnapped and disarmed the fighters, and others willingly gave up their arms. The head of USCENTCOM, GEN Lloyd Austin, was forced to acknowledge in testimony to Congress that only four or five armed fighters trained by U.S. SOF remained inside Syria after the yearlong effort.[18] This number fell far short of the goal of raising a 3,000–5,000-man contingent in a year, as part of a plan to produce 12,000 fighters in five years.

The Syria Train and Equip program was suspended, but restarted in 2016 after revision to focus more narrowly on training individual fighters to spot targets and call in air support for established groups whose leaders had been vetted and to focus on areas where extremists did not hold ground, such as in the south. Efforts were also made to encourage Syrian Arab fighters to join the YPG in a Syrian Democratic Forces coalition and to provide them training and equipment. U.S.

---

[17] Interview with former DoD official with role in overseeing Syria policy, March 11, 2016.

[18] Thomas Gibbons-Neff, "Only 4 to 5 American-Trained Syrians Fighting Against the Islamic State," *Washington Post*, September 16, 2015.

officials stated that 3,500 Arab fighters were recruited by mid-2016, but news reports indicated that the fighters still struggled for sufficient materiel support.[19] The focus of military efforts was the Islamic state, as the United States had resumed diplomatic efforts to broker negotiations and a ceasefire with the Assad regime, with Russian support, under the terms of the 2012 Geneva communique in which the parties had agreed to a transitional government with full executive powers. Previous talks in 2014 broke down amid various disputes, including over Assad's participation in such a government.

Proposal Formation and Stakeholder Analysis

Proposals were not lacking nor were high-level supporters of such proposals. As noted above, CIA Director Petraeus put forward a proposal to support Syrian opposition forces with the support of Secretary of Defense Panetta and Secretary of State Clinton in late summer 2012, but President Obama declined to approve it. In her 2014 memoir, Clinton described the debate:

> Petraeus presented the plan to the President. He listened carefully and had a lot of questions. . . . The president asked for examples of instances when the United States had backed an insurgency that could be considered a success. . . . Petraeus and I argued there was a big difference between Qatar and Saudi Arabia dumping weapons into the country and the United States responsibly training and equipping a nonextremist rebel force.[20]

However, it appeared that sufficient, convincing evidence was not provided to sway the President.

Senior U.S. military leaders did not adopt a strong or consistent stand in favor of supporting Syrian fighters. At various times during 2012 and 2013, senior U.S. military leaders voiced varying degrees of

---

[19] Liz Sly, "The Last Remaining Pentagon-Trained Rebel Group in Syria Is Now in Jeopardy," *Washington Post*, May 27, 2016.

[20] Hillary Clinton, *Hard Choices: A Memoir*, New York: Simon and Schuster, 2014, p. 463.

skepticism or concern about the risks of military options, including arming local fighters. For example, in a March 7, 2012, prepared statement for testimony to the SASC, Defense Secretary Panetta described DoD's uncertainty about the Syrian opposition and its prospects:

> It is not clear what constitutes the Syrian armed opposition—there has been no single unifying military alternative that can be recognized, appointed, or contacted. While the opposition is fighting back and defections and desertions from Syrian government armed forces are on the rise, the Syrian regime continues to maintain a strong military. For us to act unilaterally would be a mistake.[21]

Panetta also raised the prospect of fueling a Syrian civil war, and he noted there was no international consensus in support of intervention. The administration came down in favor of pursuing diplomatic paths for regime transition, as Panetta's statement noted: "Although we will not rule out any future course of action, currently the Administration is focusing on diplomatic and political approaches rather than a military intervention."[22] By late summer, Panetta supported the Petraeus proposal, but subsequently agreed with the President's reasons for not approving it.[23]

As of February 2012, Chairman Dempsey stated that a lack of information about the Syrian armed opposition led him to oppose advocating support for it. He said that it was "premature to take a decision to arm the opposition movement in Syria, because I would challenge anyone to clearly identify for me the opposition movement in Syria at this point."[24]

By May 2013, when the Senate Foreign Relations Committee passed a bill that authorized military aid to the Syrian opposition,

---

[21] Leon Panetta, with Jim Newton, *Worthy Fights: A Memoir of Leadership in War and Peace*, New York: Penguin Press, 2014.

[22] Panetta, 2014.

[23] Michael R. Gordon and Mark Lander, "Senate Hearing Draws Out a Rift in U.S. Policy on Syria," *New York Times*, February 7, 2013.

[24] "U.S. Military Chief Dubious About Arming Syrian Rebels," CNN, February 20, 2012.

Chairman Dempsey reconsidered the earlier reticence he had voiced inside the administration regarding the Petraeus proposal. He told Congress:

> My military judgment is that now that we have seen the emergence of al-Nusra and Ahrar al-Sham notably, and now that we have seen photographs of some of the weapons that have been flowing into Syria in the hands of those groups, now I am more concerned than I was before.

Dempsey added he would support arming the rebels "if we could clearly identify the right people."[25]

Finally, despite the CIA director's advocacy of arming the Syrian opposition, the agency also supplied analysis that fed the President's doubts about the viability of this option. As he stated to an interviewer: "Very early in this process, I actually asked the CIA to analyze examples of America financing and supplying arms to an insurgency in a country that actually worked out well. And they couldn't come up with much."[26] The President concluded there were low odds of success via this option:

> It is very difficult to imagine a scenario in which our involvement in Syria would have led to a better outcome, short of us being willing to undertake an effort in size and scope similar to what we did in Iraq. And when I hear people suggesting that somehow if we had just financed and armed the opposition earlier, that somehow Assad would be gone by now and we'd have a peaceful transition, it's magical thinking.

The most notable public case in recent decades was the successful effort to dislodge the Soviet Union from Afghanistan in the 1980s.

Ultimately, the President reached his decisions based on his assessment of all of these inputs. He provided an extensive public accounting

---

[25] Josh Rogin, "Senate Moves Toward Arming Syrian Rebels," *The Daily Beast*, May 22, 2013.

[26] David Remnick, "Going the Distance," *New Yorker*, January 27, 2014.

of his reasoning to the *New Yorker* in 2014, although it is worth noting that these interviews occurred before the Islamic State overran large parts of Iraq and Syria and declared its caliphate. The article quotes his assessment of the group at the time, which he likely revised at a later date:

> "The analogy we use around here sometimes, and I think is accurate, is if a jayvee team puts on Lakers uniforms that doesn't make them Kobe Bryant," Obama said, resorting to an uncharacteristically flip analogy. "I think there is a distinction between the capacity and reach of a bin Laden and a network that is actively planning major terrorist plots against the homeland versus jihadists who are engaged in various local power struggles and disputes, often sectarian."[27]

While the President authorized more-aggressive measures against the Islamic State after it launched attacks in Paris and elsewhere in 2015, his view of the Syrian internal conflict and the way forward did not appear to evolve greatly from the views he stated in 2014, as follows:

> The truth is that the challenge there has been, and continues to be, that you have an authoritarian, brutal government who is willing to do anything to hang on to power, and you have an opposition that is disorganized, ill-equipped, ill-trained, and is self-divided. All of that is on top of some of the sectarian divisions. . . . And, in that environment, our best chance of seeing a decent outcome at this point is to work the state actors who have invested so much in keeping Assad in power—mainly the Iranians and the Russians—as well as working with those who have been financing the opposition to make sure that they're not creating the kind of extremist force that we saw emerge out of Afghanistan when we were financing the mujahideen."[28]

Thus, the President's views about Syria may have been too deeply set for anyone to alter. In addition, he held a skeptical view about U.S.

---

[27] Remnick, 2014.

[28] Remnick, 2014.

ability to influence Middle East conflict. In his *New Yorker* interview, the President stated his willingness to challenge transnational terrorists who aim to attack the United States, but also his ambivalence about whether the United States possessed the tools to deal with the underlying causes of turmoil in the Middle East.

The President appears from these statements to have maintained the view that no better options were available to him than the courses he pursued, but one of his senior advisers did reach the conclusion that a number of more-proactive measures might have produced more results. Former senior defense official Derek Chollet concluded that an earlier start to training, maintaining a presence in Iraq after 2011, initiating airstrikes in Syria sooner, and being "more creative" (i.e., more aggressive) with target selection would have achieved more effects in the Syria campaign. "None of these steps would have been the kind of game-changer many critics suggest, but even a modest improvement would be good enough," he wrote.[29]

Decision and Outcome Analysis

The debate over whether to support armed indigenous fighters revolved around three central questions: What were the groups' military prospects? Were they extremists or moderates? And would they be able to keep weaponry from falling into the wrong hands? Interviews with special operations personnel and other officials suggested that additional information, analysis, or options provided at certain junctures might have contributed significantly to the decisionmaking process. Several missed opportunities, and the reasons for them, were identified. Nonetheless, given the President's deliberate decisionmaking pace and general skepticism regarding this particular form of military force, it is not evident that additional input would have produced different decisions.

---

[29] Chollett, 2016.

"Some Options Have a Time Stamp on Them"
Only after the 2013 chemical weapons attacks were U.S. SOF asked to formulate proposals for training, advising, and assisting the Syrian opposition, according to a senior SOF officer.[30] This officer argued internally for early help to the resistance before extremists became more organized, but said that he was told to "stand down" by USCENTCOM. He attributed this to "a dominant trend to the policy thinking now that waiting longer preserves options." However, he assessed that "now, for the moderate opposition to win would be hard if not impossible. Some of these options have a time stamp on them," he concluded.[31]

While the questions about the orientation and capability of opposition forces were certainly germaine to the policy deliberation process, the argument for supporting these forces became gradually less convincing as they weakened for lack of support. Their ability to serve U.S. interests, even if only to force the Assad regime into serious negotiations, diminished. The prospect that extremists from the opposition forces might take over following Assad's departure, or at least greatly increase their hold on swaths of the country, further reinforced the arguments against supporting the opposition. Faced with a possible choice between Assad and al Qaeda–backed elements, many in Washington would opt for the former.[32]

Ensuring the timely development of an array of options for policymakers' consideration appears to be one of the most important lessons from this experience. The central location for full examination and development of military options in the Middle East area of responsibility is USCENTCOM. For options that are doctrinally part of SOF missions, such as support to resistance or opposition movements, their expertise would appear to be vital to developing viable options. A retired special forces officer noted that USCENTCOM does not have a special operations section in its J-5 and J-3 directorates, which reduces

---

[30] Interview #37.

[31] Interview #37.

[32] Interview with former senior U.S. intelligence official, May 17, 2016.

the ability of SOF to apply their expertise daily to develop P&O.[33] Because the Special Operations Command Central (SOCCENT) has multiple duties and limited manpower, its personnel often engage with USCENTCOM sporadically and by phone rather than side by side. Finally, this officer noted that although the SOCCENT commander is the designated officer to provide special operations' advice to USCENTCOM, his views are often overshadowed by those of the four-star USSOCOM commander, whose headquarters is on the same base as USCENTCOM and CT forces.

Comprehensive Assessment Lacking
The path to decisions included the assessment that not enough was known about opposition figures to confidently proceed to support the resistance. This was a point made numerous times by Chairman Dempsey. U.S. doctrine for supporting indigenous resistance forces, known as UW, calls for a deliberate assessment of potential forces' leadership, their military skills, organizational structure, willingness to work with the United States, and long-term goals. That assessment provides policymakers with the information they need to decide whether to proceed with this option. A U.S. military officer assigned to SOCCENT said that no such assessment was conducted as of late 2013.[34] The lack of thorough assessment of the viability of the resistance and the requirements for a successful program would come back to haunt SOCCENT when it was ordered to develop a train-and-equip program in 2014.

The Free Syrian Army's leadership comprised primarily defected Syrian soldiers and, at the time, represented some 75,000 fighters, according to one U.S. military officer interviewed for this report.[35] The Free Syrian Army was in actuality an umbrella group of smaller factions led by local leaders in their geographic home areas. The army was

---

[33] Interview, May 20, 2016.

[34] Interview with special operations officer, May 20, 2016.

[35] Interview with special operations general officer, April 1, 2016.

criticized by some observers and rebels as ineffective and insufficiently supportive of the fighters on the ground.[36]

Joseph Holliday concluded his analysis in a detailed report for the Institute for the Study of War by arguing that the diffuse nature of the armed opposition should not in itself disqualify it from receiving backing. He noted that "revolutions proceed in phases rather than all at once, and delaying policy decisions before the opposition has coalesced around a viable alternative government is tantamount to insisting that the revolution succeed fully before it receives practical or military assistance."[37] He recommended that the administration establish closer ties with key elements of the armed opposition to make more-grounded judgments and provide options for the future.

Lacking a full assessment of the viability of supporting the moderate opposition, the United States reportedly relied instead on regional partners to arm and fund the Syrian opposition.[38] This may have paradoxically pushed the administration toward greater action in 2013, because regional partners' approach to arming groups favored the more Islamist factions.

The State Department's nonlethal program to support the civilian opposition might have been enlisted in a more-coordinated way to supply information and analysis and to detect and encourage coherent local opposition movements. The model for UW is to identify and support a charismatic, authentic local leader inside the country, and this program would have been an ideal vehicle for such an effort. A USAID interviewee described his role in vetting and developing political leadership during the mujahedeen war against the Soviet occupation of Afghanistan in the 1980s.[39]

---

[36] Joseph Holliday, "Syria's Armed Opposition," in *Middle East Security Report* 3, Washington, D.C.: Institute for the Study of War, March 2012, p. 17.

[37] Holliday, 2012, p. 38.

[38] Emile Hokayem, "How Syria Defeated the Sunni Powers," *New York Times*, December 30, 2016.

[39] Interview with retired USAID official, January 20, 2016.

Lack of Adequate Plan and Training Concept

Following a comprehensive assessment and a policy decision, doctrine calls for the development of a written plan with phased objectives, along with a detailed but realistic training concept. A written plan for the Syria Train and Equip effort was never developed.[40] The goal of training 3,000–5,000 fighters in the first year was too ambitious, particularly given the extensive vetting requirements. The training course envisioned was far too long for a cadre that had left the battlefield and traveled outside Syria, without any logistical assistance. The decision to supply U.S.-made arms as a means to exercise control further hamstrung the groups' ability to fight and resupply themselves. The more-onerous and unrealistic that the U.S. programs became, the more attractive the extremists' ready pay and supply became. In addition, the United States did not incorporate a robust psychological-operations effort to bolster the moderates and counter the jihadists' appeal.

A U.S. officer involved in support to the Syrians said that more-effective and robust outside support might have bolstered Syrian opposition leadership by assisting with resupply hubs, more weapons and ammunition, and better logistics mechanisms for quickly getting supplies to forces in the field. Efforts to improve campaign planning also ran aground on disagreements or indecision about whether the objective was to place pressure on the regime and achieve discrete tactical objectives or, more ambitiously, to take and hold territory.[41]

There remains the question of what types of support, and at what level, might have enabled the Syrian resistance to mount a challenge to Assad sufficient to summarily force him out or to get him to make a negotiated departure via the transition process envisioned by the Geneva agreement. Brookings analyst Ken Pollack argued in a paper that U.S. efforts to remake the Croatian army were pivotal in the Yugoslav Wars. Based on that experience, he estimated that a successful effort in Syria would require a two-to-five-year effort to produce suffi-

---

[40] Interview with special operations officer assigned to SOCCENT, May 20, 2016.

[41] Interview with special operations general officer working on the issue, April 1, 2016.

cient well-trained troops, U.S. advisers to accompany them, and tanks and other significant materiel.[42]

Negative Views of Unconventional Warfare

Perhaps the most-important factor affecting the consideration of support to Syrian fighters is the skepticism and a basic confusion about this option. One retired officer who worked at USCENTCOM stated that USCENTCOM J-3 had a very negative view of UW and asked him to refrain from using it, saying "UW is a toxic term."[43] The fact is that the administration, like many U.S. administrations before it, takes a wary view of waging war on a government through this means. In those cases where the U.S. government has taken this approach, it normally does so through a presidential finding to authorize a covert operation, which then is conducted without acknowledgment. This was true in two now-public cases, the U.S. backing of the mujahedeen who fought the Soviet occupation of Afghanistan in the 1980s and the Nicaraguan "contra" rebels who fought the Soviet-backed Sandinista revolutionary regime in the same decade. The post-9/11 era includes the case of U.S. support to Afghanistan's Northern Alliance, headed by the charismatic leader Ahmed Shah Masood, which was publicly justified as part of the U.S. defense against al Qaeda's attack.

President Obama indicated that he viewed the record of UW as poor, although defenders of UW as an option point to its utility in the specific cases just mentioned, as well as others. The first case resulted in the Soviet departure from Afghanistan, but also the rise of extremist forces, including al Qaeda. The Nicaraguan contra movement began as right-wing paramilitaries with an unsavory reputation but morphed into a peasant army that helped pressure the Sandinistas into an election which they lost. The Northern Alliance played the major role in ousting the Taliban and today is part of the Afghan government.

---

[42] Kenneth M. Pollack, "Building a Better Syrian Opposition Army: The How and the Why," Washington, D.C.: Center for Middle East Policy at Brookings Institution Analysis Paper No. 35, October 2014.

[43] Interview with special operations officer, May 20, 2016.

Any consideration of support to resistance or opposition forces requires clarity about the factors that make such a movement successful. A retired special forces officer who has participated in these operations cited four characteristics of a successful insurgency: a charismatic leader (or leaders) who leads from within the country, a unifying cause or ideology that draws fighters, a bottom-up approach to developing the insurgent organization, and the need for an insurgency to develop competence through confidence targets.[44] All of these characteristics require patience and a less directly controlled approach than makes most U.S. government officials comfortable; efficient approaches that minimize risks are greatly preferred.

The United States has increasingly relied on an array of local forces for various purposes in recent years. This has led to a significant confusion about the use of indigenous forces that many interviewees remarked on. The term *unconventional warfare* refers to support of an indigenous resistance or opposition movement that is motivated by its own goals and leadership. The use of surrogates or proxies recruited purely to help the United States achieve its goals is a very different endeavor. This difference was not sufficiently illuminated as the U.S. policy proposal morphed in 2013 from supporting the existing Syrian opposition, whose primary goal is to unseat Assad, to the raising of a counter–Islamic State force. Various concepts that were developed but not employed relied on this same idea of developing Syrian proxy forces to seize chemical storage sites or peacekeepers to secure borders.[45]

Small forces might be raised for these discrete, tactical purposes, but the creation of a force capable of pressuring the Assad regime into a political transition would require an approach much closer to UW, according to numerous interviewees. Advocates of opposing Assad more forcefully, including through this means, continue to make their case. But a very different approach would be required, including devolving such tactical decisions as approval for resupply missions from the White House to the field, according to the practitioners inter-

---

[44] Interview, March 8, 2016.

[45] Interview with retired special operations officer, June 10, 2016.

viewed. In sum, without a decision to accept greater risk, supporting a resistance movement may remain an unviable option.

Summary of Lessons

While the administration debated Syria policy options for years and attempted some programs, the "policy window" opened and closed at various times. To some degree, this was due to a larger uncertainty on the part of administration officials over whether any approach to Syria's conflict could effectively address the complex conflict that involved both resistance to the Assad regime's repression and the Islamic State taking advantage of that to root itself deeply within the country. The growth of the Islamic State and burgeoning violence, which issued in the worst refugee crisis since World War II, forced continued scrutiny of military options, including those that relied heavily on SOF. The principal early proposal, offered by CIA Director Petraeus, was not approved, and policymakers' attention shifted to the narrower goal of removing chemical weapons. Then the administration sought proposals narrowly focused on removing the Islamic State, which resulted in the Syria Train and Equip program, which was belated, being slow to get off the ground, and unsound in concept, according to many UW experts.

Two fundamental lessons may be drawn from this complex series of events. For various reasons, special operations leaders and other SOF advocates were unable to present SOF capabilities and proposals for their employment in a manner that sufficiently addressed decisionmakers' concerns. That may have been an impossible task, in this particular case, but the evidence suggests that, at a minimum, policymakers and perhaps conventional force commanders in senior military positions may not understand the specific requirements for successful employment of SOF. It is the duty of special operations leaders to educate and inform as well as to develop technically proficient proposals. At the end of the day, the President will make decisions based on the information provided to him and his own best judgment.

More effort should be made to ensure that senior officials understand the requirements for successful special operations, in particular UW. In particular, policymakers may not grasp the vital connections among persistent presence, early assessments, and validated options. To obtain full answers to the basic questions about the Syrian fighters' political and ideological orientation, their military capabilities, and their ability to keep control of materiel supplied to them, U.S. policymakers and senior military commanders must direct and authorize robust intelligence collection and assessments to include contact with the fighting groups. An early proposal to contact Syrian expatriates was turned down. These assessment and preparatory tasks were not given to SOCCENT until 2013, by which time the situation had evolved in a less propitious direction. The repeated efforts by SOF to collect information and develop assessments were not supported, in part because senior military officers told them to "stand down" and "do not bring me options that involve unconventional warfare."

GCCs may also possess insufficient understanding of special operations, impeding proposal development at that level. The small size and multiple duties of the theater special operations command staff limit their ability to work on a daily basis with the intelligence, plans, and operations staff sections of the GCCs. Without robust special operations expertise inside the GCC, insufficient development and advocacy of special operations options may result. In addition to senior SOF advocacy of options, the development of a greater understanding of special operations requirements and capabilities within the GCCs can generate effects over time. One remedy suggested is to place more SOF personnel within the relevant staff sections at the GCCs.

Proposal socialization within the policy community through informal contacts and backchannels may be helpful. Formal proposals for use of SOF are normally pursued through one of two channels, the GCC or the Joint Staff Deputy Director for Special Operations. The latter office is the conduit for short-notice concepts of operations, primarily for CT or other urgent contingency operations. The channel has been used for advocacy of options in addition to the combatant command channel. One Joint Staff interviewee suggested that SOF should make use of other channels in the Joint Staff and the building to discuss ideas; for example, a regional bureau director who had a close relationship with the chairman suggests that route for sending ideas to the chairman of the Joint Chiefs of Staff. This path risks raising the ire of the GCC, but if relationships are developed ahead of time, such trial balloons can be floated in a confidential manner. A retired officer who worked in the Joint Staff noted that the national mission forces have routinely cultivated and used such informal networks through one or more assignments in key policy offices.

Presidential views will ultimately be determinative. Strongly held presidential views may not change, or they may only under dire circumstances. The main lesson of U.S. policymaking on Syria may not be the dearth of options, but rather the fundamental reluctance of the commander in chief to pursue military options in Syria, even as leverage to enhance diplomatic strategies. The rise of the Islamic State led the President to take increasing steps to confront it militarily, but he continued to hope that Assad's patrons would place pressure on the regime to agree to a political transition. He sought convincing evidence that support to resistance fighters could work, but no sufficiently compelling case was made. The subject remains an open one, given the ongoing conflict and the continued survival of moderate fighters, albeit heavily intermixed with Islamist fighters of various stripes. So long as the conflict continues to have regional and global effect on U.S. interests, the U.S. government will likely revisit its options and evaluate their relative risks and merits. Thus, U.S. SOF views may be solicited in evaluating these options.

CHAPTER FIFTEEN
Findings and Recommendations

In this chapter, we present eight overarching findings that represent the synthesis of the individual case study lessons. We use the findings to develop an opportunity and decision-analysis framework that can be applied to future decisionmaking. The overall findings are also analyzed to derive recommendations for specific steps that the special operations community may consider for DOTMLPF changes to improve development of narrative, proposal formation, and interagency engagement. These recommendations are developed to address the sponsor's request that RAND Arroyo Center examine how the Army and Army SOF, as part of the joint SOF, might better articulate their value proposition and better contribute to formation of Army, joint, and DoD policy.

Findings: Synthesis of Case Study Lessons

The case studies of the previous chapters yielded lessons drawn from each decisionmaking episode. This chapter synthesizes the common lessons that correlate across the cases to a strong degree into the eight findings summarized below. The findings involve both formal and informal processes that affect decisions. Many of the processes and dynamics examined here are governed by laws or regulations, but, to a large degree, formal and informal policymaking practices are adopted in variable forms by the principal agent or agents seeking to promote a particular course of action. The study team found that these eight elements were most often associated with a successful outcome.

Identify Whether a Propitious Policy Window Exists

The case studies all start with the description of an event or other catalyst that created an opportunity for the policy entrepreneur to put forward a proposal. These "demand signals" for the military community can arise from a new threat or crisis that would appear to require U.S. action; in some cases they arise from a failure of on operation or a policy, leaving a problem that is still to be resolved. In some cases, a leader or influential figure may discover or formulate a better way of conducting everyday business that is so valuable or revolutionary that it, in effect, creates its own policy window. The literature on agenda setting, which includes these concepts of policy windows, focusing events, and policy communities, has been shown to apply to national security and foreign policy decisions.[1]

The case studies suggest the importance not only of correctly identifying a policy window that is propitious for putting forward a proposal regarding the use or development of SOF, but also correctly determining when there is no window and thus when it would be advisable to wait. For example, the Korean War provided an opportunity for successfully advocating for psychological operations capabilities, but the opportunity for pushing for UW came later, when the deactivation of the Rangers created more personnel openings. The classic opportunity for Special Forces arose when President John F. Kennedy visited Fort Bragg, and the community was prepared to advocate for its capabilities to a president who had already identified the need for such a force. The SASC waited for the right opportunity to advance the Nunn-Cohen legislation creating USSOCOM. In the 1990s, an existing policy consensus around the need to combat narcotrafficking provided the foundation for support to counternarcoterrorism and the FARC in Colombia. Richard Clarke's advocacy of using SOF for CT fell on deaf ears before 9/11, but those attacks created a substantial consensus for expansion of SOF. Section 1208 authority

---

[1] Michael J. Mazarr, "The Iraq War and Agenda Setting," *Foreign Policy Analysis*, Vol. 3, No. 1, January 2007; and Julia M. Macdonald, "Eisenhower's Scientists: Policy Entrepreneurs and the Test-Ban Debate 1954–1958," *Foreign Policy Analysis*, Vol. 11, No. 1, January 2015.

received wide support as it became known that special forces lacked the ability to support their Northern Alliance allies in toppling the Taliban. Some of the GSN initiatives may have incurred opposition because they were launched at a time when the military departments faced painful budget and personnel cuts.

Understand and Leverage Established Processes to Initiate Proposals and Pursue Objectives

A corollary finding suggests that proponents should not rely on formal process alone. However, bypassing established procedures will likely antagonize superiors and other power centers. The best practice appears to be to work within the system while actively cultivating allies in key nodes of the bureaucracy. During the 2006 QDR process, USSOCOM commander GEN Doug Brown and his deputy and successor, VDM Eric Olson, worked assiduously within the established procedures to gain support for the historic multiyear SOF expansion. ASD/SOLIC Michael Vickers and his staff pursued institutionalized development of IW capabilities through creation of DoD Directive 3000.07. USSOCOM commander ADM Bill McRaven used established processes to gain combatant command authority over the theater special operations commands through the "Forces For" memorandum. In most cases, USSOCOM and/or SOLIC are the principal representatives within the established process charged with initiating and advocating policy-level proposals regarding SOF.

Conducting Rigorous Proposal Development and Validating Its Substance Are Key Indicators of Success

This finding includes related elements. The first one underscores the importance of conducting rigorous analysis internally. In the case of the GSN, the initiatives (such as USSOCOM gaining authority over TSOCs) that were more successful tended to be those that relied heavily on broad stakeholder input and were justified by rigorous, often exhaustive processes. We heard repeatedly from DoD and congressional officials that the need for RSCCs, USSOCOM-NCR, and LP 308 was unclear and unevenly messaged. Second, stakeholders may require education in special operations. In some cases, the relevant audience lacks sufficient understanding of the requirements for successful special operations, and this basic knowledge deficit must be addressed. For example, proposals to conduct early assessments and development of options such as in Syria may have been rejected because senior officials did not understand that this spadework is essential to providing sufficiently validated options for policymakers.

Third, providing evidence of a policy gap greatly strengthens a proposal. In the case of Section 1208, battlefield reports were used to illustrate the need. Expert external validation can provide potent support for change: The Holloway Commission, which documented the failures of SOF in Operation Desert One, laid the groundwork for creation of USSOCOM. Fourth, internally produced publications can also create the theoretical and evidentiary basis to strengthen proposals, but they need to be solidly constructed and address stakeholder concerns in accessible language. Fifth, public debate can be helpful in creating a consensus behind proposals. For example, the series of articles in AFJI yielded a steady stream of quality publications.

Map Stakeholders and Incorporate Them from the Outset to Solicit Input and Encourage Buy-in

This finding encompasses a number of observations including the need to show stakeholders how they may benefit from a proposal, solicitation of their input, a willingness to bargain, and strategies for dealing with the opposition. For example, support for the QDR recommendations to expand SOF was built ahead of time by OSD's expert cell, congressional testimony, and the Downing report. In the GSN effort, USSOCOM attempted to engage stakeholders, but the message often fell flat: The broader U.S. government audience felt like they were being briefed on what USSOCOM had already decided, rather than consulted as a collaborating party. Further, USSOCOM officials noted that the GSN efforts may have been more effective if they had more closely involved ASD/SOLIC and other key DoD offices. The bid to assign TSOCs ultimately prevailed because the GCCs were eventually convinced that they would benefit or at least not lose in the process.

Building a large tent can bring in additional supporters and at least provide a forum for identifying key issues that may need to be finessed. The IW tiger team included all relevant stakeholders from both OSD and the services, and all participants were afforded a clear understanding of their equities and roles in implementing the desired changes. Perhaps the most successful case of gaining support by providing benefit was the SMU community's transformation, which hinged on gaining full interagency support from the intelligence community. GEN Stanley McChrystal gave stakeholders a reason to participate by cultivating relations and sharing his intelligence. He also made an intelligence community representative one of his deputies, a level of commitment that helped cement a vital (if sometimes contentious) relationship.

A similar strategy may work in reverse for the GCCs, which are perhaps the most important stakeholder for SOF. While senior military leader interactions can persuade GCCs of the benefits of SOF proposals, a bottom-up strategy to working with the GCCs may have a more powerful and permanent effect. That would entail assigning more SOF personnel to the GCC's relevant staff sections to provide constant education and suggestions for proper employment of special operations capabilities. Proposals developed within a staff may receive a warmer welcome than those originating outside.

Cultivate Networks and Advocates at All Levels
Presidential support is a valuable asset, but paradoxically, it may not be sufficient. President Franklin D. Roosevelt's support for William Donovan led to the creation of OSS, but Donovan realized that, unless he made peace with Army Chief of Staff GEN George C. Marshall and became a valued part of the military, his organization would never have the access and resources it needed. The demonstrated value of OSS, combined with Donovan's willingness to subordinate OSS to the Joint Chiefs, finally sold Marshall on the value of special warfare. Donovan was also careful to hire subordinates, including the President's son, who understood broader Washington politics to manage what today would be called the interagency process.

President Kennedy's support for special forces did not obviate the need for support from the Army as well. Passage of the Nunn-Cohen amendment relied on leadership from a small but critical group of legislators, whose staffs developed ties with key OSD proponent Neil Koch. GEN (ret.) Wayne Downing developed close ties with senior George W. Bush administration officials, and GEN Peter Schoomaker developed a close relationship with Secretary Donald Rumsfeld. While General McChrystal invested time in building a wide array of partnerships and in pushing internal change in his organization, the support of Secretary Rumsfeld and GEN John Abizaid were vital to the SMU community's expansion in resources, manpower, and authorities. Sustained support by the White House and senior State Department officials was instrumental in the long-term SOF operations in Colombia. In another case of a long-term SOF mission, in the Philippines, funding and policy support was maintained because it fell under the CT umbrella of Operation Enduring Freedom.

Occasionally, high-level advocates may be recruited explicitly to break through resistance. This can be a controversial use of leverage, and it incurs risk. Perhaps the most contentious element of the IW directive process was Vickers's enlistment of McChrystal and the CTCC as the arbiter of disagreements that the established process could not resolve. Proposals can also be socialized with senior or other influential officials through informal back-channel contacts. Proposals are usually pursued formally through the combatant command or via the Joint Staff Deputy Director for Special Operations, but outreach can increase awareness of options. As this can be risky for officers expected to follow the chain of command, such socialization is best conducted through established relationships.

Finally, the contrary case of presidential or White House opposition may prevent any SOF proposal, no matter how soundly crafted, to fail to receive consideration. For example, the public record of President Barack Obama's statements suggests that his strongly held views about Syria and U.S. interests therein led him to resist military options and continue to seek Russian assistance in pressuring Syrian President Bashar al-Assad. An interviewee reported that, because of opposition in the White House, Chairman Martin Dempsey told subordinates not to bring him any more proposals for supporting Syrian fighters.[2]

---

[2] Interview with retired officer assigned to the Joint Staff, June 10, 2016.

The dramatic contraction of special forces after the Vietnam War may have been another case in which no set of arguments for the utility of SOF would have prevailed.

Provide Subject-Matter Expertise to Congress and Develop Relationships with Staff Through Authorized Engagements

Official liaison offices manage the U.S. military relationship with Congress; ASD/SOLIC is the DoD interlocutor on special operations policy matters. SOLIC's purviews and duties should be thoroughly understood, and a collaborative approach is usually preferable. The office should be treated as a vital source of counsel and feedback for all SOF matters pertaining to Congress. Contacts from congressional members or staff in search of information should be viewed as vital opportunities to increase their knowledge base. This is particularly true of staff who are relied on by members and committees for most of the substantive work. An effort by special operations leadership, with support from the services' personnel divisions, to place more serving (or reserve) SOF personnel into congressional offices would pay enormous long-term benefits to the special operations community. It would create a resident source of knowledge in a branch of government that touches virtually every aspect of SOF manning, training, equipment, employment, and funding. The role played by Jim Locher, formerly at OSD and then on the congressional staff, in the creation of USSOCOM and SOLIC cannot be overstated. Opportunities to brief staff, host congressional delegations, and provide testimony to Congress should be considered among the most valuable opportunities to shape the policy environment for both short- and long-term objectives. As such, they deserve extensive, diligent preparation and rehearsal.

Address Bureaucratic Rivalry with Deliberate Strategies to Promote Synergy and Avoid Zero-Sum Outcomes

For various reasons, some stakeholders are at least partly institutional rivals of SOF. While rivalry can be exacerbated by personalities or the personalization of issues, usually chronic tensions are explained by overlapping roles and missions or power dynamics such as competition for resources. Two particular tensions came to light in the case studies. First, CIA and SOF have competed and collaborated since their founding. The central lesson of the cases is that both communities have unique capabilities that are strongly synergistic for special warfare—and UW in particular. Recommendations for addressing this rivalry to gain greater synergy are described in the subsection titled Recommendation 2 below.

The other chronic competition is between SOF and the military services, primarily because they compete for funds and, to some degree, missions. All SOF depend greatly on the services for manning (and funding for personnel), non-SOF-unique equipment, and a host of operational and institutional enabling functions, from combat service support to education. To the degree that SOF seek to become a fifth service, that competition will increase. However, a more-productive approach in the current situation is to encourage the services to see their respective SOF elements as niche capabilities from which they can gain value in a wide (and increasing) range of contingencies. In turn, SOF can gain credibility with the services by assisting them in developing SOF-like capabilities (such as advisory formations) that will provide SOF with force multipliers that will, at times, augment their own formations. The support of senior military leaders for key initiatives is often just as vital as the support of senior civilian leaders, and, in the case of development of capabilities, it may be determinative. Thus, in the wake of Vietnam, as counterinsurgency fell out of favor, the SOF repositioned as long-range reconnaissance forces to preserve their utility to the Army and thus some end strength. Also, as conventional military leaders are likely to hold most of the combatant command positions, in that capacity, their voice in operational employment of SOF can be powerful.

Pursue Incremental Change as Part of a Long-Range Plan
Significant gains can be made at times through leveraging current authorities in creative ways. That was the lesson of the Alamo Scouts' creation, and it pertained as well to the case of Plan Colombia. Existing authorities can often be used for new ends, or at least as bridging solutions. A close corollary is to accept partial gains because they do represent gains. Section 1208 may not have funded UW or supported indig-

enous surrogates for non-CT uses, but it did provide a way for SOF to use its own funds in increasing amounts for partnered approaches in dozens of countries. Interviewees stated that USSOCOM believed more support to the TSOCs was still required, but that, through the achieved changes, USSOCOM established a precedent and the basis for additional changes. The signing of the IW directive created the forcing function for pursuing needed changes; follow-on decisions and implementation would be required to achieve the intended objectives. Continuity of personnel increased the momentum in that direction.

Plan Colombia is another case in which momentum for further progress was built over time. The U.S. military and U.S. country team established a track record of compliance, transparency, and results. The U.S. military scrupulously complied with conditions imposed by Congress, including force caps, Leahy vetting requirements, and active scrutiny through congressional visits and engagement in Colombia and at USSOUTHCOM. A succession of USSOUTHCOM commanders provided detailed testimony to Congress, and the U.S. country team provided briefings to visiting delegations.

Finally, the SMU community made evolutionary change, adapting after painful lessons in Somalia, the Balkans, and the early days in Afghanistan. The leadership adopted a deliberate effort to change the internal organizational culture by enforcing the open exchange of information, empowerment of subordinates, development of outside contacts, and self-criticism. Despite the secrecy of the organization, operational results were circulated to key stakeholders.

Opportunity and Decision Analysis Framework

This section distills the above findings into an opportunity and decision analysis framework. U.S. military doctrine lays out many standard practices for development of concepts of operations and proposals. This framework (Table 15.1) builds on those basic practices to incorporate insights from SOF's various engagements with policy-level personnel gleaned in the case studies. In particular, it would be advisable to direct that policymakers' points of reference, language, and particular concerns be incorporated into the initial assessment and proposal-framing process. This should ensure that proposals would include evidence and rationales to address the areas of importance or concern to the policymaker, in addition to those required for military purposes.

Table 15.1
Decision Analysis Tool

1	Scan environment for emerging or festering threats to U.S. interests. 1a. Identify white space of unmet needs. 1b. Identify remedies for any SOF capabilities inadequate to meet such threats.
2	Analyze policy demand signal (if any).
3	Seek permission to conduct assessment and explore options.
4	Assess technical feasibility through policy lens.
5	Assess value proposition and acceptability through policy lens.
6	Conduct future constraints test (ability to achieve outcome with projected available resources).
7	Weight opportunity costs and downside risks.
8	Seek support for assessment among stakeholders.
9	Assess feedback including criticism or rejection; reconsider or reframe.
10	Pursue long-term strategies and take calculated risks.

Recommendations

The findings of this research represent the most important factors influencing the outcome of the decisions studied. We examined SOF's ability to act appropriately on the implications of these findings to ensure that they were conveying their requirements and proposals in the most effective manner, consistent with their assigned responsibilities. The study team also received numerous inputs from the stakeholder and SOF interviewees, suggesting gaps in the ability to act effectively. The team distilled four areas in which SOF, and Army SOF in particular, could focus their attention to develop institutional responses and routine practices that will enhance their ability to undertake two activities: Convey SOF requirements to decisionmakers and provide sound options for employment of SOF as appropriate to address national security challenges.

Recommendation 1: Develop "Plain English" Explanations of Special Operations Terminology and Narrative

The special operations community has, for the past decade, sought to refine its ability to communicate its unique requirements and capabilities in a manner that is well understood by interagency and external audiences. This endeavor is part of a more general effort to address what the community perceives to be a lack of understanding among GCCs, the interagency community, and Congress regarding the utility and value of certain types of special operations. The sponsor requested that we specifically address the requirement for a persuasive and widely comprehensible SOF narrative.

This perceived need arises from various sources. First, the special operations community is fairly new, compared with the military services. Its small size and relative secrecy have also contributed to the lack of familiarity. Evolving special operations law and doctrine enumerate a wide variety of special operations core activities and operations, themselves varied, evolving, and not readily understood by the layman. The current list, in Joint Publication 3-05, *Special Operations*, is:

- Direct action
- Special reconnaissance
- Countering weapons of mass destruction
- Counterterrorism
- Unconventional warfare
- Foreign internal defense
- Security force assistance
- Hostage rescue and recovery
- Counterinsurgency
- Foreign humanitarian assistance
- Military information support operations

- Civil affairs operations.[3]

SOCOM attempted to provide a more-readily understood characterization by describing SOF as operating via a "direct approach" (i.e., the unilateral, kinetic, and usually lethal application of force) and/or an "indirect approach" that pertained to working with or through indigenous forces or populations in many cases (although not always) in a noncombat mode.

In Army Doctrinal Publication 3-05, *Special Operations*, Army SOF developed a new dichotomy of "special warfare" and "surgical strike," which were roughly analogous to the indirect and direct approaches.[4] These were intended to be more descriptive and precise terms that could migrate from Army into joint doctrine. Because of disagreements within the joint community, this terminology was not adopted into the latest version of Joint Publication 3-05. In particular, the Army doctrine's use of special warfare as terms pertaining to Army SOF—although it does have historical precedent—causes some confusion with the formal name of Naval Special Warfare, the Navy component of SOF.

Another broad lesson concerns IW. Coining new terms and migrating them into doctrine does not always lead to greater comprehension or acceptance. While IW has now been adopted into joint doctrine, it was not used in the 2008 QDR or subsequently, and it has now been overtaken in current policy and military dialogue by "hybrid warfare" and "gray zone" conflicts or challenges. These two latter terms represent new efforts to gain broad support among stakeholders or at least repel fewer audiences. The official adoption of IW did not necessarily overcome all objections. However, the doctrinal term *irregular warfare* did achieve the objective of identifying a type of warfare that the U.S. military must be able to fight successfully, and the IW directive provides a means to pursue that goal.

---

[3] Joint Publication 3-05, *Special Operations*, July 16, 2014.

[4] Army Doctrine Publication 3-05, *Special Operations*, Washington, D.C.: Headquarters, Department of the Army, August 2012.

This lesson regarding terminology is particularly relevant to consideration of the terms that the special operations community uses, and those terms that it wants to place into wider circulation. The question must be asked: To what end? The purpose of propagating a given term should be clarified, and then a deliberate plan to gain acceptance fashioned. Army SOF in particular continues to believe that their capabilities employing special forces, Civil Affairs and Military Information Support Operations (formerly known as psychological operations), are not widely understood, and this is compounded by the general unfamiliarity with SOF's core missions of UW and foreign internal defense.

We recommend that Army SOF not promulgate a new doctrinal term but use several basic, readily understood terms and illustrate their proposals by reference to specific previous Army SOF missions and operations. An overarching description of one of SOF's major roles might be "supporting indigenous or partnered forces," which is the common element of both UW and foreign internal defense. Working with partner forces in an indigenous approach, furthermore, is readily tied to current defense guidance and the national security strategy, which emphasizes U.S. reliance on other nations and friendly forces as a cost-effective and force-multiplying approach to the national defense, and a critical element in creating a broad international alliance of nations that are united in abiding by and supporting a rules-based international order.

Furthermore, the indigenous approach does not exclude the option of using precision targeting methods and unilateral forces when circumstances require. It is important to note that Army SOF include the Ranger Regiment, which has become closely identified with the CT mission in the past 15 years but has a long history as a light-infantry force employed in various ways. Indeed, it is more helpful to present all special operations capabilities as readily combined and tailored to the specific circumstances of a conflict environment, political constraints, or the nature of the threat. Special operations capabilities can therefore be understood as applicable in a wide range of scenarios, including nonstate actor threats and state threats against which stealth and proxy or indigenous forces are required. Of course, special operations have continuing utility in the more traditional form, as adjuncts to major combat operations in certain niche roles such as special reconnaissance and other behind-the-lines operations.

This characterization of special operations, moreover, reverses a certain tendency to associate SOF with one single mission, CT, which unduly limits the understanding of the utility of these forces. A decline in the perceived threat of terrorism would thereby put at risk SOF as currently sized and funded. Similarly, while hostage rescue and render-safe capabilities are vital, depicting them as the primary missions risks the downsizing of the force and its restriction to primarily tactical formations. The trend has, in fact, been in the opposite direction, as in the latest campaign against the Islamic State, where SOF have played a wide variety of roles and, together with their multinational SOF coalition partners, form the majority of the forces deployed in the campaign.

Special warfare and surgical strike do not need to be jettisoned from the vocabulary, as they are in Army doctrine, and do fill a descriptive purpose. In keeping with the broader objectives outlined above, the emphasis going forward might be usefully placed on the complementary and often-combined application of these two Army SOF capabilities. At least for Army audiences, these two terms may have ongoing value. For the wider policy audience, however, this study recommends that the terms *special operations, indigenous approach*, and *precision targeting* may have the greatest resonance. The specific proposed or current application can be illustrated or explained by reference to previous analogous operations. Thus, by referencing operations in the Philippines, Colombia, Balkans, Afghanistan, Iraq, and now Syria—and other operations as they are declassified—the public can become more familiar with the history of special operations.

Finally, the history of the term *unconventional warfare* deserves particular attention, as does a promising new development. Although UW is a doctrinal and statutory mission for special forces, it is not widely embraced or well understood in the larger U.S. military and policymaking community. Hence, a 2010–2011 effort to write a follow-on directive for UW did not come to fruition, and an oft-stated need for specific authorities for funding UW has gone unmet. One reason cited was that Vickers moved on to another position and no ardent champion took his place to move it forward.

Some interviewees suggested that different approaches might have better prospects. One official noted that a Joint Staff tabletop exercise on UW found that combatant commanders responded well to a more-general inquiry from SOF to discuss how the community could help prepare the environment and prepare options for the commander's consideration.[5] Given the aversion to the term *unconventional warfare* among the policy community and the conventional military forces, the special operations community has begun to use the term *support to resistance* as a more sympathetic—and accurate—term, since SOF will most often be supporting others' resistance rather than conducting UW itself. This flexibility in terminology is a good example of the community adapting to gain buy-in from key stakeholders so that it might be able to carry out vital missions. In the case of Europe, many stakeholders support the term *resistance* and even incorporate it into their national plans and doctrine. It is also critical to distinguish this term from the current, widespread use of indigenous surrogates to wage U.S. CT operations. As one senior U.S. military official explains, "There is a fundamental difference between our network and their network. An effort centered around *their* network is the UW approach."[6]

Recommendation 2: Further Develop the SOF-CIA Relationship and Reframe the Conduct of Unconventional Warfare

Interviewees described an intensive evolution in the years since 9/11 toward greater familiarity and synergy between SOF and the CIA than at any previous period in their history. The search for Osama bin Laden and other key terrorist figures has been one focal point for the development of this recent collaboration. This is not surprising from one vantage point, in that both communities trace their lineage and missions to OSS. The potential synergy extends beyond manhunts and is particularly strong in the mission of UW. The historical case study on the Vietnam-era collaboration notes that the CIA possesses unique

---

[5] Interview with Joint Staff official, January 20, 2016.

[6] Interview, April 1, 2016.

assets and skills for Phases 1–3 (preparation, initial conflict, infiltration) of UW, and that special forces have primacy in terms of capabilities for planning and execution of Phases 4–6 (organization, buildup, and employment).

Thus, a cooperative approach readily suggests itself, which is that these forces enjoy the greatest success if they combine efforts in the conduct of UW. The historical record also suggests that most often the President will prefer to authorize a UW mission under Title 50 authorities as a covert operation via a presidential finding. That finding may direct that the mission be carried out by DoD (USASOC), but again history suggests that the default entity is likely to remain CIA. Presidents have daily interaction with the CIA, and the agency has refined the art of developing and maintaining relationships in Washington.

However, the conduct of UW may be most successful when experienced senior military officers at the O-6 level or above are in command of the planning and operations, certainly at the point where the campaign becomes military in nature and of a scale that would severely strain the agency's capacity. The officer in command can play this role in either entity, but the CIA would need to grant this authority to plan and execute a campaign and make the appropriate organizational adjustments.

The case study of the expansion of the SMU community makes clear such adjustments are possible, as McChrystal made an intelligence community officer his deputy. A similar adjustment could yield a senior CIA officer in charge of a task force conducting UW under Title 50 authority with an O-6 or above SOF officer detailed to the CIA as deputy for military operations. Yet, the SMU community case study makes clear such adjustments are likely to be resisted on the basis of legal or other grounds so would need significant policy-level support.

A final adjustment may increase the utility of special operations for policymakers in a turbulent era, without creating friction in the SOF-CIA relationship. Many special operations rely critically on the ability to conduct advance force operations or operational preparation of the environment. The need to conduct such operations inside countries of interest to obtain information or create infrastructure is now part of the unclassified Joint Doctrine 3-05 on *Special Operations*;

this definition and explanation were promulgated openly in part to help educate policymakers and Congress as to the vital nature of this activity.

Without these early activities, it is not possible to compile full, honest, and realistic assessments of conditions, indigenous forces, and enemy formations, and without this ground truth, few viable options will be developed. The lack of authority to conduct such assessments reduces the number of sound options that can be provided to policymakers and increases the risk of any plan that is forwarded without it. The permission to conduct such assessments can be provided to SOF without a finding as a traditional military activity. Such proposed deployments will be sensitive because of their ability to interfere with bilateral relationships and other departments' and agencies' prerogatives, so special operations leaders need to prepare detailed proposals with provisions for notification and consultation.

Recommendation 3: Prepare SOF to Interact at the Policy Level
Perhaps the most important single focus of attention for Army SOF, considering the effects it could have for all other SOF activities, would be revisions to its personnel, leader development, and education practices to permit, incentivize, and leverage SOF interagency knowledge and experience. The first step would be to ensure that the most talented special operations officers serve two or more tours in Washington in a range of policy-relevant interagency assignments. Currently, the majority of SOF officers serve in only three locations: SOLIC, the Joint Staff J-3 special operations directorate, and the Army G-3 special operations directorate. Other opportunities should be sought in the OSD, the Joint Staff regional directorates, and the State Department's regional bureaus, as these are the locations where detailed policies and plans are discussed as the primary responsibilities. In addition to competing for deputy director of the Joint Staff's regional directorates, a new special operations J-5 directorate would be helpful in integrating SOF perspectives throughout the plans process. A formal program has been instituted in recent years whereby DoD and the State Department exchange personnel to serve as senior advisers and thus increase

interagency coordination. In addition, the White House NSC staff is a major locus for policy deliberation and interagency coordination.

The model for implementing this recommendation is the position of director for CT in the White House, which has been held by a special operations officer since 9/11. Most often the director has been a Naval Special Warfare officer who continued on in his career to become a flag officer and senior commander. Serving under senior civilians creates a powerful future network that Naval Special Warfare officers have used to gain a hearing for an urgent issue or even generate support for proposals, as a number of interviewees noted. The one time an Army SOF officer occupied this position, he was not promoted to general officer.

Holding such positions provides three benefits to SOF. First, and very critically, it provides irreplaceable on-the-job training in interagency policymaking, which can inform the entire community about the policy issues that any military proposal will need to address. Second, it provides the community an opportunity to showcase the talent in its ranks and leave a lasting positive impression of SOF. Third, it provides the officer an opportunity to form networks throughout government that will serve him and the community well in the informal interactions that accompany most formal decisionmaking processes.

A large number of interviewees stressed the importance of SOF's gaining greater knowledge of and connectivity with the interagency community. While no specific example cited might be of critical importance, the evidence suggests a cumulative cost to the organization. The teaming of SOLIC and USSOCOM to produce the IW directive was an effective partnership, one official noted, but he added that it was not a routine occurrence. He suggested that SOF may not sufficiently appreciate the policy expertise at SOLIC and the Joint Staff. Another interviewee who served in the Pentagon observed that SOF do not routinely reach out to engage the relevant functional or regional offices at the joint staff or OSD to seek information and exchange views. At times, proposals and white papers do not contain sufficient knowledge of non-SOF military structures and processes or civilian policy issues. Other initiatives such as USSOCOM's previous extensive "strategic appreciation" exercise were criticized as redundant to intelligence community analytic products and processes. Numerous interviewees attributed these lapses to insufficient experience in Washington and a failure to seek out the expertise of those who work in the relevant offices. Various former SOF operators now working in civilian capacities lamented the failure of SOF officers to apply their training and insight in establishing rapport and gaining influence from their daily work of interacting with the U.S. bureaucracy.[7]

Investing in such opportunities requires a commitment to use that officer's experience in subsequent positions. This sounds obvious, but both formal Army career promotion requirements and Army SOF's informal proclivity for routing their officers into a fixed path need to be adjusted to motivate these interagency tours. Familiarity with Washington can also be an enormous boon for SOF officers to compete for senior Joint Staff and interagency positions such as in the Joint Staff directorates or as associate director for military affairs at the CIA.

Finally, this practice in the interagency community and internationally of sending officers out to assignments in non-SOF commands yields the same powerful benefits. Reducing staffing at SOF formations to enable more officers to serve in these positions would pay enormous long-term benefits in strategic-level knowledge for SOF, visibility and credibility for SOF, and the consequent understanding among a wider audience of what special operations can contribute to national security objectives.

Recommendation 4: Emphasize Pathways to Innovation and Excellence

The special operations community, given its small size, has understandably focused on operations over institutional knowledge and processes during its first decades. The increasing use of SOF around the globe would put pressure even on a historically large force. However, that same expanding use creates a long-term requirement for the community to build the processes that will continue to develop its unique areas of military expertise. The nature of special operations, with a premium

---

[7] Interview, March 25, 2016; interview, March 10, 2016; interview, February 9, 2016; and interview, June 10, 2016.

on flexibility of formations and agility in approaches, necessitates not only innovative materiel solutions but innovative thought leadership.

The implications of such a requirement are significant prioritization of and investment in knowledge-management systems, theoretical and applied research, and enhanced educational opportunities for operators. There are some excellent programs, including the master's degree program at the Naval Postgraduate School and the Army Strategic Studies doctoral program at Fort Leavenworth. In addition, senior service colleges and fellowships provide needed time for in-depth research and improved communications skills. National Defense University provides a program specialized in IW with a high proportion of international students at the College of International Security Affairs; the college also runs a satellite graduation program at Fort Bragg. The length of some programs may push promising officers out of the current promotion track, in another sign of the undue rigidity of the personnel model.

Increasingly, senior leaders at the Pentagon and services are recognizing that knowledge is the coin of the future force, and SOF should associate themselves prominently in these initiatives. SOF should also lead in pressing for personnel reforms that prioritize the acquisition of this knowledge. In addition, SOF should be in forefront of promoting a climate of experimentation and innovation, grounded in sound practices. Openness to new ideas and an emphasis on crossfertilization are highly compatible with the core values of the community and can be productively highlighted to lead the force away from isolating practices and into a future of greater engagement.

Conclusion

The special operations community and Army SOF, which constitute roughly half of the entire SOF, have undergone tremendous change since their origins in World War II and particularly in their historic expansion following the 9/11 attacks. The community has contributed to the achievement of national security objectives in an extraordinary number of ways, many of which remain unknown to the general public. This presents something of an impediment to the community's objective of promoting greater understanding of its capabilities and requirements by those at the policy level of government, in Congress or among the public.

The key to improved use of SOF is through improved understanding on the part of decisionmakers. Achieving that goal requires SOF to understand the interagency process and their appropriate roles in it. To their credit, SOF have invested time and effort in educating their officers, creating new courses to improve and adapt their tactical and operational acumen, and managing their growth while maintaining the high standards that an elite force requires. The recommendations made here, if implemented, should contribute to the further education and development of special operations forces, improved interagency understanding, and greater successes in the employment of special operations.

Bibliography

5th Special Forces Group Headquarters, *U.S. Army Special Forces Participation in the CIDG Program Vietnam, 1957–1970*, Houston, Tex.: Reprint by Radix Press, 1996.

"Administrative History," Records of the Office of War Information, Record Group 208, 208.1, June 13, 1942. As of December 21, 2016: http://www.archives.gov/research/guide-fed-records/groups/208.html#208.1

Ahearn, Dave, "Team Leaders Q&A: Improving SOF Support to Geographic Combatant Commands, Col. Stuart W. Bradin Chief Global SOF Network Operational Planning Team SOCOM," *Special Operations Technology*, Vol. 11, No. 2, March 2013, pp. 10–23.

Ahern, Jr., Thomas L., *CIA and Rural Pacification in South Vietnam*, Washington, D.C.: Center for the Study of Intelligence, 2001, declassified 2006.

———, *Undercover Armies: CIA and Surrogate Warfare in Laos, 1961–1973*, Washington, D.C.: Center for the Study of Intelligence, 2006, declassified 2009.

Alexander, Larry, *Shadows in the Jungle: The Alamo Scouts Behind Japanese Lines in World War II*, New York: NAL Caliber, 2010.

Army Doctrine Publication 3-05, *Special Operations*, Washington, D.C.: Headquarters, Department of the Army, August 2012. As of August 2, 2016: https://fas.org/irp/doddir/army/adp3_05.pdf

Associated Press, "Green Beret Chief Held in Slaying of a Vietnamese," *New York Times*, August 6, 1969. As of July 27, 2016 (subscription required): http://search.proquest.com/docview/118605248?accountid=25333

Bank, Aaron, *From OSS to Green Berets*, New York: Simon and Schuster, 1987.

"Battle of the Aleutian Islands," History.com, 2009. As of March 25, 2016: http://www.history.com/topics/world-war-ii/battle-of-the-aleutian-islands

Beittel, June S., "Colombia: Background, U.S. Relations, and Congressional Interest," Washington, D.C.: Congressional Research Service, 7-5700, RL32250, November 28, 2012. As of December 21, 2016: https://fas.org/sgp/crs/row/RL32250.pdf

Birtle, Andrew J., *U.S. Army Counterinsurgency and Contingency Operations Doctrine 1942–1976*, Washington, D.C.: Center of Military History, U.S. Army, 2006. As of July 27, 2016:
http://www.history.army.mil/html/books/us_army_counterinsurgency/CMH_70-98-1_US%20Army_Counterinsurgency_WQ.pdf

Boykin, William G., "Special Operations and Low-Intensity Conflict Legislation: Why Was It Passed and Have the Voids Been Filled?" Carlisle Barracks, Pa.: U.S. Army War College, April 1991.

Brown, Anthony Cave, *The Last Hero: Wild Bill Donovan*, New York: Times Books, 1982.

Brown, Harry S., "The Command and Control of Special Operations Forces," thesis, Monterey, Calif.: Naval Postgraduate School, December 1996.

Builta, Jeffrey A., and Eric N. Heller, "Reflections on 10 Years of Counterterrorism Analysis," *Studies in Intelligence*, Vol. 55, No. 3 (unclassified extracts), September 2011.

Bumiller, Elisabeth, "Panetta Warns of Dire Consequences to Military from Budget Cuts," *New York Times*, February 6, 2013. As of June 26, 2016:
http://www.nytimes.com/2013/02/07/us/politics/panetta-warns-of-dire-consequences-to-military-from-cuts.html

Bureau of Western Hemisphere Affairs, "Fact Sheet: U.S. Relations with Colombia," Washington, D.C.: U.S. Department of State, November 19, 2013. As of July 26, 2016:
http://www.state.gov/r/pa/ei/bgn/35754.htm

Chollet, Derek, "Inside Obama's Syria Choices (A Guide for Dissenting Diplomats)," DefenseOne.com, June 16, 2016. As of July 19, 2016:
http://www.defenseone.com/ideas/2016/06/defense-obamas-syria-choices/129230/

Clancy, Tom, Carl Stiner, and Tony Koltz, *Shadow Warriors: Inside the Special Forces*, New York: G. P. Putnam's Sons, 2002.

Clinton, Hillary, *Hard Choices: A Memoir*, New York: Simon and Schuster, 2014.

Clinton, William J., "Communication from the President of the United States: A Report on Continued U.S. Contributions in Support of Peacekeeping Efforts in the Former Yugoslavia," December 17, 1997.

Cohen, William S., "A Defense Special Operations Agency: Fix for an SOF Capability That Is Most Assuredly Broken," *Armed Forces Journal International*, January 1986.

Cole, Ronald H., *Operation Just Cause: The Planning and Execution of Joint Operations in Panama February 1988–January 1990*, Washington, D.C.: Joint History Office, Office of the Joint Chiefs of Staff, 1995.

Coleman, David, "U.S. Military Personnel 1954–2014," historyinpieces.com, undated. As of January 9, 2017:
http://historyinpieces.com/research/us-military-personnel-1954-2014#fnref-5821-fn1

Collins, John, "U.S. Special Operations—Personal Opinions," presented to the 1st Battalion, 1st Special Warfare Training Group, Camp Mackall, N.C., December 11, 2008.

"Colombia: The Ties That Bind: Colombia and Military-Paramilitary Links," *Human Rights Watch*, Vol 12., No. 1 (B), February 2000. As of July 26, 2016:
https://www.hrw.org/reports/2000/colombia/

C/S, Patrick, "Planning for the Alamo Scout Training Center," memorandum to General Krueger, November 1, 1943.

Culp, W. W., "A Recommended Plan for the Program for Training of Scouts," memorandum to General Krueger, October 30, 1943.

Department of the Army, Office of the Chief of Psychological Warfare, Washington, D.C., Summary Sheet for Chief of Staff, Subject: J. Lawton Collin's Conference at the Infantry Center, April 5, 1951, from COL Edward Galvin, Acting Chief of Psychological Warfare (summary sheet prepared by LTC Russell W. Volckmann), April 16, 1951, Record Group 319, Army-Chief of Special Warfare, 1951–54, TS Decimal Files, Psy War 337 (April 16, 1951), National Archives.

Department of the Army, Plans and Operations Division, Washington, D.C., Summary Sheet and Study to Chief of Staff, subject: A Study of Psychological Warfare, from LTG A. C. Wedemeyer, Director of Plans and Operations, February 10, 1948, Record Group 319, P&O Division, 1946–48, 091.3–091.7, Section I, box 28, P&O 091.412 TS (January 15, 1948), National Archives.

———, Plans and Operations Division, Washington D.C., Memorandum for the Chief of Staff, 18 March 1948, from LTG A. C. Wedemeyer, Director, Plans and Operations, Record Group 319, Plans and Operations Division, 1946–48, 091.3–091.7, Section I, box 28, filed with P&O 09.412 (November 30, 1948), National Archives.

Department of Defense Directive, "Military Support for Stability, Security, Transition, and Reconstruction (SSTR) Operations," Washington, D.C.: U.S. Department of Defense, number 3000.05, November 28, 2005.

———, "Irregular Warfare (IW)," Washington, D.C.: U.S. Department of Defense, number 3000.07, December 1, 2008.

———, "Irregular Warfare (IW)," Washington, D.C.: U.S. Department of Defense, number 3000.07, August 28, 2014.

Downing, Wayne, "Special Operations Forces Assessment," memorandum for the Secretary of Defense, Chairman, Joint Chiefs of Staff, November 9, 2005.

Dozier, Kimberly, "Bin Laden Raid Commander Seeks Global Expansion," Associated Press, January 26, 2012.

Escuela Superior de Guerra [Superior School of War], *Centro Regional de Estudios Estrategicos en Seguridad* [regional center for strategic security studies], undated. As of June 26, 2016:
http://www.esdegue.edu.co/node/4465

Feickert, Andrew, *U.S. Special Operations Forces (SOF): Background and Issues for Congress,* Congressional Research Service, 7-7500, RS21048, September 18, 2013.

———, *U.S. Special Operations Forces (SOF): Background and Issues for Congress*, Congressional Research Service, November 2015.

Finlayson, Andrew R., "A Retrospective on Counterinsurgency Operations: The Tay Ninh Provincial Reconnaissance Unit and Its Role in the Phoenix Program, 1969–70," *Studies in Intelligence*, Vol. 51, No. 2, 2007.

———, *Marine Advisors with the Vietnamese Provincial Reconnaissance Units, 1966–1970*, Quantico, Va.: History Division, U.S. Marine Corps, 2009.

Flynn, Michael T., Rich Juergens, and Thomas L. Cantrell, "Employing ISR: SOF Best Practices," *Joint Forces Quarterly*, Vol. 50, 2008.

"Frank Pace Jr., Former Secretary of the Army and Executive, Dies," *New York Times*, January 10, 1988. As of April 15, 2016:
http://www.nytimes.com/1988/01/10/obituaries/frank-pace-jr-former-secretary-of-the-army-and-executive-dies.html

Future Authorities That May Be Necessary for Special Operations Forces to Adequately Conduct Counterterrorism, Unconventional Warfare, and Irregular Warfare Missions: Report to Congress, Washington, D.C.: Office of the Assistant Secretary of Defense, U.S. Department of Defense, September 5, 2012.

"The Future of Special Operations: Proposed Changes in the Unified Command Plan," *Global Security Forum 2012, Conference Proceedings,* Washington, D.C.: Center for Strategic and International Studies, April 2012.

"GEN J. Lawton Collins's Conference at the Infantry Center," April 5, 1951.

Gibbons-Neff, Thomas. "Only 4 to 5 American-Trained Syrians Fighting Against the Islamic State," *Washington Post*, September 16, 2015.

Gibson, James Bryant, "Super-Rangers: The Early Years of Army Special Forces 1944–1953," thesis, Chapel Hill, N.C.: University of North Carolina at Chapel Hill, 2008. As of July 27, 2016:
https://cdr.lib.unc.edu/indexablecontent/
uuid:0fdd22e8-4d9d-4c49-b5aa-a047046fad38

Goldberg, Jeffrey, "The Obama Doctrine," *The Atlantic*, April 2016.

Gordon, Michael R., and Mark Lander, "Senate Hearing Draws Out a Rift in U.S. Policy on Syria," *New York Times*, February 7, 2013. As of July 27, 2016: http://www.nytimes.com/2013/02/08/us/politics/panetta-speaks-to-senate-panel-on-benghazi-attack.html

Green, Andrew, "National Security Council Directive 4-A," in Jan Goldman, ed., *The Central Intelligence Agency: An Encyclopedia of Covert Ops, Intelligence Gathering, and Spies*, Vol. 1, Santa Barbara, Calif.: ABC-CLIO, 2015, pp. 266–267.

———, "National Security Council Directive 10/2," in Jan Goldman, ed., *The Central Intelligence Agency: An Encyclopedia of Covert Ops, Intelligence Gathering, and Spies*, Vol. 1, Santa Barbara, Calif.: ABC-CLIO, 2015, pp. 267–269.

Greenert, Jonathan, "House Appropriations Subcommittee on Defense: Hearing on President Obama's Fiscal 2016 Budget Request for the Navy," February 26, 2015.

Guardia, Mike, *American Guerrilla: The Forgotten Heroics of Russell W. Volckmann*, Havertown, Pa.: Casemate Publishers, 2010.

Guerilla Operations in Vietnam Territory, National Security Action Memorandum No. 28, March 9, 1961. As of July 18, 2016: http://www.jfklibrary.org/Asset-Viewer/T6F6HW7rs0i_yrHDA0I4vg.aspx

Headquarters, Department of the Army, U.S. Army South, U.S. Military Group Colombia, "Colombia Joint Task Force Consultative Team Report," September 17, 2012.

Hokayem, Emile, "How Syria Defeated the Sunni Powers," *New York Times*, December 30, 2016.

Holliday, Joseph. "Syria's Armed Opposition," in *Middle East Security Report* 3, Washington, D.C.: Institute for the Study of War, March 2012. As of July 27, 2016: http://www.understandingwar.org/sites/default/files/Syrias_Armed_Opposition.pdf

Joint Chiefs of Staff, Special Operations Review Group, *Holloway Commission Report*, 1980.

Joint Publication 3-05, *Special Operations*, July 16, 2014. As of August 2, 2016: http://www.dtic.mil/doctrine/new_pubs/jp3_05.pdf

Kelly, Francis J., *Vietnam Forces: U.S. Army Special Forces 1961–1971*, Washington, D.C.: Center of Military History, Department of the Army, CMH Pub 90-23-1, 1973.

Kennedy, John F., "Green Berets," John F. Kennedy Presidential Library and Museum web page, undated. As of April 14, 2016: http://www.jfklibrary.org/JFK/JFK-in-History/Green-Berets.aspx

———, *A Compilation of Speeches During His Service in the U.S. Senate and House of Representatives*, Washington, D.C.: U.S. Government Printing Office, 1964, pp. 1002–1003.

"Krueger of the Sixth," *Newsweek*, February 4, 1946.

Krueger, Walter, *From Down Under to Nippon: The Story of Sixth Army in World War II*, Washington, D.C.: Combat Forces Press, 1953.

Kugler, Richard, *Operation Anaconda in Afghanistan: A Case Study of Adaptation in Battle* (Case Studies in Defense Transformation, Number 5), Washington, D.C.: National Defense University, Center for Technology and National Security Policy, 2007.

Lamb, Christopher J., and Evan Munsing, *Secret Weapon: High-Value Target Teams as an Organizational Innovation*, Washington, D.C.: National Defense University Press, March 2011.

Lister, Charles R., *The Syrian Jihad: Al-Qaeda, the Islamic State and the Evolution of an Insurgency*, Oxford: Oxford University Press, 2016.

Locher, III, James R., *Victory on the Potomac*, College Station, Tex.: Texas A&M University Press, 2002.

———, "Congress to the Rescue: Statutory Creation of USSOCOM," *Air Commando Journal*, Vol. 1, No. 3, Spring 2012.

Macdonald, Julia M., "Eisenhower's Scientists: Policy Entrepreneurs and the Test-Ban Debate 1954–1958," *Foreign Policy Analysis*, Vol. 11, No. 1, January 2015, pp. 1–21.

Marcella, Gabriel, *Plan Colombia: Strategic and Operational Imperatives*, Carlisle, Pa.: Strategic Studies Institute, U.S. Army War College, April 2001.

Marks, Thomas, *Colombian Army Adaptation to FARC Insurgency*, Carlisle, Pa.: Strategic Studies Institute, U.S. Army War College, January 2002.

Marquis, Susan L., *Unconventional Warfare: Rebuilding U.S. Special Operations Forces*, Washington, D.C.: Brookings Institution Press, 1997.

Marrero, Ramon M., "4th Battalion, 7th Special Forces Group Activates," *Paraglide*, October 25, 2012.

Martinage, Robert, *Special Operations Forces: Challenges and Opportunities*, testimony before the U.S. House of Representatives House Armed Services Committee, Subcommittee on Terrorism, Unconventional Threats and Capabilities, Washington, D.C., March 3, 2009.

Martinez, Luis, "Gen. Martin Dempsey Lays Out U.S. Military Options for Syria," ABC News, July 22, 2013. As of July 27, 2016:
http://abcnews.go.com/blogs/politics/2013/07/gen-martin-dempsey-lays-out-us-military-options-for-syria/

Mazarr, Michael J., "The Iraq War and Agenda Setting," *Foreign Policy Analysis*, Vol. 3, No. 1, January 2007, pp. 1–23.

McChrystal, Stanley, *My Share of the Task: A Memoir*, New York: Penguin, 2014.

McRaven, William H., "Purple Note," in *USSOCOM, Global Special Operations Forces Network Operational Planning Team: A History*, 2011, p. 34.

———, "Posture Statement of Admiral William H. McRaven, USN Commander, United States Special Operations Command, Before the 113th Congress, House Arms Service Committee, Washington, D.C., March 6, 2013.

Mejía, Daniel, *Plan Colombia: An Analysis of Effectiveness and Costs*, Washington, D.C.: Brookings Institution, 2016.

Memorandum to Assistant Chief of Staff, G-2, G.H.Q., S.W.P.A., APO 500, "Naval Amphibious Scout Training Center," from Headquarters Alamo Forces, Office of the Chief of Staff, COL G. H. Decker, Deputy Chief of Staff, November 7, 1943.

Mullen, Michael G., "Transcript of Q&A with Defense Writers Group," June 10, 2008.

Myers, Richard, "Reducing Demands on Special Operations Forces," memorandum to Secretary of Defense, September 26, 2002.

"Nation: Green Berets on Trial," *Time*, August 22, 1969.

Naughton, James M., "White House Confirms That Nixon Was Involved in Decision to Drop Charges Against Green Berets," *New York Times*, October 2, 1969. As of October 2, 2015 (subscription required):
http://search.proquest.com/docview/118676596?accountid=25333

"NSC 68: United States Objectives and Programs for National Security: A Report to the President, Pursuant to the President's Directive of January 31, 1950," Washington, D.C., April 7, 1950. As of June 16, 2016:
http://www.citizensource.com/History/20thCen/NSC68.PDF

Nunn, Sam, Barry M. Goldwater, and James R. Locher, III, *Defense Organization: The Need for Change: Staff Report to the Committee on Armed Services, United States Senate*, Washington, D.C.: U.S. Government Printing Office, October 16, 1985.

Office of the Secretary of Defense, U.S. Department of Defense, Establishment of Regional Special Operations Coordination Centers, April 16, 2014.

Office of the Vice Commander, U.S. Special Operations Command, "Global Special Operations Forces Network Concept of Operations," memorandum to Directors for Force Structure, Resources, and Assessments, May 1, 2013.

Ospina, Carlos, and Thomas A. Marks, "Changing Strategy Amidst the Struggle," *Small Wars and Insurgencies*, Vol. 25, No. 2, 2014, pp. 354–371.

Paddock, Jr., Alfred H., *U.S. Army Special Warfare: Its Origins*, revised ed., Topeka, Kan.: University of Kansas Press, 2002.

Panetta, Leon, with Jim Newton, *Worthy Fights: A Memoir of Leadership in War and Peace*, New York: Penguin Press, 2014.

Petraeus, David, and Michael E. O'Hanlon, "The Success Story in Colombia," Brookings Institution website, September 24, 2013. As of August 1, 2016: https://www.brookings.edu/opinions/the-success-story-in-colombia/

Polk, J. F., "A Plan for the Organization and Training of the Scouts," memorandum to Gen. Krueger, October 31, 1943.

Pollack, Kenneth M., "Building a Better Syrian Opposition Army: The How and the Why," Washington, D.C.: Center for Middle East Policy at Brookings Institution Analysis Paper No. 35, October 2014. As of December 21, 2016: http://www.brookings.edu/~/media/research/files/papers/2014/10/building-syrian-opposition-army-pollack/building-a-better-syrian-armyweb.pdf

Powell, Colin L., with Joseph E. Persico, *My American Journey*, New York: Random House Ballantine Publishing Group, 1996.

Public Law 108–375, Ronald W. Reagan National Defense Authorization Act for Fiscal Year 2005, October 28, 2004.

Public Law 110-181, National Defense Authorization Act for Fiscal Year 2008, Sec. 1202, Authority for Support of Military Operations to Combat Terrorism, January 28, 2008.

Public Law 110-417, Duncan Hunter National Defense Authorization Act for Fiscal Year 2009, Sec. 1208, Extension and Expansion of Authority for Support of Special Operations to Combat Terrorism, October 14, 2008.

Public Law 111–84, National Defense Authorization Act for Fiscal Year 2010, Sec. 1202, Expansion of Authority and Modification of Notification and Reporting Requirements for Use of Authority for Support of Special Operations to Combat Terrorism, October 28, 2009.

Public Law 111–383, Ike Skelton National Defense Authorization Act for Fiscal Year 2011, Sec. 1201, Expansion of Authority for Support of Special Operations to Combat Terrorism, January 7, 2011.

Public Law 112-81, National Defense Authorization Act for Fiscal Year 2012, Sec. 1203, Extension and Expansion of Authority for Support of Special Operations to Combat Terrorism, December 31, 2011.

Public Law 113-66, National Defense Authorization Act for Fiscal Year 2014, Sec. 343, Limitation on funding for United States Special Operations Command National Capital Region, December 26, 2013.

Public Law 113-291, Carl Levin and Howard P. "Buck" McKeon National Defense Authorization Act for Fiscal Year 2015, Sec. 1208, Extension and Modification of Authority for Support of Special Operations to Combat Terrorism, January 3, 2014.

Public Law 114-92, National Defense Authorization Act for Fiscal Year 2016, Sec. 1274, Modification of Authority for Support of Special Operations to Combat Terrorism, January 6, 2015.

"Quadrennial Defense Review," U.S. Department of Defense website, undated. As of December 27, 2016:
https://www.defense.gov/News/Special-Reports/QDR

Remnick, David, "Going the Distance," *New Yorker*, January 27, 2014. As of August 1, 2016:
http://www.newyorker.com/magazine/2014/01/27/going-the-distance-david-remnick

Robinson, Linda, *Assessment of the Politico-Military Campaign to Counter ISIL and Options for Adaptation*, Santa Monica, Calif.: RAND Corporation, RR-1290-OSD, 2016. As of December 21, 2016:
http://www.rand.org/pubs/research_reports/RR1290.html

Rogin, Josh, "Senate Moves Toward Arming Syrian Rebels," *The Daily Beast*, May 22, 2013. As of July 27, 2016:
http://www.thedailybeast.com/articles/2013/05/22/senate-moves-toward-arming-the-syrian-rebels.html

Rumsfeld, Donald, "Subject: Afghanistan," memorandum to Gen. Myers, October 17, 2001.

———, "Subject: Reducing Demands on Special Operations Forces," memorandum to Gen. Myers, September 26, 2002.

———, "Subject: Marine Special Operations Command," memorandum to General Doug Brown, February 7, 2005.

———, "Your Attendance at the NSC Meeting," note to MG Stan McChrystal, July 1, 2005.

———, "Stan McChrystal," note to VADM Staser Holcomb, September 29, 2005.

———, "Subject: Marine Special Operations Component (MARSOC)," memorandum to Gen. Pete Pace, November 4, 2005.

———, "Stan McChrystal's Chart," note to Gen. Peter Pace and Eric Edelman, January 5, 2006.

Schmitt, Eric, "Elite Military Forces Are Denied in Bid for Expansion," *New York Times*, June 4, 2012.

———, "C.I.A. Said to Aid in Steering Arms to Syrian Opposition," *New York Times*, June 21, 2012. As of August 1, 2016:
http://www.nytimes.com/2012/06/21/world/middleeast/cia-said-to-aid-in-steering-arms-to-syrian-rebels.html

Schmitt, Eric, and Thom Shanker, "A Commander Seeks to Chart a New Path for Special Operations," *New York Times*, May 1, 2013.

Schofield, Matthew, "Few Military Options for U.S. in Syria, General Says," *McClatchy Newspapers*, March 6, 2012. As of August 1, 2016:
http://www.mcclatchydc.com/news/nation-world/world/article24725533.html

Schoomaker, Peter, "Testimony to Senate Armed Services Committee," 1998.

"Secretary of Defense Leon E. Panetta Submitted Statement on Syria, Senate Armed Services Committee," March 7, 2012. As of July 27, 2016:
http://www.armed-services.senate.gov/imo/media/doc/Panetta%2003-07-121.pdf

Selva, Paul J., "Theater Special Operations Command and Control Doctrine, Organization, Training, Material, Leadership and Education, Personnel, Facilities, and Policy (DOTMLPF-P) Change Recommendation," Washington, D.C.: U.S. Department of Defense, March 11, 2016.

"Senators Unveil Congressional Resolution on Syria," Senator John McCain website, March 28, 2012. As of July 27, 2016:
http://www.mccain.senate.gov/public/index.cfm/2012/3/post-5a07266e-c08f-eb13-dfdf-8f5c3a3b41a6

Serafino, Nina M., *Global Security Contingency Fund: Summary and Issue Overview*, Washington, D.C.: Congressional Research Service, 7-5700, R42641, April 4, 2014a. As of June 28, 2016:
https://www.fas.org/sgp/crs/row/R42641.pdf

———, *Security Assistance Reform: "Section 1206" Background and Issues for Congress*, Washington, D.C.: Congressional Research Service, 7-7500, RS22855, April 4, 2014b. As of January 6, 2017:
http://www.dtic.mil/cgi-bin/GetTRDoc?AD=ADA601565

Shifter, Michael, "Plan Colombia: A Retrospective," *Americas Quarterly*, Summer 2012.

Shultz, Jr., Richard H., *The Secret War Against Hanoi: The Untold Story of Spies, Saboteurs, and Covert Warriors in North Vietnam*, New York: Perennial, 1999.

———, "Showstoppers," *Weekly Standard*, January 26, 2004.

Simpson, Charles M., *Inside the Green Berets: The First Thirty Years*, Novato, Calif.: Presidio Press, 1983.

Singlaub, John K., with Malcolm McConnell, *Hazardous Duty: An American Soldier in the Twentieth Century*, New York: Summit Books, 1991.

Sly, Liz, "The Last Remaining Pentagon-Trained Rebel Group in Syria Is Now in Jeopardy," *Washington Post*, May 27, 2016. As of August 1, 2016: https://www.washingtonpost.com/world/middle_east/the-last-remaining-pentagon-trained-rebel-group-in-syria-is-now-in-jeopardy/2016/05/27/91de194a-1c5f-11e6-82c2-a7dcb313287d_story.html

Sorley, Lewis, *Thunderbolt: General Creighton Abrams and the Army of His Times*, Bloomington, Ind.: Indiana University Press, 2008.

Southworth, Samuel A., and Stephen Tanner, *U.S. Special Forces: A Guide to America's Special Operations Units*, Cambridge, Mass.: Da Capo Press, 2002.

Spencer, David, "The Sword of Honor Campaign in the Cauca Valley: 2011–2013 Colombian Conflict Focus of Effort," *Small Wars Journal*, May 31, 2013.

Springer, Greg, *The Element of Surprise*, Ft. Bliss, Tex.: U.S. Army Sergeants Major Academy, 2010.

Stewart, Richard W., *The United States Army in Somalia, 1992–1994*, Washington D.C.: Center of Military History, CMH Pub 70–81–1, 2002.

Tenet, George, "DCI Statement: Current and Projected National Security Threats, State of the Director of Central Intelligence George J. Tenet Before the Senate Armed Services Committee Hearing on Current and Projected National Security Threats," Central Intelligence Agency website, speeches and testimony archive, February 1999.

Thomas, Evan, and Bruce van Voorst, "Drums Along the Potomac: The Military Establishment Is Besieged by Some of Its Staunchest Supporters," *Time*, October 21, 1985.

Thomas, Jim, and Chris Dougherty, *Beyond the Ramparts: The Future of U.S. Special Operations Forces*, Washington, D.C.: Center for Strategic and Budgetary Assessments, 2013.

Ulrich, John, *Defense Drawdowns: Analysis with Implications*, Carlisle, Pa.: U.S. Army War College, 2012.

United States Code, Title 10, Section 161, Combatant Commands: Establishment, October 1, 1986.

United States Code, Title 10, Section 167, Unified Combatant Command for Special Operations Forces, December 19, 2014.

U.S. Department of Defense, *Quadrennial Defense Review Report*, Washington, D.C., February 2010. As of December 27, 2016: http://www.comw.org/qdr/fulltext/1002QDR2010.pdf

U.S. Department of Defense, Sec. 308 Special Operations Security Force Assistance, draft legislative proposal, 2012a.

———, Sustaining U.S. Global Leadership: Priorities for 21st Century Defense, Washington, D.C., January 2012b. As of July 16, 2016: http://archive.defense.gov/news/Defense_Strategic_Guidance.pdf

U.S. Government Accountability Office, *Plan Colombia: Drug Reduction Goals Were Not Fully Met, but Security Has Improved, U.S. Agencies Need More Detailed Plans for Reducing Assistance*, Washington, D.C., GAO-09-07, October 2008.

U.S. House of Representatives, 113th Cong., 1st Sess., Department of Defense Appropriations Act, Washington, D.C., H.R. 2397, July 30, 2013.

———, Limitation on Establishment of Regional Special Operations Forces Coordination Centers, Sec. 1245 of National Defense Authorization Act for Fiscal Year 2014, Washington, D.C., H.R. 1960, July 8, 2013.

"U.S. Military Chief Dubious About Arming Syrian Rebels," CNN.com, February 20, 2012. As of December 29, 2016: http://www.cnn.com/2012/02/19/us/syria/

U.S. Senate, 112th Cong., 2nd Sess., National Defense Authorization Act for Fiscal Year 2013, Washington, D.C., S. 3254, June 4, 2012.

———, 113th Cong., 1st Sess., Limitation on Funding for Regional Special Operations Coordination Centers, Sec. 342 of National Defense Authorization Act for Fiscal Year 2014, Washington, D.C., S. 1197, June 20, 2013.

U.S. Special Operations Command, "Enabling the Global SOF Network," draft paper, March 2012a.

———, The Global SOF Network, pre-decisional draft paper, March 2, 2012c.

———, "Enabling the Global SOF Network," briefing slides, March 13, 2012b.

———, Special Operations Forces 2020: Enhancing the Global SOF Network, 2013a.

———, "Special Operations Forces 2020: You Can't Surge Trust," briefing slides, 2013b.

———, *Global Special Operations Forces Network Operational Planning Team: A History*, 2014.

———, "Joint DOTMLPF-P Change Recommendation for Theater Special Operations Command Headquarters Command and Control," September 2015.

Votel, Joseph L., "Advanced Policy Questions Delivered to the 114th Congress, Senate Armed Services Committee," Washington, D.C., March 9, 2016.

Waller, Douglas, *Wild Bill Donovan: The Spymaster Who Created the OSS and Modern American Espionage*, New York: Free Press, 2011.

Warner, Michael, *The Office of Strategic Services: America's First Intelligence Agency*, Washington, D.C.: Center for the Study of Intelligence, 2000.

Westmoreland, William Childs, *A Soldier Reports*, Cambridge, Mass.: Da Capo Press, 1989.

White House, "Statement by Deputy National Security Advisor for Strategic Communications Ben Rhodes on Syrian Chemical Weapons Use," Washington, D.C., June 13, 2013. As of January 2, 2016:
https://www.whitehouse.gov/the-press-office/2013/06/13/statement-deputy-national-security-advisor-strategic-communications-ben-

Winnefeld, Jr., James A., "Global SOF Network 2020 Concept of Operations," memorandum for the Under Secretaries of Defense, Military Service Vice Chiefs, and Combatant Commanders, Washington, D.C.: U.S. Department of Defense, October 16, 2013.

Young, William G., David Stebbins, Bryan Frederick, and Omar Al-Shahery, *Spillover from the Conflict in Syria: An Assessment of the Factors That Aid and Impede the Spread of Violence*, Santa Monica, Calif.: RAND Corporation, RR-609-OSD, 2014. As of December 21, 2016:
http://www.rand.org/pubs/research_reports/RR609.html

Zedric, Lance Q., *Silent Warriors of World War II: The Alamo Scouts Behind Japanese Lines*, Ventura, Calif.: Pathfinder Publishing of California, 1995.